Anchors of the Soul

A Novel

By

Carol Egmont St. John

ISBN: 1-4107-1657-0 (e-book)
ISBN: 1-4107-1658-9 (Paperback)
ISBN: 1-4107-1659-7 (Dust Jacket)

Library of Congress Control Number: 2003090384

This book is printed on acid free paper.

Printed in the United States of America
Bloomington, IN

1stBooks - rev. 06/05/03

Acknowledgments:

Thank you to my writing groups and reading groups where I have found inspiration and trust. Thank you to my husband who sat through twenty versions of chapter one. Thank you to Pat and Phil Dunn and my daughter, Jill Buchanan, who gave me the opportunity to face a challenged culture. Thank you to my other daughters, Leslie, Tamie and Heather who teach me daily that the generation gap is not as wide as I feared. Thank you to Jean Phillips, Al Petrillo, Barbara McNichol, Joan Frank, Terry Olson, Marty Schuyler, Glenda Martin, Joanne Michos and Susie Williams, who responded to my words and gave me permission to proceed. And thank you to my teachers at Northeastern University whose nurture and brilliance encouraged me to write a little and then a lot.

Finally, thank you dear reader for opening this page.

Carol Egmont St. John

Dusk

at the edge of day
we understand the promises
some broken some fulfilled
some still fallow or waiting for
another chance another possibility

we send them to the scalloped
edges of earth
push them into pink and yellow clouds
to be washed and ironed
and returned like myths
to the starry well of sky

Carol St. John

One

Gwen

Cloud cover and salty air augment the sound of the siren careening down the street. When it stops abruptly in front of our house I look up to see a red pulsating light on the living room wall. It's strange they should park here, we have no emergency. Then again, Granite Shores Police are known for using their sirens for any reason at all. Tim says they will blast them to clear the streets just to get home on time for dinner. I imagine today it's the Police Fund Drive, that annual extortion of Granite Shores' citizens forced to contribute to the Police Benevolent Fund. In this town, you wouldn't want your car stickerless when you miss a stop sign.

I don't intend to turn around and disturb the tidy pile of luncheon invitations balanced on my lap. "Tim, is anything serious going on out there? For heavens sake, they don't have to leave that awful light on."

"It's Hank Richman's patrol car," he says. "He's getting out."

"Well, he needn't bother. I will not contribute one cent to this year's fund drive. Not after they took Mildred's car and handcuffed her right there on the street for driving an unregistered vehicle. Such a public humiliation, an unnecessary thing to do to anyone, but to a seventy-two year old woman, that was just too much! Another example of the misuse of power in a town too small to keep the police entertained."

Another car pulls up. A second door slams. *Now, who could that be?* I wonder.

As if he's read my mind, my son tells me, "It's Mac from the plant."

Twitches of trouble travel up my legs. I hope there hasn't been an accident or a theft, or anything worse. I put the invitations on the coffee table, glance outside, and catch the two men nodding to each other soberly at the gate. They walk up the brick walk, shoulder to shoulder, grim as pallbearers.

Tim heads for the door to greet the men and I follow.

"Hi, Mac. Come on in.

"May I help you, Sheriff?" Tim asks. He sounds more and more like his father these days.

"Afternoon, Tim. How ya doin'?" says our sheriff.

"Good enough. Is there anything we can do for you?"

Hank nods. Mac remains silent.

Failing to remove his hat, the sheriff inspects my living room. His eyes graze over the Chippendale breakfront, across Wyeth's sketches of Baryshnikov and stop at the dear bronze nude by the window facing Spain. He looks at my invitations on the table, actually touches one of them and then, just as rudely, asks me to sit down. Does he want to tell me something I cannot hear on my feet?

1

Mac is noticeably uncomfortable.

Obliging the law, I sit on the edge of the divan and wait.

Wendy, annoyed by my arrival, unfurls her feline self and disappears; dandelion fur dances in the solitary slant of sun she leaves behind.

Mac sits across from me. "Have you heard from Nial?" he asks.

"No. Nothing. I mean, not since he left. Why? Have you?"

"And you, Tim? Have *you* heard from him? You're named as his co-pilot on the flight plan."

"I decided to stay home this time around. Had to finish up some course work," Tim explains. "Why? What do you want to know?"

"Your father failed to record the fact that you weren't going with him. When did you two talk last?"

"Day before yesterday. He never calls us from Nicaragua. We don't expect him to. It's too complicated."

One might wonder why an incorrect flight plan should compel two men to come to our house in the middle of an ordinary spring day.

"Mrs. Townsend," Mac says gently, his voice much too paternal, "I'm afraid we have bad news."

I really do not want to hear this. I can't seem to breathe.

"Nial's plane sent out a Mayday signal, yesterday, and that was the last anyone has heard from him. The Coast Guard and shipping lines are searching the waters along the Mosquito Coast, but no luck so far. At least there's no visible sign of an accident."

What is he trying to tell me? Am I hearing what I think I'm hearing? Perhaps it's the lack of oxygen to my brain that makes it hard to discern. "You're saying there's no sign of an accident? Am I to assume this is good news?"

"Not exactly," Sheriff Richman says. I note his jacket is too small. His pants too short. Nial never liked him. Dimples and sweat dapple his puffy face. Without a neck, he looks like a ball, not a sheriff. I should tell him about Mildred and what I saw for myself. I don't like his chubby officiousness. I don't like bullies in uniforms, period.

He is saying something about a storm. Something about the Coast Guard. There is no reality here. It would be better if they left now.

Mac interrupts. "But you know there are many possibilities to consider, Mrs. Townsend. It's a difficult coastline. The waters are filled with islands and the shore is mostly jungle. Hard to navigate. Right now, all we can do is be patient and hope for the best."

The words get lost between the men's mouths and my ears, and the intrusive red light continues to bounce off the walls. At least the sound is off. I have an aversion to loud noises; the wail of an ambulance, the shriek of a police car. They bring back fears caused by a war that never began or ended—the so-called cold war. It hovered over my little girl head and sent me scrambling under my school desk more times than I wish to remember. Such nonsense. The piercing, urgent bells only served to instill us with a sense of impending doom.

Mac says to Tim, "All we have right now, son, are questions. Your father's whereabouts is a mystery."

Mystery and misery were synonymous to me as a child.

I started out watching war's misery. Pictures of hungry, homeless children in Europe were deeply imprinted on my mind; those, and the Jews huddled in a boat waiting for a homeland. The mystery was why. Why did these things happen?

One Sunday I asked my pretty Sunday School teacher why God made people suffer.

"It's a mystery," Miss Jolie had said, with her easy Presbyterian smile. "Something terrible happens to someone everyday, everywhere. We have to prepare ourselves so we're right with the Lord when *our* time comes."

I began to dread the suffering she deemed inevitable. Was sure my comfortable beginnings would demand all sorts of reparations. That's why it did not escape me when I was twenty-two and suffered a devastating loss, that my time had come. The mystery was over. Not only did my baby girl die in her crib but I was left to live with the knowledge that had I been paying closer attention..."

"...Mrs. Townsend?" the sheriff wants to know something. I can't imagine what.

"Is it necessary to leave that awful light on, Sheriff?" I ask.

"Yes, Ma'am it is."

When they leave, Mac suggests that Tim call Dr. Bomson. He mentions I should call a close family member.

Poor lost Mother won't do.

I sit as still as possible waiting for the dream to end. Waiting for something to correct what I think I heard. Meanwhile, Tim is on the telephone trying to reach the farm in Nicaragua.

At day's end, Dr. Bomson comes to the house and delivers a variety of pills. He gives me Zoloft for the daylight hours. "Take the blue pill in the morning, and the pink one at night, all you need to handle is one day at a time," he suggests, as if a few pills will make everything bearable.

***

Five weeks go by, during which I listen to the answering machine regularly to hear Nial's voice. It confirms to me that he is very much alive. Who could deny his warm greeting, "Hello, there! This is the Townsend residence. If you're calling Nail, hang up. If it's Nial or Tim or Gwen, we'll get back to you."

It is too bad that Leslie Wingart calls my hanging on to his voice, *morbid*. She needs to know, along with everyone else, that I am waiting for Nial to be found and will not, absolutely will not allow the worst to be true.

But I'm afraid, on a day to day basis, things are getting fuzzier. I can't remember items at the store and found the iron in the refrigerator yesterday.

3

My garden is dry. I don't keep standing appointments. In fact, I have to admit, the most I've been asking of myself is to get out of bed.

Thor, the dog that Nial loves more than his own son, has the patience of Job. He waits, head hunched between his big black toes, staunchly resolved to greet Nial at six each night. And Nial's things have gravitated to Thor's hiding place under the front stairs. I found the pile; a dirty sock, an old shoe, broken sunglasses—he is doing the same thing I am, waiting out the storm until it's over. Thor, Storm God. Protector of the household. Was Nial's naming him prescient?

Of course, all our dogs were named after gods. Our first black lab we called Ajax. He was a powerhouse of a creature, a stallion without a mane. Nial gave him to me for my birthday and I remember thinking that it was a strange gift, comparable to awarding me a tackle box. But Ajax turned out to be far more interesting than the hooks and flies of a tackle box. He was an imperious guard dog and a comfort to me when Nial was gone—when the baby and I were left to rattle about the house all day.

Then there was Zeus. A beauty and a beast. He was a nomad at heart despite his royal ties; a golden retriever who'd rather search than find.

Oh dear, and those trips to the court to pay for his adventures.

"Charge?" the bailiff would ask—

"Dog Without Leash," the courtroom reporter would announce.

"Dog Without Leash AGAIN?" Judge Levinson would ask.

The last time we were fined, I left the courthouse to discover Zeus waiting for me, tail wagging, smile stretched across his yellow face. I pretended not to know him, hoping I could just get to the car before we were ticketed again. We made it that day, but ultimately a careless Corvette hit him and his journey ended, tragically, on a road he thought he owned.

He was followed by Apollo, a golden lab and a sun god indeed. We shortened his name to Pollo but he answered to anything at all. He was Tim's best buddy and perfectly willing to be yours upon request. Pollo drowned in Little Quarry across the road where Tim was playing ice hockey with the neighborhood boys. Pollo didn't know he wasn't one of them. He ran and slid between their blades like a pro. I will never forget the horror of his spill and Nial crashing through the ice to get to him. Pollo rose halfway out of the water and then fell back, as though pulled by some primeval monster from below. The fear and question in that dog's expression! And then he went down, sinking so far beyond reach Nial knew there was no hope of saving him. And the poor man had to retreat from the frigid water while the rest of us stood there watching, helplessly. My darling boy was sobbing, trapped in his ice skates just beyond the lifeless hint of gold. I stood on shore screaming, warning Tim not to go any closer to the water, to be careful of the thin ice.

We didn't know it, but Francis Serra had run home for an ax. When he returned we all held hands and stretched from the shore to the center of the ice. Frannie hacked away, and yet soon it was clear, even his ax couldn't penetrate the thickness of mid-winter ice. Pollo was frozen in place until

4

spring arrived. When they brought his body from the water, Tim wept and vowed he would never swim in the quarry again. I don't think he ever has.

Two

Serena

Nothing's changed and everything's changed. Autumn is right on schedule and yet the shorter the days—the longer they seem. Purple asters have replaced the black-eyed Susans along the roadsides and the Queen Anne's lace is drooping, her white bonnets gone brown and wrinkled. You can hear the crickets playing frantically for a soulmate. I wonder who will play for me?

Nial Townsend hasn't been found. Some say he's dead, but I don't believe it. He may be lost or hiding, but he's not dead. I'd know because I pay attention in ways others don't. My Wiccan sensors are tuned. They pick up clues, like the sign I got this morning that told me it's time. Time to do something I should have done long ago—time to meet Nial's wife.

Gwen Townsend's life and mine are more entangled than she could ever imagine and yet she hardly knows I exist. I need to let her know Townsend Cove is not her exclusive territory. From now on, she's not only going to recognize me, she's going to gain some respect for the roots I have here. She might be surprised to find out mine go a lot deeper than hers. She might be surprised about a lot of other things.

I got the message to introduce myself during my fall vigil out on Clemen's Point. I go there every year to catch a view of the monarchs gathering for their flight south. The sandy paths reminded me of how fast things happen in late September. Overnight, the beach plums had turned orange and the maple leaves were painted red and yellow. A good wind and they'll be on their way to compost.

At the curve of the road, I stopped to look for butterfly wings. About ten yards beyond the winterberry and honeysuckle was a stand of sumac, dark red, against a field of grass so white you'd think it was snow. I couldn't tell right off if the thinning branches were wearing dead leaves or butterflies. Then they began to flutter. I stood still as a heron and watched as, one by one, the orange and black wings opened and lifted. Soon there were clouds of butterflies rising and falling from the brush and circling the dunes like muted blackbirds. I'd guess there were thousands, stretching, sweeping, over, under, around—some settling on my head and arms only to take off again; a touch and go dance before their long trip to Mexico.

I asked myself what it is that tells them when to meet and where to go? What mechanism operates inside their tiny heads that says, "Now!"? And that was the moment I realized *now* applies to me as well.

I decided to act quickly; and here I am, eleven hours later, on this empty beach, hoping Gwen Townsend will show up. Even the air is excited, clear and gutsy. She makes an art of her exclusivity, so our meeting has to seem natural, like a coincidence. It helps to know her rituals—how she walks the dog right before dark and watches the sunset from the stretch of sand in front of her house. All I need is patience. She's as predictable as the tides.

Penny Loaf Island is in my view, only half a mile away. I push away memories of things I learned there and study, instead, how its jagged edges of pine turn black against the sky, watch the rocks at its hem darken into silhouette. Masts sway like golden crosses on the water. The green and red markers of my lobster pots bob to the jangle of loose halyards. It's a scene I never get tired of, part of my blood.

Then I hear the heavy latch on the garden gate clank and turn to see Gwen Townsend and her dog heading for the beach. Thor, that most magnificent of black dogs, bounds past her. Stalks of sea grass glow like so many candles lighting her way as she walks down the makeshift path of wooden planks across the dunes. On the beach she stops to watch the sun lower itself into the horizon.

When I was a little girl, I saw the eternal in the reach from shore to sky and promises in the Eucharistic offering of the sun to the sea. But, Pop soon taught me the sea didn't swallow the sun, and the horizon is not the great distance it appears to be from the water's edge. At zero degree altitude, it's only five miles out. Even on the clearest day, distance is an illusion.

Gwen sits, adjusting herself in the curved waist of a tree trunk the tide delivered this summer. In the last light it looks like a glittering throne. And she's queenly, despite the sag in her shoulders. Of course, she's lonely. I can almost see the wall around her. I have no trouble imagining her loneliness because of my own. Our empty nests sit behind us, facing one another—hers, from its granite ledge looking down; mine, from the pier, looking up.

Barefooted, I walk toward her, across a perilous spill of small stones and shells. I don't stop to put on the sandals that dangle like loose claws from my hands. She pretends she doesn't notice me moving her way, even though I must look dark and strange against the flaming sky, especially when a stiff breeze puffs out my loose skirts and hair. I would imagine billowing swirls of cloth flapping like sails have to be hard to ignore, but she does her best.

When I'm close enough for it to be obvious my intention is to approach her, she deliberately looks away.

It's understandable. I'm on Townsend land, trespassing on what she considers to be her private beach, interrupting her privacy. And she has every reason to consider me suspect. The story of Nial Townsend's disappearance has been all over the news. I might be another reporter as far as she knows, the CIA, a nosey neighbor or a nut case. I can't blame her for her attitude. But I also expect her to be too proper to point these things out. She'll probably wait, try to obliterate me and use silence as a form of dismissal, but I can't let it work, not tonight.

My size ten feet gnarl her smooth sand as I move a little closer. "Mind if I join you?"

7

I almost jump when she answers. "I don't suppose it matters." Her long neck reaches away and she manages to hide behind her right hand, which has come up to her face like a blinder keeping me out of her vision.

We're not meant to be friends. I have no high expectations about what she'll think of me, but forces brought me here, at this moment, to take whatever steps I can to connect. What I did and why I did it is something she doesn't need to know. Nial and I were no less an act of nature than water falling over rock.

I move closer, close enough to smell the lavender of her. "Sunset is a reminder, isn't it? It tells us things will get brighter no matter how dark it gets."

She ignores me.

I could recite a litany of my losses for her, but figure she's only interested in her own. "I've been through hard times, too—enough to know healing comes, especially if you help," I say.

She refuses to look my way, although I notice she's dropped her hand and seems to be looking at the water's edge where Thor is joyfully chasing gulls into the air.

"Such a shiny evening, even the wings of the gulls seem to shimmer," I try.

Nothing.

I won't give up.

Pulling my skirts beneath me, I lower myself to squat on the sand beside her. If I choose silence maybe she'll eventually say something. But patience is not one of my best attributes. Five minutes go by, maybe one, when I realize it's too uncomfortable for me to remain like a stray dog at her feet.

"Name's Serena," I say, and reach my hand toward hers. This forces her to acknowledge me. When she does, whew! Her eyes take in everything—fast. They check my big feet and hopeless hair. Scan my ears and fingers for gold. Check out the gold button in my nose and ask how dare I be here at all.

She's managed not to see me my entire life (that sin of omission thing) even though I've been right in front of her face. Even though I've known her family, her husband and son better than she has. Go ahead, look at me Gwen Townsend, I'm not intimidated by you.

Before I say the wrong thing, I remind myself all that matters is my mission. Squaring my shoulders and pulling back my hair, I bare my face with its angles and pride. I won't cower no matter how much she'd prefer to see me do just that. I'm my father's daughter, tough-skinned and strong-armed, and I am not going to apologize for my hands. What could she know about hands like mine? They're used, no-nonsense, functional hands. I can save my own life with them.

"Serena," she repeats.

"Serena Tesorerio."

"Have we met?" she asks.

8

I couldn't tell her how many times I've watched her, watched them. "I'm your neighbor. I live in that little house, over there, at the end of the dock. The one with the red door."

It's funny to watch her surprise as she looks out to the dilapidated shacks at the end of the fishing pier. She must be asking herself if anyone could actually live in them. I'm sure she's never given it a thought. They're simply part of *her* landscape, built for tools, gear and the like—things foreign and dirty to her. But she hasn't wondered about the fishermen who come and go on a regular basis. We're of no concern to her. I'd lay money on it.

"I had no idea anyone lived there. I always assumed those buildings were uninhabitable. But you don't actually *live* there?" She looks from me to the wharf as if she is seeing it for the first time.

"My whole life! At least from April to December. Pop was a lobsterman, I was his stern man. We crabbed down on the Keys during the winter. Lived on the Serena Marie coming and going. That's my lobster boat down there." I nod toward the Serena Marie sitting like a smile on the water, not that she gives a damn.

"That would explain my not recognizing you. It's likely I would have, if you were here year 'round."

"Seems so," I say. *Bitch*, I think.

"You know, I used to watch you play croquet back there on your lawn," I tell her. "I was six the first time I saw your family knocking those big balls around. I would watch you play on Sunday afternoons after Pop and I brought in the catch.

"Those days are long gone..." she says. "But how...?"

"I knew the peep holes in the stone wall. I watched you all the time. I wanted to play, too."

"Peep holes?"

"After Pop caught me, he started taking me downtown to play what he called Guinea croquet."

She gives me a blank look.

"Bocci ball," I explain.

"But you watched us?"

"I used to look through the spaces between the rocks. I was more boy than girl in those days. Pop even called me Sam. The thing was, the game looked too easy to cause the excitement you guys made of it. I used to think I could beat the whole gang."

I should stop here, but like a jerk I tell her about the night they'd left the hoops up and the equipment out. How I'd knocked the balls around by myself. You'd think I'd hit her.

"You actually climbed over our wall during the night?"

"Yup."

"You scaled our wall?" she asks again, then shakes her head as if I did it yesterday. "What we don't know is probably a blessing."

I try to explain I was just curious. (It's a little late to apologize.) But she seems shaken.

My words must remind her of those family moments when life was exactly as it was supposed to be for the Townsends. Exclusive and perfect. All that easy happiness tucked in by tall everythings: walls, flowers, trees, people—the whole perfect picture—on a manicured carpet of green grass no less. And them, perfect, too, pretty and rich, with their crisp clothes and sun-streaked hair. It was hard to imagine they could ever be unhappy, much less miserable. God, life has a wicked set of surprises.

"Father used to make sure that Tim won the game by knocking everyone else out. Tim was my baby and didn't have a prayer. Did you know him?" she asks.

"I remember your father. It's been a long time, now, since he died, hasn't it?" He was my idea of a gentleman, through and through, always dressed up and in charge. I liked the old man and his ever-ready bow tie. I don't tell Mrs. Townsend, though. I think I've already told her too much.

"Seven years and I still miss him," she says.

We feel a gust of cool air. She undoes the pink sweater that's tied around her neck and sticks her arms in the sleeves. Her long fingers tremble as she searches for a button and a hole. Thor's now in the Atlantic having his evening swim. I'm looking for words to stretch our conversation.

Instead of telling her I'm sorry about her father, I tell her her how to get over it. "My father's dead, too. We all have to move on," I say. "Pop died three years ago, and I don't hear his voice as much as I did at first; he's moving on just like yours, just like everything. Look at the beach glass." I pick up a piece. "This stuff was once a medicine bottle and now what's left could decorate a work of art. Look how nature transformed a piece of glass into a precious jewel. I've got myself a whole collection. My favorites are these tiny blue pieces." I hand her the glass nugget. "Been collecting them since I was a little kid."

She puts it in her sweater pocket and looks out to the horizon again.

"What? What in the world...isn't that a whale?" she asks.

I know better—whales don't come into the harbor—but I follow her gaze to see what she's seen.

Out in the bay, right where an apricot light is teasing the water, there's a huge dark shape. I wonder if it's a submarine surfacing when a geyser erupts from its back. It can't be, but it is. It *is* a whale. I can imagine the sound, its putrid smell. Then he breaches, comes all the way out of the water and dives, leaving only a footprint for evidence.

"Holy shit!" I hear myself say as I stand up and move toward the water to have a better look. "I think it's a sperm whale!" I want to call the Coast Guard or Bob Teague, the Harbor Master. But more importantly, magic is taking place and I want to tell Gwen Townsend. A whale in the harbor is beyond belief.

She stands up. "You see the smooth circle? That's the footprint," she explains, as if I've never seen one before.

"Wow!" I shake my head. "This is awesome! It's one of those times when you can believe in miracles or blow it off like so much spume." She should realize this means something—this phenomenon taking place at the very moment we're together.

But, she's cool as a clam, as snooty as I expected. How could a person not be blown away when a whale shows up in their backyard? We stand side by side expecting another view and minutes go by without a show. Then, just as she turns to leave, the whale reappears. I grab her arm with my left hand and point with my right. When it breaches, I can feel the thrill that passes through her. I think, *she gets it! A whale at twilight has to be heaven sent.* "Look at its tail suspended in the air like a victory sign. It's a message," I say.

"What do you think it means?" she asks. She sounds genuinely curious.

"Well, Pop would have said that the squid are running and the whale is just chasing its dinner—but that's not what I think. I think it's got to have some kind of spiritual meaning. You know sperm whales are rare, just off the endangered species list. And I'm pretty sure this is a sperm whale; you saw the size of its head. I've seen others, but not under these circumstances. One of them coming into the harbor, it's well—it's unheard of—it's too weird not to be important."

"What kind of message do you believe it brings?" she asks.

"It depends.

"Moby Dick was a sperm whale," she points out.

"Yup. Man's will against nature's. Could be that's what this is about."

"I would have described *Moby Dick* as a story about obsession," she says.

I think, *obsession?* I suppose that makes sense, but nature versus man is the obvious reason. Too bad Pop isn't here to argue with her; they didn't call him *The Professor* for nothing. I don't need to argue with her. "You might be right. Anyway, *your* whale isn't Melville's; yours is about something else."

"And what would you propose?" she asks.

Sarcasm rules her voice. It won't stop me. "That whale we just saw is one third head, mostly brain. Maybe it has something to do with using your head."

"Hmmm. I don't see the connection yet," she says. Her words come out in little cartoon clouds.

Even though I know she won't see it my way, I add, "Sometimes we forget there are higher orders of intelligence. We think we should have it all under control." I'd also like to tell her she doesn't know everything about everything, straight out.

"She must be lost. Surely that's the best reason for a whale to approach us—that is, if they're as intelligent as you say. Certainly no self-respecting whale would put herself in the lap of danger," she says

"Himself. It's a he. Only the bulls swim alone. The cows and their calves are playing with the whale boats just three miles out, giving the whale watchers their money's worth. But, no matter, trust me, whales aren't foolish, they're smart."

"Perhaps," she says. Her hand wipes stray hairs from her face and I see the wedding band Nial gave her twenty seven years ago. It looks too thin for her long fingers.

She needs educating. Fortunately, I'm the one to do it.

"I wouldn't put down the whale so easily. We couldn't hold a candle to the whale if we were in the sea. The whale sings, talks, even analyzes, and after it takes what it needs, it moves on. Not like us. We're never satisfied."

My hands are doing that thing again. The Italian in me talks in sign. I tie my arms in a knot on my chest and continue. "Whales aren't just something bigger than we are; they're more evolved and spiritual. They're survivors." (These are my Superwhale lines, the same words I've recited on Salty Sal's Whale Watch for the last five years.) "They're larger than the largest dinosaur, hungrier than any other living thing and smart enough to find the two thousand pounds of food a day they need to keep going. They're worthy of our respect." Old Sal would be proud of me.

"Perhaps", she says distractedly

"Hey, whales were smart enough to kick off their legs and take over the oceans instead of the land. And they never had to resort to killing their own kind like we do."

She nods, I see her search the water for another sighting. Thor is now leaping at dragon flies. Dogs know how to have fun.

"There was Jonah, Jonah and the whale," she says, mostly to herself.

"I know a little about Jonah. Jonah traveled in a whale's belly, didn't he? I wasn't as interested in that stuff as I should have been. I get Bible stories mixed up with fairy tales. Like, Jonah and Pinocchio."

The sun has almost disappeared. It only shines in the gold edges of a few mauve-colored clouds. We watch the Regina Maris coming in, her hull low in the water. Must have been a good catch.

Frankie will be happy.

Gwen says, "As I remember, a storm came and swept Jonah off his ship. He was swallowed by a great fish and lived in its belly for three days and three nights until he was delivered to dry land."

"Did the whale belch him up or did he build a fire like Pinocchio did?" I ask.

"I couldn't say. I've certainly never put the two stories together before, or at least on the same level. Pinocchio's just an Italian folk tale after all. It's not endowed with a sacred message."

I would love to tell her it's all the same thing, but I don't. This conversation is more than I'd hoped for. Our connection has been sealed by the appearance of a miracle, something so unforgettable it insures her memory of our meeting. Who knows, she may even go so far as to ask herself why it happened. She may even wonder if her husband was scooped up by a great fish and planted on a foreign shore.

As I shake the sand off my skirts I grab one more chance to have my say. "There's meaning in everything if you look for it. The universe is talking to us all the time. We just have to listen in a new way. If we do, we'll get the answers to our questions. Most of us just don't take time to notice."

She nods. Not what I expected. Then she takes a deep breath and exhales slowly in a misty sigh that sounds like there might be room for another thought.

So, I give her my dream theory. "Look at the language of dreams. If a whale showed up in your dream, it would be just as significant as it is in the harbor, because dreams aren't accidents; they're metaphors with deep meanings. They're the Goddess talking. All our answers are delivered to us."

"I see. You put meaning into everything, not merely in extraordinary events such as a whale leaping out of the harbor? You actually believe the entire world is conspiring to talk to you, awake or asleep?"

The tone of her voice says it all. I've said too much.

"Well, the whale was kind of in your face," I remind her.

"Hmmm. Yes. And yours."

She calls, "Thor! Come. It's time to go home." His legs barely touch the ground as he runs to us.

He comes to me first, his tail wagging the rest of him. Dogs never forget their friends.

"Nice dog," I say

"He's my sweet old boy." Her lips are tight as she turns to leave. I know Thor's really Nial's shadow. Nial's sweet old boy.

I look at her back. She's writing me off before we even get started. I'm as empty inside as the space she leaves between us.

Then she remembers her manners and turns back around. We're standing on even ground and her eyes look straight into mine. "It has been interesting meeting you," she says.

She's not quite as tall as I had thought, and in this half-light her eyes are a deep blue, as beautiful as the beach glass in her pocket.

"I suppose I don't have to introduce myself?"

"No. I know you're Gwen Townsend. I imagine you'd like me to call you *Mrs.* Townsend?"

"Yes. That's right. Well, goodnight, Selena. I must say I am surprised we haven't met before this."

"Serena. Don't be. Pop made sure I knew my place. It's only since he's gone that I've made my own rules."

"Yes, well, goodnight then, Serena," she says, and off she goes toward the captain's great stone house.

I stand and watch her retreat up the stairs. Her straight pale hair is caught by the wind and she easily sweeps its silky strands from one side of her head to the other, an act enviably foreign to my own kinky mop. She's almost beyond hearing distance when I call out, "Maybe Jonah needed to go some place that scared him shitless. What do you think?"

A seagull swoops down and barks at me. "Je-er-rk," he screams."

I can't take it back. All I can do is watch her walk to the house without a backward glance.

Dammit, why do I slip into boy talk whenever I'm nervous?

At least we've met, and I'll make sure we meet again. Maybe tomorrow.

One thing's for sure. That whale proves Nial is alive. Meeting Gwen proved a few other things, too. She had never laid eyes on me. I'm not surprised because I've always suspected I was invisible in her world of somebodies and somethings, but you might have thought she'd recall some frizzy-headed moppet around and about the place, especially during those years when I fished with my father. After all, I was growing up alongside her precious son who was almost my age.

But, it isn't hate I feel. How could I? I'm just sad, sad for her, sad for me. We've both lost the people we've loved most in the world.

On my way back to the wharf, I turn and look up at the house. Gwen is out on the deck looking down at me. She picks up a mug she must have left standing on the porch rail. I can almost see Nial's hands wrapped around it, see him standing there looking out to sea, waving at Tim, at me, at a friend on a yawl.

I stop myself. He's been missing for five months now. That's reason enough for some people to believe he'll never come back. But there are no remains and the presence of sharks is just too easy an explanation. He was always prepared—too smart for such a horrible death. The information in the papers has been sketchy. They reported that his plane went down violently. But I'd like to know from what evidence? Who checked? The coast where his plane went down is impenetrable and unfriendly, at least that's what they say. My guess is, not enough was done to find him. I know what happens around here when there's an accident and the Coast Guard kicks into action. But down there, in Central America, where things are even harder and there's less accountability, I'll bet they don't make the same kind of effort. He's alive—he must be—and someone has to go to Nicaragua to find him. It can't be me. It won't be his son. It will have to be his wife.

Three

Gwen

"Maybe Jonah needed to go some place that scared him shitless. What do you think?" she calls over her shoulder.

I think I hear her laugh.

She's a brash one and those purple skirts and the jingling bracelets! I should think she'd be more comfortable with a band of gypsies on the coast of Spain than here. Of course, here, she's one of a kind, and I suppose she likes that, typical for a girl her age.

The fisherman's wharf looms dark against the slashes of light still playing on the water. It looks far from here, but that's no reason to relegate it to a foreign land. I think I'm guilty of having done just that. No matter how many times I've looked at shacks from the rear of the house to the beach, I've never so much as thought about what is going on inside their walls. Never considered learning the names of the fisherman who moor their boats so near to ours; never stopped to chat; never felt comfortable walking out there. Even when we bought lobsters directly off the boats at a local's price, I felt no need to introduce myself to them. In fact, I left the bartering up to Father or Nial or Tim. More often than not, it was Tim who served as the go-between for the family and the fishermen. Serena didn't mention it, but she and Tim must have met at some time or other.

And how could it be that I have exactly no recall of this young woman? If she had really fished with her father as a child and stayed by his side as an adult, why had I not noticed? With her wild red hair and those long legs, it would take blinders not to see her.

Her story about climbing the granite wall is stunning. It's fourteen feet high, for heaven's sake!

And to think that wall has represented generations of security ever since Captain Townsend built it back in 1832. Nial's great grandfather's great grandfather was not only a ship captain but the quarry master in the days when granite was to the cape like oil to Texas. The progeny of the Finns who cut the stone are still populating this place, and share the pride that Townsend stone helped build the skyscrapers of New York and the curbstones of Washington.

Salvage, the rocks that didn't make it to the ships, was used to build this house and our neighbor's houses. Thousands of blocks of granite were stacked to build the wall that for one hundred and fifty years has kept the sea at bay behind our house. And here is that young woman telling me she climbed it. How could any six year old have scaled a fourteen foot wall? If a child did it, who else may be capable of invading our privacy?

Although the wall's original purpose was to protect the apple and pear trees in that first seaside garden, lately, I've taken comfort thinking it's protecting me. I've obviously been deluding myself into believing I have any privacy left.

The lawn between the house and the wall has always been a hallowed ground for us. The scene of marriages, picnics and family affairs. Except for that terrible time when we poisoned the groundhog. Blumpy, Tim named him. I never should have let that name stick, but it seemed so appropriate for the roly-poly creature who appeared amidst the lilies and the columbine each spring. Tim saw him as a wild pet. Cliff, our gardener did not find him as charming. Tim cried his eyes out when he found his little Blumpy in the rose garden, stiff as a rake, mouth and eyes staring into eternity, his four fat legs stretched out in front of him—no longer able to dash to his tunneled kingdom beneath the earth.

I am like that poor beast. I can't run either. I'm at such a disadvantage, knowing there's gossip, knowing people are watching me with questions and answers of their own. Lola's Place went quiet when I came in the door the other day. Then the unnatural conversations the girls tried to make while I had my facial, nonsense about John John Kennedy and Winona Ryder. Why did I go there in the first place? Because I can't bear to look in the mirror? Who cares what I look like? And sitting there those long hours, suffering that ridiculous chatter about Harrison Ford's love life! Watching Mabel Goetz soak her feet and her fingertips at the same time. I will not be doing that again for a while.

I still reach my arm across the bed to touch Nial; the hole is huge where he should lie. His absence fills every room...as does unfinished business. Thor still waits at the door at dinnertime ready to greet him. The slipper I've placed in his dog bed is small compensation. He's not satisfied.

But the worst moments are about small things, like the dead sparrow the cat brought into the house and put in Tim's room last Saturday. It devastated me.

Tim's on the road west. I'd like to know where, *exactly* where. He's finding himself, he says. I can only pray the same instinct that moved him away will bring him back. This house, this town, it's all his heritage.

Wendy is Tim's cat. He brought her home in his bookbag one day—it must have been thirteen years ago—when he was still mine. His arms were striped with her scratches but he had to have her. I've had her declawed since then, turned her into a house cat. Well, almost, she did manage to catch that bird. Perhaps a nail or two has reappeared. Regardless, Wendy has become stealthy and neurotic. I love her yellow coat and am grateful for her little annoyances, but when she hides in the broom closet, or jumps with all four feet off the ground, she reveals a paranoia I sense may reflect my own.

It is hard to be here, in Granite Shores—hard to be anywhere on the planet right now. Yesterday, Mrs. Ogilvie knocked on my door to report that the Wallace's young girls had picked a few of my chrysanthemums. I told her I hoped they took stems long enough for their bouquets. Petty crimes are all we have here. God forbid anyone would want to announce a baby girl with pink balloons on a fencepost. Balloons on a fencepost provoke fines. Cars are impounded for being parked on crosswalks, working men frisked and arrested for unpaid parking tickets. The police blotter, with its petty crimes, is the most read column in the *Granite Shore Gazette*. All told, it listed three hundred and forty reports last year. Other than domestic violence, the most serious was a hold-up at the Exxon gas station where a young man's finger pointing into his cloth pocket was described as a dangerous weapon.

Local news would more aptly be described as gossip. Normally, I accept rumor and exaggeration as the price one pays for small-town charm, but right now I'm at its mercy and I'd prefer Manhattan.

The mug from my morning coffee is balanced on the deck rail. I can almost see Nial's long fingers wrapped around it, the angle of his arm as he'd stand there wearing one of his white woolly fisherman sweaters and looking out to sea like some ancient mariner—his wonderful forehead furrowed in a concentration I knew not to interrupt. I pick it up and lean into the rail. Serena is still in sight and I catch her looking at me. Strange, so strange, I have never seen her before. I don't wave to her. *Go somewhere where you're scared shitless.* Her words echo in my head. Another example of the audacity and ignorance of youth. Little can she know how I feel when I wake in the morning having to face one more day's emptiness.

My son's withdrawal has managed to make things worse. Where are you Tim? You had it all and you couldn't appreciate it. Why not? Is there such a thing as too much love? Was there a thing you wanted that you didn't get? Now where are you? Surely not at my side. Nor were you with your father at the end. But at least I can be grateful, for that.

It is now so many months since Nial disappeared. I would love to believe he will rise from the sea regurgitated by some breaching whale. Despite the fact that he has officially been declared lost, I can't let him go. It's part of the reason I struggle to keep the case open. It mustn't be over until I have more explanations, more facts. Although, I don't know what it would take for me to believe in his death. I suppose if spring doesn't follow winter, or the harbor becomes a desert ...I might know then.

I haven't *felt* him die. At least, there has been no moment when I knew his soul went somewhere else. But I remember the portents of trouble that preceded the accident, the ones I had refused to see at the time. There was the day when the alarm failed and Nial didn't care. A day when he buried his head in the pillows and said, "Call in for me." Of course I assumed he was ill, a rare circumstance, but I chose not to worry. It was when he added, "It's just not fun anymore," and didn't go in again for the rest of the week—only then that I felt anxious. In all the years of our marriage, I couldn't remember his having any resistance to work. I was actually jealous of his business, saw it as the *other woman*, until that week when he seemed empty and tired.

I tried to do something to help; suggest we go on a vacation, take an exotic trip to a place where no business meeting could possibly interrupt. He wouldn't look at the travel brochures I put out, or the travel ideas from the University Club. I found them all in the waste basket. He scoffed at the idea of going around the world on the Concorde, birdwatching in Patagonia, floating down the canals of France on a barge. He said I was pestering him with play while he was weighing serious business decisions. That's when I realized I was being insensitive. Wanting to travel *was* selfish on my part.

Like most couples, we had some problems along the way and we didn't discuss them as thoroughly as we might have. For example, the night Tim called from the police station and Nial didn't look up from his newspaper. I thought he was cold and accused him of having a hard heart. But, later, it occurred to me, why wouldn't a father be angry at a son smoking grass on the village green? A boy who was so indulged and adored; a boy who claimed he didn't ask to be born and who didn't honor a father who spent his entire adult life building a future for him.

Nial was my rock. He had been dedicated and present for so long I was able to deny the fact that things were changing. Even though my body lay, night after night, ignored by the man who used to leave me weak with satisfaction, I said nothing. Then it became weeks, soon months and still I remained silent, wondering if it was my fault for knowing so little about how to arouse him. One night when I reached over to touch his shoulder he said, "Please Gwen, for God's sake, I'm just about asleep." Whatever the situation was, I believed words would only exacerbate it.

This old house is hollow now. Even the stones echo loss. The wide hallways and chandeliered ceilings speak of some other time. There's antiquity on every surface, in the mahogany of the Chippendale, the Heppelwaite's curly maple; all the furniture I once coveted enough to move from Grandmother's New York brownstone more than a quarter of a century ago, is meaningless.

I am too, living in the dust of a disappeared family: the dust of a young man's anger, an infant girl's crib, a husband's restlessness, parents going and gone. My own dust. I tremble at the thought and go inside to get ready to climb under the covers of my lovely, lonely bed.

The red button on the answering machine blinks in the dark. I know what calls are waiting. Lily wants me to play bridge. The lawyers would like to work out some kinks in the papers piling up at the office. MCI wants me to change my telephone service. It's time for the Red Cross blood drive. Am I going to subscribe to the Boston Ballet? I cannot care, but I must stop that light.

I rewind the tape and extinguish the voices choking the line.

Four

Serena

The wind's up. I turn my top skirt up around my shoulders like a shawl.

Tiny's boat is tied up. He's unloaded and not in sight. Good. I'll have the shack to myself.

My sweats hang on a hook on the back of the door. I put them on after I take a pee in the privy at the end of the wharf. God, it's disgusting. They always think it's my job to clean up that stink hole. Well, they can shove it.

I've got an uncomfortable feeling. It isn't fair. I know that. I'm invading Gwen Townsend's world for my own agenda. She doesn't need me. Far from it. But, dammit, the only world Mrs. Townsend can see is the one in her face or on her plate. They're all like that, the Townsends, the Lowrys, the Mortimers and the Harveys. I grew up intimidated by them just for being whatever they think they are. Mostly for being rich.

Pop used to tell me it was a waste of energy, that God had worked it out so we all got a fair share of the good and the bad if we lived long enough. Well, I try to tell myself, now it's Gwen's turn and she's getting her fair share. But, I know life in the great house hasn't prepared her for a world that doesn't work. It's a world that, in justice's strange way, my entire life prepared me for. I was pulled from my dead mother's body, for God's sake—a lousy beginning, but it could have been worse. I could have died inside her, or been born without a brain. There it is—I can always think of something worse than what was doled out to me. Pop taught me that, too. Pop said survival's in my genes.

It *was* a mysterious thing to see the whale at that very moment, right when I needed to say something, anything, to the woman. I'd often thought about how I'd walk right up to her and let her know I exist, but how could I have ever imagined a whale at my service?

My sweats are cold and damp. Hell, I'll put them on anyway, body heat should take care of them. Mrs. Townsend's probably drinking sherry and contemplating her nails from the comfort of her featherbed.

She isn't all that bad. I've watched her long enough to know how she was with her family, how she tended her garden. I could tell she loved her father and mother. She probably tried to be an ideal daughter, then an ideal wife, and she probably treated Tim just like her mother treated her. Nial never said a word against her. I wished he had. The Blond Family, so predictable in their waspy ways. Everything right. Everything wrong.

When I was a kid, viewing them through the holes in the wall was like viewing life in a foreign country. Sometimes I'd imagine I was one of them, Gwen's daughter. That was until I decided I definitely didn't want Tim as a brother. No, I wanted more of him than that. I liked it when he put down his

19

mother. I'd enjoy his criticisms of her dull routines, his need to escape from her control over him. It made it easier not to care if he introduced me to her.

But the story about living on the wharf in the fishing shack, that was going a little too far! And she bought it—proof just how little she knows about anyone beyond her garden.

The shack I call home was built 150 years ago by Italian fishermen. Cured by fish blood and gull guano, it's one of three in a row at the end of the public pier. The stilts that hold them came from the same stand of trees that built the masts for Champlain's sails back in the sixteen hundreds.

I saw the weathered trio in at least a century of American paintings: Fitz Hugh Lane, Edward Hopper, Winslow Homer and God knows who else. Pop thought it would help me own the beauty of the harbor if I were exposed to as many aspects of it as possible. "But, Sam," he said, "Remember this, no matter how many Homers or Kiplings try to explain this place, no one owns it or understands it as well as the fishermen."

Then he'd launch into one of the harbor's mythical stories and you'd think he'd lived through it himself.

It's nearly dark, now. The glow of Boston flickers along the southern horizon. Portugal lies somewhere way out there. I light the kerosene lamp and sit down at the table where today's *Gazette* lies open.

It's almost over—the summer, its festivals, wooden boat races, umpteen fireworks. Fort Winthrop's bad music no longer spills over the water from the bandstand. The paper is focusing on the candidates for the upcoming elections. Pretty soon the whale boats will be calling it quits and the boys will be making their annual treks down to Key West. There's a photo of Marino's Marina. They're hauling up sailboats daily. Most of the summer lobstermen are gone. It's good when they leave. Seems more down-home to those who hang around 'til Thanksgiving or see it through winter, when lobsters are at their best.

I'm cold. I should have known damp sweats wouldn't work.

There it is again, Nial's name in bold type. Yet another newspaper article about him. They're relentless. It says his estate is in probate court. It's held up on account of back taxes and settlements on the part of his company's debts. His real estate holdings are under investigation, and the banks are defending the huge loans they'd sent his way. I wonder what all that means to the Lady Guenivere? Can she take over? Does she know anything about her husband's work?

Tim hadn't thought much about it, that was for sure. It was as if he and his mother lived at his father's feet. As if both of them were born to be cared for by the great Nial Townsend. They just bought what they needed, ate their steak tartar, and picked up tickets for the next cruise, the next concert or tennis match.

Shit. This is a ridiculous rag of a newspaper! I can't even read to the end of an article. The news seems empty and untrue since Nial disappeared. I can't blame Gwen Townsend for hating the Townsend stories. They make Nial sound like a runaway thief. After all he did for the town, too.

I was probably rude to her, a know-it-all, no better than she is. At least I take the advice I offer. They're the same words I tell myself, *let go and move on; healing only comes when you're open to it.* I'm trying to trust the Goddess, the ebb and the flow. But I'm still searching for something beyond belief, for the knowing beyond knowing. Does a person have to die before she gets it?

The Pultzgratz is coming in. The damn size of her sets things rocking and rolling. Her huge motor rattles these pilings and walls, but they've endured far worse threats. I run to catch the broken crates and tool boxes reverberatiing in a noisy shuffle, but the cardboard box from Frankie's Liquors stays in place. That's our makeshift library of magazines and discarded paperbacks which always holds a wide range of reading materials—anything from *Build Your Own Poop Deck* to *Summerhill.* Outside the door, there's a tub of nets wants attention. Maybe it will do me a favor and wriggle right into the sea.

This room has changed little over time. A table and four chairs sit between two salt-encrusted windows. I have no idea how many years they've been there, but I remember nothing else. On the side wall, there's a moldy stained mattress on a wire spring metal bed frame that I've draped with comforters and pillows to resemble a couch. Resting on some old lobster pots are a few kerosene lamps. Calendars hang on the walls, collector's items dating back to 1948. I light the Franklin Stove and it makes the room feel cozy. Then I lean back and watch the flames dance. I place my feet as close to the heat as I can get without igniting them.

I doubt if Gwen Townsend will ever knock on the door, but, if she does, there's no way she'll be able to appreciate the history—the long nights I sat in here, a girl among men, listening to fish stories, feeling safe and protected from any storm. So many nights, my pop, Whitey, with his pipe in his teeth and a book on his lap, would read to me until I fell asleep, my head cradled in his arm. His stories became my dreams.

The Serena Marie was Pop's boat. Twin engines, double hulled and built just up Route 133 in Ipswich. Pop used to say she was the *Unsinkable* Serena Marie. It's weird to navigate a boat with your own name on it, but I have no choice. I inherited the name with the boat. Changing the name of any boat is playing with fate.

The bed is comfortable no matter how old. I stretch myself out long and luxuriously on top of the covers that hide the ancient mattress. It is silly to stay here when I could go to Grandma's with all the creature comforts, but there is something about the shack, some reassuring quality that makes what I said to Gwen almost true. It *is* a home to me with memories, good and bad. Bad when Frankie Haskell came home early with a thousand pounds of swordfish only to find his wife fucking Harry Travaglione. Scary to see him staggering into the shack, falling over his boots and crying in his beer like that. Bad when we watched the town pier burn right into the harbor, fireboats spraying futile streams into the flames. Bad when the Jenny McGee didn't come home, or the Andrea Gale or the Judith Marino. Bad

21

when we saw the wreaths of so many father's and sons floating to our docks. But, tonight, I want to remember the good. The good was in the arms of my father.

"Tell me about the night that I was born Poppa," I used to ask, and he would recite it like it was written in the Bible.

"On the night that you were born, we were out on Jeffrey's Bank, Thomas Haas, Frankie Haskell and me. St. Peter loaded our nets with fish, so many fish that we had to head home. The winds came up and we were pushed toward land. The Phyllis A. made a record fifteen knots that night, but when we pulled into the harbor the wind went totally still, and there was your grandma, like an old world vision, standing on the pier waving a kerosene lamp into the dark."

He would always pause here. He'd look up as if he was staring at the stars and telling it for the first time.

"I knew, as sure as I knew we had one hell of a catch, that your Momma had a little girl waiting for me. Grandma cried all the way to the hospital. She couldn't speak. I saw the moon smiling over Cape Ann and the Big Dipper and the Little Dipper and stars I'd never seen before. I thought it was as serene a night as we knew in New England."

"And then?" I'd ask.

"And then, 'Serena,' I said to Grandma. 'Serena, that's what we'll call her.' Grandma just nodded."

He made a point not to tell me that my arrival in the world cost me a mother and took the only woman he ever loved. He could no more tell me this than his own mother could speak of it. I guess he'd hoped the truth would reveal itself some day, when I was old enough to understand. He'd tried to postpone it, but I learned about it on a day when I was only eight years old.

Pops was on the bridge that afternoon, having a smoke. He had put the boat on automatic pilot. I decided to entertain myself in the cabin. I rummaged around under his berth looking for the box he had hidden, *the off limits box*. It looked like a treasure chest with its brass trim on the corners and fancy lock, and had always fascinated me... mostly because I had learned early on it held things I shouldn't see. He normally kept it on shore and hidden from sight, but when we started packing for the trip south, I saw him hide it in the blanket bin.

My fingers found it easily and I after pulled the box out of its hiding place and turned the clasp, to my surprise, it opened. Out spilled photographs, news articles and letters I'd never seen before. I saw the name Kirsten Haas Tesorerio and a picture of my mother beneath it. As always, I examined her photograph looking for signs of myself. Then I heard something and saw my father's yellow boots on the top step coming down the ladder into the hold. I tucked the article into my shirt pocket, buttoned it down, and shoved the box back into the bin where it belonged. He didn't notice.

We moored the boat late in the afternoon in Jamestown Harbor. The new Navy aircraft carrier, Enterprise, was in port at Quonset Point. The waters around the ship were busy with sightseers but the sea was calm and the air warm for that time of year.

"A boat knows its own name and lives up to it as best it can," he said. "This Enterprise is named after the most decorated ship in WW II, which was named after the five Enterprises that preceded it—the first being back in the American Revolution. But, I hate to think what this monster can do," he said. "She's got enough nuclear warheads to blow up China." He pointed toward land. "Come on, Sam. Let's hit the beach and walk the streets where history was made!"

With our backs to Quonset Point, we headed toward the crowded waters of Newport, motored around Goat Island and tied up alongside Bannister's Wharf. The smell of clam cakes navigated us to one of the few stands still open. We bought a baker's dozen and ate them at a picnic table while a gadzillion gnats began eating us.

Afterwards, he took me for a walk from Washington Square up to the Old Colony House and over the cobblestones of Touro Street. Our first stop was a small white building that looked like most of New England's early churches. This one had a date on it. 1763. "The first temple in America, built way back in 1763," Pop said. "Oh, Jesus, look at that!"

"What's that?"

"It's a swastika, a hate symbol. It just doesn't go away."

"But they can paint it away, can't they, Pop?"

"There's some things you can't erase, Sam."

Our next stop was the Quaker Meeting House. We went inside and I didn't want to say it, but it didn't impress me much. I liked St. Ann's church better, with its dark corners, and niches for gilded saints. I loved the gold on the walls behind the altar, and outside, a roof that sparkled like a second sun. I loved the other Catholic church, the Portuguese church where my friend Teresa went, just as much. There, the Blessed Mother looked out above the harbor, hugging a boat instead of a baby, bright blue domes on either side marked her spot. We didn't go there often because Grandma said it was hard enough for her to be an Irish woman in an Italian neighborhood, never mind the Portuguese on the other side of town.

I loved that day, holding hands with Pop on the old streets of Newport, him going on about religions and war and making them seem one and the same. He said things like, "Right and might lead to *catastrophe*."

I remember writing that word in my journal. *cat has trophy*. "Religion makes fools of us..." he said.

I didn't point out we were Catholic, or that Grandma was trying to turn me into a nun.

His hand squeezed mine as we explored the hilly narrow roads and he talked about Americans who had walked there first. He told me stories about families from the Vanderbilts to the Kennedys. I listened to every word from his mouth as though he was God Himself, the true wise one.

Pop especially loved the structure of language. I do, too. It's no wonder I didn't think like other kids. Pop encouraged this. The boys on the pier talked like their fathers, and, according to Pop, their fathers had no respect for the English language. He said they were perfectly happy breaking down what took twenty thousand years to build.

I suppose this contributed to the way I performed in dancing school where I heard my own music and did my own choreography. I had learned to think for myself. It would explain why the teacher gave me a solo in the recital. Of course, Grandma insisted it was because I was best.

I'll never forget how, on the night of the dance recital, Pop sat right in the front row, sitting taller and prouder than anyone else. He clapped so loudly when I finished the dance, I ran off the stage with my ears as red as the nail polish Grandma Bridgit had put on my fingernails.

They probably sent me to dancing school to turn me into a girl. Grandma hated that my nickname, among Pop's fishermen friends, was Sam. She said Serena was a beautiful name and suited me much better. She must have been worried about my tomboy tendencies because she would make an event out of buying me dresses for Sundays and festivals. Silly dresses with ruffles and bows that I hated. Every now and then, she would scold Pop and tell him I had to be dressed like a girl even if I didn't like it, and I didn't. Well, except for Holy Communion and the white dress and veil with a crown of flowers. Then, I might as well have been Mary herself. It was okay to be a girl in a magical dress at a magical altar on a magical day.

Getting there and sitting through catechism classes had not been easy. It didn't matter that I knew history, loved Tolkein and C.S. Lewis, or that I could tie a line, cut a wave and recite a litany of Italian cuss words. Father Francis wasn't much interested in these facts, but it made a difference to me. I refused to pretend to be a sweet little thing in catechism class when I knew I could hold my own in a man's world.

Those overtaught parochial school girls had so little imagination, they thought to covet was a sin. I was a coveter from way back, and refused to be ashamed of it. I wanted to be as a smart as Pop and as strong. I wanted to swim like Shirley Babashoff and win the gold and then grow up to be as beautiful as Gwen Townsend.

I was a girl watcher, fascinated by the ones who hung out on the boulevard skirting the harbor, girls who knew lots about hair, giggles and wiggles and could walk normally in a pair of too-tight jeans. From a distance I wondered how I could possibly be like them, especially when Pop's friends referred to them as Twats and Cunts.

The day I found out my mother died giving birth to me, I understood that I came into the world at a high cost. From then on, I figured it was my job to make it up to Pop. He tried hard to be a father and a mother, and Grandma did her best, too, but she was *a bit daft* (Pop's words) and strange about Mary and the saints. It was as if they sat at the table with us. She walked and talked to them and wanted no less from me. Her idea of death was to be blessed by the angels and carried home, being spared the *cruelties* of earth.

Pop would tease her. "What a beautiful table you've set, Ma. Are Jesus, Mary and Joseph comin' ta dinner tonight?"

"Go on with ya' now," she'd say. "You'd best be getting on yer knees to thank St. Peter for yer bounty, taint right to make fun o' yer old Ma."

He said I should try to understand that she came from the world of fairies and sprites, with the saints just more of the same.

Once, she made me wash my mouth out with soap because I said *geez*. "It's short fer Jesus and you'll not take his name in vain in front of yer Grandmother, young lady," she scolded.

Whenever Pop was gone, she'd haul me off to church where we'd light candles and say rosaries. I tried my best to make her happy and didn't really have bad feelings about the nuns or the priests, but Pop would get angry and puffed up if I told him where we went and what was said. So, I didn't tell him the part where Father Francis told me my soul would go to purgatory and I'd not be seeing my poor dead mother in Heaven if I didn't pay closer attention to my lessons.

I prayed to be smart and tried to remember to memorize the Catechism. I talked to my mother because I knew she was in Heaven watching, making sure Pop and I were all right. She told me I should stick close to him; he was my real father, not Father Francis. I didn't need anyone to tell me Sister Agnes wasn't my real sister, either. She used to pull at my ears when I was looking out the window at the clouds piling up on the sea. I hated the sound of her ruler clicking as she walked up and down the aisles.

About this time, I decided not to go to school any more. Quitting school at age eight is not easy. The only way I could get away with it was to get sick, so I did. I had stomach aches, headaches, sore throats and dizzy spells. I was sick so often that Dr. Bomson made me stop eating certain foods and took blood samples, ran urine tests and all the rest. He finally gave my illness a name. Looking deep into my throat, he said, "I suspect we have a case of school phobia, here." I got real scared until Pop explained it meant I didn't want to go to school.

It was true! It amazed me! Dr. Bomson could see how much I didn't want to go to school by looking in my throat. I wondered if he could tell I wanted to go fishing with Pop, instead. I already knew how to read and write, knew my numbers and more science than Sister Katherine ever would. I told Pop he should be my teacher and then I could go to Florida with him and live on the Serena Marie all year.

Pop and Grandma fought it out in front of me. She said the ocean was no place for a young girl to spend her days. He said the ocean was a perfect place for any young person to be; it was the good Lord's schoolroom.

She said I should be living with her.

He said he was going to try home schooling for a year.

She said that he would have me a heathen before the year was out.

I was smart enough to say exactly nothing. Truth was, I was well on my way to being a heathen already. And as soon as Pop won the right to home school me, I forgot to be sick.

He loved teaching and I loved learning. We studied wind and weather, maps and great books. He read poetry to me, then I wrote poems to him. It wasn't long before I learned how to use the sextant and operate the ham radio. We got a computer and spent a lot of money on computer programs. It was much more fun than school had ever been. I learned the world in little pieces attached to the places we visited and the people we met. By the next spring, I had to prove he was able to home school me and my journals became evidence of ways he found to bring history to life. His teaching proved to be more than a fun way for us to talk, because I ended up making top scores on the achievement tests, although the grades didn't really matter to either if us.

I could take better care of Pop, too. We lived in Massachusetts in the summer and Florida in the winter. The best part was, I didn't have to worry about the long stretches when I used to have to live with Grandma. It worked better when my time with her lasted just a few days here and there.

My other grandmother, Grandma Haas, didn't like us. She told everyone Whitey Tesorerio (my pop) was responsible for ending all her dreams--that he had stolen her little girl and she was not interested in raising his. She didn't want anything to do with me, and when we met on the street, it seemed like meeting someone I hardly knew. Pop referred to her as a mean old hag; he said my mom had been grateful to get out of her house. I wished we could become friends because I wanted to know more about my mother, but it wasn't going to happen. Grandma Haas remained as cold and as separate as Finland.

It was my luck that Timothy Townsend became my friend and helped me discover my female self. I was only thirteen when he and his dad puttered up to me in their Boston Whaler and asked if I wanted a lift. "No way, I'll race you to the far side of the island," I said—forever the jock.

"What have we here, a mermaid?" his father asked. "Better tell me your name so I can identify you for the Coast Guard when they scoop you up!"

"Sam Tesorerio," I yelled over his motor. "Watch for it in the next Olympics!"

They actually did show up on the island. I made a joke of it and asked what had taken them so long. We spent hours that day looking for beach glass and talking about things like striped bass and battles we had heard about, legendary and real, with bluefish. We gave awards in special categories to sea critters we knew. The starfish won for Most Boring. Tim nominated the sea squirt for the Most Pathetic. I'd never known about the sea squirt until he told me how it wanders the sea searching for just the right hunk of coral. But, once it finds the perfect one, it plants itself, loses its nervous system and, gross as it is, eats its own brain.

Tim and I were connected to one another as easily as we were to the water world we grew up in.

"You know what?" I asked him on the way home.

"Speak. You little squirt. What?"

"I hate the taste of lobster!"

We both laughed.

It was a weird confession since lobster was my lifeline. I had more to confess, but something in me reserved certain facts. I couldn't tell him I'd been a Townsend stalker since I was too young to read, and I would never have told him I saw him in a bib when he was at least nine years old, or that I dreamed I was at the same table and refused to eat.

The summer of the first kiss came a year later, when I was fourteen. Everything changed then. Tim was home for summer vacation from Endfield, a prep school on the western side of the state, and I was preparing to go to public high school with the Townies. I was scared to death. Pop and I went to the school and all I saw were bundles of kids attached to one another like mussels on rope. I couldn't see myself walking in the front doors or making conversation between classes. I dreaded having to go on the lunch line and sit at a table with kids I didn't know. I didn't have the right clothes. I was too tall. My hair was too red and hopelessly curly. I didn't know their music, their language, their attitudes. I couldn't do it. I couldn't.

"Tesorerios don't say can't," Pop said.

It was a hot day, early in June, when I saw Tim, about a foot taller than when I'd seen him last, looking as if he had been stretched from either end like salt water taffy. He was waving to me from the dock. "Hey, you have anything that will feed five on board?"

"How about ham sandwiches?" I yelled, squinting at him from the bowsprit. "Some people out there are catching stripers but it isn't us, and the blues aren't running yet."

"How many lobsters have you got?"

"Four!"

"How big?" he asked, starting to scratch everything but his butt.

"One-and-a-half to two-pounders. The shells are a little soft, but they're fresh and should be delicious."

"Hey, Sam, it is you, isn't it? The little squirt?"

"Sam, yes."

I wondered what was wrong with him? He seemed so distracted.

"Well, hey, where did you come from?"

"You know I'm always here, I'm the First Mate. Neptune's daughter."

"The Serena Marie?" he said, looking at the boat as if he'd never seen it before. "Oh, yeah, sure. This is your boat."

"My father's."

"Whitey is your dad? Man, sure! I forgot. Right."

He was acting very strangely. I thought it could have been because he was in a hurry, but he stayed put.

"Sam, you're the Sam of the Penny Loaf Island, right?"

"A few minutes ago I was."

"Yeah, but you've changed a lot, and you, well, you..." he shifted his weight from one foot to the other, got distracted by some boat setting anchor, "You look different," he said.

27

It was true. My legs had stretched to a thiry-three inch inseam. I looked at his elastic arms and legs and thought how he had changed, too; he'd become a wire re-creation of his father.

"How we grow, right?" he said.

"I guess."

"Want to take a moonlight cruise over to the island some night?" he asked. Then not waiting for my answer added, "I mean, like, how about tonight?"

I'd never been alone with a boy and the idea of a date was not in my mind. Dates were about dressing up and going somewhere, about dances and parties and things that I hoped would somehow become real. But so far, they had nothing to do with me.

That evening when Pop went into town, Tim motored out to my end of the wharf and we began our adventure.

It was my first trip to Penny Loaf Island at night. We were surrounded with moonglow and a breathless kind of quiet, only the sound of slapping surf. We sat for a long time listening. Then he started to talk. He told me how he had to take a job at the Yacht Club for the summer or he'd have become his mother's slave.

"Tim, could you get those draperies down? Tim, would you just move those bushes in the side yard to the front?" he mimicked. It was always something, he said. "Tim, why don't you get a haircut? You aren't trying to look like a punk star, are you?" She even wanted to control his social life. "Cora's niece is visiting; why don't you take her to the movies?" She drove him crazy.

I told him I wouldn't mind having a mother to drive me crazy.

"Did your folks get divorced?" he asked.

"No. My mother died during childbirth."

"Oh. Shit. I'm sorry. Every one at my school has a couple of sets of parents. I just figured..."

"I found the obituary in Pop's stuff when I was eight years old. It was a combination of a car accident and childbirth. The guy who hit my mother was drunk and, to make matters worse, he was my uncle."

I couldn't believe I was telling him the family secrets, but I went on anyway. "Whitey sued him and he went on trial for drunk driving. I guess it pretty much messed up my uncle's entire life. It's something that's kept my family angry and separated ever since."

"Man! That's tough. Must have hurt your father big time, too. I mean your mom dying and all."

"Pop's hair turned pure white when Kirsten died. That's when everyone started calling him Whitey. He never talks to me about it, though."

Tim kept his eyes on his toes while I spoke. And even though he wasn't looking at me, I figured he was listening. "Whenever I ask Grandma to talk about my mother or tell me about her and my father, she makes it sound like a love story. She wants me to believe Kirsten and my father were the perfect couple. She says my mother loved me so much that when she gave out her last breath, a lucky star appeared above my head and it has been there ever since. Grandma's Irish. *Full of the Blarney*, Pop says. She's a nice lady, but, lately, I don't know, I would give anything to have a mom around. A girl needs a mom now and then."

"Yeah, I guess," Tim said. "Like it would be tough for a guy not to have a dad."

His mind seemed to go somewhere else. I chose to be quiet, too. Our breath became part of the sea music and I thought that maybe this was what it felt like to be a teenager, tingly and happy. A little nervous about what might happen next. All I knew about sex was what I'd seen in movies and had read in novels and magazines, and in that book Teresa found in her mother's bedroom.

Teresa was my best friend. I met her because she lived next door to Grandma's condo. Teresa and I confessed everything to each other which, despite our small lives, managed to fill dozens upon dozens of hours. Superstitions and suspicions ruled our heads, and we spent a lot of energy trying to find out what other people knew. We identified words like douche bag, cocksucker, phallic and cunnilingus. Finding definitions made us laugh and gag with disgust at the same time. I couldn't see Teresa as much as I wanted to, but knowing her helped me face going to the high school. And Grandma liked her because she was named after one of her favorite saints, the one with the stigmata. I guess to Grandma, blood was proof of goodness.

When the day came that I bled and had to acknowledge my own sex, I was at Grandma's house. She didn't have any sanitary napkins and was at church, so I called Teresa who had been menstruating since she was eleven. I told her I had to go to the store.

"For what?" she asked.

I said, "You know."

She didn't know but she came immediately because that was how it was with us. I told her my news and we set out on our quest. We had to pass Al the Barber's storefront. Everyone knew Al the Barber was a pervert. We never walked by his shop until his eyes were directed at the back of the store, then we'd race past, relieved each time that we'd escaped his scrutiny. At Seaman's Café, we stopped and got a Coke. I wondered if Morris Seaman could tell I was changed. I was painfully aware of the wad of tissues stuck between my legs.

We crossed Rogers Street where remnants of the trolley tracks had escaped layers of blacktop. I tripped and felt the wad loosen between my legs. I prayed the elastic on my panties would hold as I took tiny tight steps into the drugstore.

Teresa and I looked up and down the aisles for people we might know, then faced the shelves offering pastel boxes with too many names and sizes. Teresa told me virgins used pads instead of plungers, and I had to ask which ones would be right for me. Was I a *Light Day*, a *Maxi*, *Extra-long*, *Scented* or *Plain*? Just as she was going to tell me, Tiny Haskell walked in

29

and we stuck our heads into the shelving for cover. From there, we crawled, then scrambled to the door and made our way back out onto the street. I preferred waiting for Grandma to come home than let Tiny know I was a girl who bled.

If I'd had a mother, I might have been ready. It might have been a happier moment. But it was mostly mortifying instead.

If I'd had a mother I could have told her about Tim, and told her how warm it was when he kissed me on the lips, and how exciting it was and different from my father's kisses or any kiss I'd ever dreamed of. In fact, even though Tim's first kiss seemed more like a question, we kissed again and again, and each time I let my lips stay longer and more attached. I loved kissing him. But Bridget would never have understood.

The night of the first kiss I took back my name. From then on I called myself Serena and, for a while, I felt like a princess ordained by her prince. I guess that was wishful thinking.

Five

Gwen

We are in the midst of Indian Summer, that last warm breath which makes it easy to deny what's to follow. The deck's wood is warm from the sun. My flower pots really should be put indoors before a frost cracks them. The harbor is still wearing its summer blues. A hand grabs my heart when I see Nial, with a summer tan, down on the beach: His old crushed khaki hat on his head. He's waving to me and I'm frozen, until I focus more sharply, and realize it isn't Nial at all. It's our neighbor, Ted Peterson. Strange, I have never noticed how much alike they look.

"Gwen Townsend, come on down from your tower and keep me company. How about a quickie around the harbor?" he calls.

"Thanks, Ted, maybe another time."

"I've got crab salad sandwiches and a bottle of Merlot."

I know Ted is trying to get me out of the house, and he's probably just as lonely as I am, his wife having left him last February. Come to think of it, I haven't seen him but once or twice since Nial's plane went down.

"Come down from your tower and join the world, Mrs. Townsend," he calls again. "It's a beautiful night and the tide's high!"

He is a known entity. A familiar man.

I leave the deck and join him below.

My unwashed hair is caught in a loose knot and my clothes are a hodgepodge—an old lamb's wool sweater, tired chinos and well-worn boat shoes. But I am seaworthy.

We climb aboard his Creelock. It's a forty-five-foot beauty. As I start to untie the lines, Ted looks over my shoulder and gives a thumbs up to someone behind me.

I turn and see Serena coming toward us. She wears her father's shirt, no doubt, tied at her waist. Her arms are held behind her as she walks, magnifying her chest soaked from sea spray. A wet t-shirt betrays any modesty she may wish to pretend. It is apparent, even to me, how these founts of womanhood overwhelm the mannish pants below. I blush at her easy sexuality.

"Hey, Serena, did you bring us some lobster after all?"

Ted asks.

She was pleased to see him. Was she a friend of his?

"You know, for Neptune's daughter, I shouldn't have had so much trouble getting these beauties," she says, revealing the two squiggling lobsters she'd hidden behind her back.

"Well, look what we have here. These ought to make a pot of steam in the hold worth the effort. I'm glad you're still here."

"I never leave before the end of hurricane season, you know that. I don't trust the Goddess *that* much," she smiles.

Ted laughs as if she has just made an extraordinarily funny joke. Her comment is simply not that amusing, but he's self-conscious. Like a school boy, perhaps. I surmise his behavior is triggered by her nipples standing hard in the wet shirt.

"Of course you know Gwen Townsend, here?" he asks, apparently remembering my presence.

"We're old friends aren't we Mrs. Townsend?" Serena says. Her voice has a conspiratorial nature to it.

Ted's eyes turn to me. They look too blue and his cosmetic smile is wrapped around too many teeth. I hear a visceral alarm sounding.

"We're about to take a quick cruise around the island," he explains. "Want to come along?"

Serena answers quickly, "Not tonight, got a hot date with a new book. Enjoy!"

Who is this woman, I wonder.

We sail around the harbor, then past the jetty into the open sea. Looking back at the city, with its spires and old world domes, I marvel at the familiar beauty of Granite Shores, but I am uncomfortably aware that I am operating in uncharted territory. I have not gone anywhere alone with a man, other than my husband, for almost thirty years. I don't know whether Ted considers himself a friend or a suitor. He must realize I am not ready for anything. As far as I'm concerned, Nial is alive and coming back to me. But, it's ironic that Ted looks so much like Nial. His broad shoulders, even the way he stands at the wheel. I am thinking too much. This could be my last moonlight sail if I don't stop.

The past three months I've put on a good front. I refused to play widow. When sad faces looked at mine and tried to acknowledge my grief, I stayed strong and positive. I told myself, when Nial's found, all that sadness will be embarrassing in retrospect. I tried to ease the concern of others. It was the terror and confusion of the unknown I was willing to bury, not Nial.

When the calls and cards stopped coming and the gossip prevailed, I went somewhere inside, where it was much darker and more bizarre than my worst dreams. I became obsessed with things. One day it would be solitaire, another polishing silver, another reading the Bible or eating chocolates, and I don't mean one or two chocolates—I ate as many as I wanted. It was obscene. I gave myself permission to watch family movies, over and over again. I played and replayed reels of my little girl baby and her proud parents, and then the films of the Christenings, Sabrina's then Tim's. Breaking a bottle of Seltzer water on the bow of Tim's whaler, dubbing it *The Avenger*, and Mother and Father always looking like the perfect grandparents, smiling and smiling for every frame. One could believe we had no bad days; we had never lost a baby we hardly got to know; had money enough to match our ideals; and a marriage that could never grow stale. I watched us at the beach. Nial so agile and boyish, no frowns or deep crevices in his forehead. Myself, silly with joy, tickling Tim, running barefoot in seafoam; Nial lifting me like a bride and taking us both under.

I reran our travel films. Laughed at the one we took in Germany aboard the ferry on the Rhine—that covey of Japanese, so many blackbirds in a row, lined up behind us taking their own photographs. Dusseldorf and Baden-Baden, pristine, ancient cities with curtained windows that sparkled along tidy streets. I remembered the morning we ordered breakfast in fractured German and got a bowl of mayonnaise and two raw eggs. Nial insisted the waiters did it on purpose because we were Americans.

Ted moors at Brace's Cove. A young couple on the beach is watching him drop anchor. I see them embrace and separate. She runs away and he chases her. Their laughter ripples over the water and covers me with a violet veil. I can hardly see them as they tumble across the wet sand.

My hand finds comfort in the smoothness of the teak rail. Such a sleek craft he has. When he emerges from the hole, he hands me a glass of wine and some crackers and cheese. I hear how his son has been working at the Yacht Club for the summer and how much closer they have become. I remember when Tim did the same. I can't speak about my son in the face of losing him to a strange desert, a humanly uninhabitable place meant for scorpions and diamondbacks.

"Tim has stopped writing," is all I venture as a response to Ted's news. What I can't say is that after Nial's plane went down, I tried to wrap myself up with Tim but he wouldn't let me. He was too distracted and unable to handle his own grief. "*I don't want to talk about it anymore! Okay?*" he yelled at me one day when I began to rerun the events of the day Nial left. Then I knew we could be no comfort for one another. He was too angry, the poor boy. So angry. I'm hurt by his behavior more than worried. He's taught me grief is impossible to share.

Sometimes I watch the oldies from Hollywood. I watched Doris Day for an entire week, trying to find every film she ever made. Then it was Ingrid and Bogie saying goodbye at the Casablanca Airport, time and again. I discovered that the more hopelessly tragic the movie, the more I loved it. *On the Waterfront, Splendor in the Grass, Les Miserables.*

Many days I didn't bother to dress. I went about making little messes around the house instead. Pulled out piles of newspapers and magazines to sort. Found clothes that needed a button, a tuck here or there, an impossible stain to remove. I searched for things that would require attention the following day.

I am stricken at the strangest moments: the school bus rattling down the street, a child delivering newspapers. The other day my car was low on gas and I burst into tears.

Songs can hurt. Last night WGBH played *Blue Moon* as I maneuvered somewhere between the shower and the bed. It evoked smoky sounds in a smoky room, dark red leather seats against tacky oak paneling, and booths where mini-jukeboxes ate quarters and played music just for us. I remembered dancing with Nial, so slow it was more like sex, a rolling of our bodies into each other, his breath in my ear, his arms and hands around me, my fingers on his neck finding little hairs to play with. How the whole length of our bodies were pressed against one another, and how I felt something hard grow, a delicious secret, keeping us on the dance floor for the next tune, and then the next. I meant to wait until we married, but that night with the scent of beer and sawdust, our chemistry delivered me to that rarified zone in the confines of his Chevrolet's backseat. For a brief phase of my life, I dropped the rules.

Ted's voice interrupts my thoughts. "You're going to have to start living again, one of these days, Gwen. It looks to me like you're pretty cloistered."

"And what have you been doing?" I ask, "Painting the town red?" I know better than to turn it on him. I should just say what's true.

"I don't know how to begin. I don't even think Nial is dead. I never felt him go."

"What do you think happened to him?" he asks.

"I'm not sure. Not sure about much these days. It's hard for me to articulate. I'm afraid of my own pathetic twaddle, feel like I'm caught in a dream."

"There are things I've been wanting to talk to you about."

Oh, this is it, he has something to tell me. I should have realized. What a ninny I am to think he was wanting my company, a sail and nothing more. My elbows are hot. I can feel splotches on my neck, in my eyes. I'm anxious, frightened, by what? More bad news? Nothing in his voice gives me reason.

"Then speak!" I cry.

Could I hurt any more? Are there worse secrets than whether or my husband is alive or dead? I can hardly imagine.

"Nial talked to me. Confided that he didn't want to worry you, but personally, I think it was more than that," Ted begins.

"A wife knows when there's something to worry about."

"I think he was afraid of losing control of things in the middle of his life. He's not the first man I've known to feel that way."

"I sensed something was wrong but...."

"He denied the signs for a long time. Too long. The rope and cordage industry went through a total change. He knew hemp was out and plastic in, but what he didn't know was how the big guys, Dupont and the foreign markets would take over the industry. Suddenly, he became a very small fish in a big pond. You know Nial didn't like that idea."

"He didn't talk to me about that."

"I think he thought he could work it out."

I can't ask Ted the questions I have to ask myself. Was it because I cherished our structure too much or made too many assumptions? We didn't need his money. I had my own money, in trust funds I rarely touched. But, of course, Nial knew that. We would have been all right no matter what happened to the business. He was prideful, had never approached me for money, never even hinted at the fact he needed financial help. Perhaps it

34

was just our history. I'd been excluded from that end of our lives from the beginning. As far as both of us were concerned, my job was relegated to the children, the house and our social calendar. It created a kind of equanimity.

"The papers, the lawyers, they imply something underhanded," I say.

"Screw them. Nothing was underhanded. No more so than any other entrepreneurial deal these past few years. Nial was awarded some big loans, and the banks were probably wrong to have let him have them. But money has been flowing easily lately; put out your hand and someone will fill it."

"You actually think Nial put out his hand?"

"Yes. I know he did."

Ted knew more than I did apparently.

"Where is the money?"

"I don't know. That's part of the problem."

"Am I obligated to pay the banks back?"

"It depends on the agreement. The business is probably the collateral. But it could be the house as well. There may be a postmortem clause. Haven't your lawyers talked to you?"

"Yes, but the terms are complicated and the language exhausts me. Would you help? Actually sit with me when I meet with the lawyers again. I nod and agree to everything they say, but I can't discern the basic facts of the situation."

"I'm not adverse to doing that."

Ted Peterson, neighbor, friend and now advisor. I am grateful, almost happy in the moment, just to lean on him.

We watch the sun set and the full moon rise. The harvest moon, orange as a pumpkin, leaves the land to darkness while it turns the sea gold. Ted brings me a blanket and wraps me in it. Then he sits near me and tucks me into his shoulder and arm. I feel comfortable. The lights of Boston glow on the western horizon and gulls are making their last rounds for the evening. The beach is empty now. The lovers must have found a less public playground. Stars ignite the sky. We are like an old couple, wrapped in our private thoughts. When he kisses me, it feels tentative at best. I guess I need more than a kiss to see if I can really feel, to know if there are kisses left inside me. I experience a warm pleasure but not what I once had. I move away, just enough not to offend. His nervousness on the pier comes to mind.

"That girl, Serena," I say.

"Are you trying to plant another woman between us?"

"Oh no. I just thought, I think..."

"She's something, isn't she?" he says, obviously relieved at my retreat.

"I've watched her grow up. Knew her father, Whitey. You must have known him too?" he asks.

"No. No, I didn't," I have to admit.

"He was quite a guy. Went to Boston University with me for a year, full academic scholarship mind you, and then fell out of his head in love with this beach beauty he met during the summer, Kirsten. I knew her family. Finns. He dropped out of school to marry her and sure enough they shipped him off to Vietnam. But she got pregnant and it kept them from extending his tour of duty. According to him, Serena probably saved his life."

"The irony was she killed her mother. No. Not really. Kirsten was hit by a car, had the baby that night and died in childbirth. It wasn't Serena that killed her; it was Old Man Haas, her drunk of an uncle. He was tried and found guilty of drunk driving. Only did time for a few years. You know him. He drives the cab that's at the train station any hour of the day. He's made his living driving after being found guilty of vehicular homicide; ironic isn't it? The world's a strange place."

Now that Ted mentions it, I do know him. Well, not exactly. What interests me most is that Serena told me the truth. She has obviously been a part of the wharf for twenty years and I have no memory of laying eyes on her.

"She's an interesting girl isn't she?" I ask.

"Ha!" he laughs. "She doesn't have to be. You could just prop her up and look at her all day. That would be enough."

"Why you dirty old man!" I nudge him with my elbow in his side.

"Serena and I met one day when I was out on the wharf looking for some fresh fish and she ran up behind me, threw her whole luscious self into me and kissed my neck. She was embarrassed, more embarrassed than me, thought I was someone else, she said. We've bantered about it ever since."

"Must have been quite a hug," I say, retreating into my head.

"Well, I wasn't exactly talking about a father/daughter hug, I can tell you that; it was more like a horny toad getting kissed by a princess."

Another difference between men and women. I would hardly feel the same way being kissed by a young man in a wet T-shirt. Or would I? What turned my mind into such a rule book? Years of programming? Years of restraint? All of my life has been about platitudes. Mind your own garden. Cleanliness is next to Godliness. Smile and the world smiles with you. Only cloth napkins. Never, never paper flowers. Who named the world? Why have I reduced it to such trivia? Does a water lily have to know its name? How many limits we place on ourselves just in the naming!

I think about Tim and realize that somehow my son has helped me feel old. He is intent on distancing himself, contrary in every opinion. I once believed we would be friends by the time he was in his twenties, but the truth is, we have very little in common right now. To be his mother is not enough to bridge the differences, it seems.

"You know, you're a beautiful woman," says Ted.

I wonder who he sees. Is it the slim line of a woman I used to be, or the rounder version I've become? I've known Ted for, what, it must be twenty-five years now. He and Helene moved next door soon after Nial and I married. They had lived in the apartment over the garage at first, then bought the main house from the Harveys when they moved to Florida. Nial has known Ted since high school.

When Helene ran off with Henry Talmadge, her boss, I thought Ted might disappear from humiliation or hunger. I don't think he had ever cooked a meal in his life. But, really, I didn't consider him much; I was too muddled and involved in my own life.

I manage a thank you.

"I always thought Nial got the pick of the litter," he says.

Pick of the litter? I imagine he means dogs, or could he be thinking kittens, soft things for petting. I am not ready for this.

We sail back to the wharf in a blue black sea rippled with moonlight. The beauty escapes me. I just want to get home and sleep.

When we approach the dock, I see Serena's kerosene lamp is burning. I offer a breezy butterfly kiss to Ted, say goodnight, and head her way. I suddenly want to talk; ask her about Tim, find out if she knows this errant son of mine.

I walk to the other side of the pier. Past splayed nets and rusting barrels. The shack is without paint except for the peeling condition of a door that must have once been red. I knock. She responds as if I do so on a regular basis.

"Come in!" she calls, and I enter. The place is barren. Not a sign of beauty, no kitchen, no bath. Of course, she doesn't live here. It is a fish house if there ever was one. How could I have taken her seriously?

She doesn't move from her nest on the cot.

"Have a seat," she says.

I walk over to sit in an old Laz-a-Boy chair, a true indicator of the decline of taste and civility, but no anachronism in this hapless place.

"How was your sunset sail?" she asks.

"Lovely," I answer. "I saw your light on and thought perhaps you wouldn't mind some company."

"I'm having trouble getting into this book. A break might help."

"What are you reading?" I ask.

"*My Mother/Myself*. It's not easy. Maybe it's irrelevant."

"Friday's book? It sounded interesting. It was featured in the *Times, Book Review*."

I don't mention the obvious, that it is an unlikely selection for a girl with no mother.

"What prompted your choice?" I ask.

"I've always been looking for evidence that I'm my mother's daughter. I grew up trying to imagine what having a mother would be like. If we'd go shopping together, confide in each other. Whether she'd love me as much as Whitey did, or if he would have loved me as much if she were around. It only makes sense we would have had something in common. She was my portal, after all."

"Of course," I agree.

"I can't help but wonder if the ways I'm different from Pop are the ways I'm like my mother."

A girl without a mother. It would make a profound difference in a young woman's life.

"I mean, not physically. My mother had blonde hair and a tiny nose, and pale blue eyes. Very Finnish. We wouldn't look anything alike. Then again, they say people who live together start to look alike. Therefore, I'm sure it's possible that if my Mother had lived, I would have had her blonde hair and little nose."

She smiles at me. It's a remarkably lovely smile; her mouth is wide, generous. Her eyes crinkle, the black lashes meeting one another in the corners.

"Maybe not your mother's blue eyes or blonde hair, but seriously, I'm sure you would have adopted her style, or her way of speaking. Doesn't the book say something about the inevitability of all that?"

"Actually, Pop said I *do* have her smile and that my walk *is* like hers. I like to think it's true. I wish there were videos back in those days. I would love to have seen more than the pictures in Grandma's photo albums— those dumb shots with the same smile from one page to the next. Grandma said they buried her in her wedding dress. Imagine how sad that must have been! I always wanted to know more about her, but the Haases and the Tesorerios don't connect. So I have to take the Tesorerio version, which leaves out her whole life, practically."

I'd like to know the details of Serena's life, too. My guess is they would challenge the norm.

She says, "I used to try to talk to Whitey about her, but his stories became more and more just that, stories. I found newspaper clippings about the car accident, but those didn't tell me much."

"Newspapers are only interested in sensationalism. They are glorified gossip. You can't rely on newspapers for the facts," I say.

She gets up, and I realize she's wearing only her panties and T-shirt. Her long tan legs take themselves to a cabinet from which she pulls two mugs and a box of tea.

"Green tea?" she asks. "It's an antioxidant."

I see her lean over and close the *Gazette*. She's obviously read the latest article.

"Fine." I reply.

Serena opens the spout of a huge water bottle under the utility sink, fills a saucepan, then plugs in the hot plate that rests on the shelf by the sink.

"From the time I was very small, I believed I had a special angel taking care of me. Of course, there have been just as many times when I've wondered where the hell she is."

"Yes. Well, of course. In my present status I am listening for angels, too, but none have shown up yet."

"Maybe you aren't listening carefully enough," she suggests.

38

The truth is, I am not listening for angels at all; I don't believe in winged ghosts.

"Sometimes, I hate to say it, but I think it was better not to know my mother. It doesn't hurt as much when you don't know someone. Plus, a made-up mom is perfect. She would never love anyone as much as she loved me. We would never argue or hurt each other."

"Tell me about your father," I ask.

"Pop was pretty consistently a great father even though he was dark sometimes, and spent long periods inside his head. He was a brain. The guys called him the professor."

"You must have been very close."

"After Whitey died, I felt like I died too. I actually couldn't feel my arms and legs one day, and went to the doctor because I thought I had some horrible paralysis. She said I was empathizing with Pop. I was imagining death. Damn, if I wasn't making something worse out of what was bad enough."

Can she possibly know my paralysis? I think as I walk over to the window.

The harbor's perspective is so different from the shack, the water churning beneath, the shore jagged and unfriendly. Penny Loaf Light is as invasive as a blinking neon sign.

"Pop used to say there's almost always something worse than what you get. That's why Pop was a survivor, that's how he did it. I practiced thinking of something worse from the time I was a kid. The only thing I could think of, worse than his dying, was his being helpless and dying a painful, slow death."

I understand this. Better than I want to believe. I have dreamed of Nial lying on a beach and calling for me; sometimes I imagine his body being eaten by sharks, impaled on rocks, caught in fish lines unable to get out. One night, I dreamed he was just a head and a torso under a tarp. I lifted it up and found him covered with maggots, but still breathing. Reverend Lavender told me to repeat, "*Hope is the anchor of the soul*" to myself over and over again when I have to blot out these dreams.

But is it hope or denial? I had prepared myself for Father's death: mapped out the arrangements, made up obituaries and announcement lists, spent hours with Mother about who to notify.

Dear Mother, so tiny in her grief, could not act on the cremation my father had requested. As usual, Nial took over and fulfilled his wishes. Father's cremation was followed by a dignified memorial service. People recited their eulogies and the minister spoke of Father's contribution to society. Despite the high level of respect Father received, I noticed a voice of intimacy was missing. The lack of it made me want to go to the pulpit and say that Father smelled like Old Spice and Captain Black Tobacco; that he had had never lifted his hand or his voice to me to cause me pain; that his dresser drawers held thirty years of cards and letters from me in a little ebony box marked "Letters from Camp." I wanted to say how I loved the way he looked over his glasses when he read something of interest; how he

39

could raise one eyebrow with a dubious look at the unconventional; how he was a refined, pigheaded and intelligent man, an archetype of male power and the source of my security and well-being. He even prepared me to let him go. I wanted to say these things but speaking in public was too terrifying and these thoughts too emotional for me to say aloud.

The death with which I absolutely could not cope had come before his. It was Sabrina's death. My first-born, born on my twenty-second birthday and looking for all the world as healthy as one could hope. She did all the things babies do...all the things but live. Her fingers captivated her attention. She tried to lift her head early on. Her eyes looked for me; her ears knew my voice. She suckled at my breast like it was always meant to be hers. Her fuzzy blonde head reflected the light.

I was exhausted from her crying, that was true, but should she have been taken from me? How could I not have heard those last gasps, or recognized her need for me? What source stopped her heart, choked her tiny throat and took her breath away? Surely, it could not have been the same source that gave her life in the first place. When Dr. Bomson came and told me waking her was no longer a choice, that some strange phenomenon with an innocuous name like crib death was the villain, I would not accept it. When I wrapped her in satin and put bows on her baby shoes, dressed her in my own Christening dress which was also my mother's, I was still praying that her sweet eyes would open and we would get another chance. But I ended up embracing her little white casket with pink and white roses instead.

She was laid out like a lovely baby doll. Many people came to the funeral. I wanted them there because I needed their tears—people crying beside me, around me, with me. All of them acknowledging death was cruel and uncompromising. I was a stone until they put the first shovel of dirt on her grave. Then I began to cry.

Nial's death is not real. I have not prepared for it as I had Father's death, nor watched it coming as I am now doing with Mother. Instead I am left numb, waiting for a call or a sign that tells me what I want to hear.

"You still here?" Serena asks.

"Just thinking."

"Want sugar?"

"No. No, thank you."

Serena hands me a mug of hot tea. I have to wait for it to cool.

"I can't stop thinking about the whale," I say.

"The messenger!" she replies enthusiastically.

"It was so bizarre," we say in unison, and laugh.

"Maybe, or maybe it just takes a huge sign to get our attention," Serena says.

"You realize that something in me wants to believe this isn't just coincidence? Part of me believes we really did receive a message."

"Yes," she says, then delivers another quixotic smile.

I suspect she may know something I don't, but will hold my questions for another day.

Six

Serena

I protest to my friend Geena over the phone, trying to ignore the squawking of two black wing gulls arguing on the railing of my deck. "You don't get it. If she doesn't go, how will I ever know the truth? This is the only way I can find out if Nial is dead or alive—I've got to get her on a plane to Nicaragua!"

Geena's silence says she's through with arguing. I defend myself, regardless. "I know, I know. Who am I kidding? I suppose it doesn't matter; nothing can erase the fact that Nial and I are over and nothing will ever be the same again. It can never be made right. I get it, Geena. But...."

"If it's amnesty you're looking for," Geena says, "give it up."

Amnesty, travesty, honesty. Are all *esty* words loaded?

I put the phone in its cradle. Have I gone too far, intruding on Gwen Townsend, whose life is as messed up as mine, who doesn't have a clue as to who I am? Can I really give a damn about her? She thinks so. What good would the truth do? It gets harder for me to be honest as she comes closer. I couldn't have imagined her friendship five years ago, or even five weeks ago. I don't want to hurt her any more than I already have. She might hate me. I don't think I've ever been hated.

I thought I knew her husband and her son in a way she didn't and that it gave me an edge when it came to rescuing them. But, maybe I didn't. Maybe I don't. Who would have imagined Tim wandering in the desert to get answers about the meaning of life? I don't expect him to find any; he's no Abraham, no Jesus. He'll be a fish out of water no matter where he goes, until he gets his relationships straightened out, and that includes his relationship with his mother, his father, and who knows, maybe, me.

Tim's exodus from my world was the first domino to fall, then, after the rest went down, he was nowhere in sight. It had been a torturous break before that, because he wasn't a complete loss, just a partial one.

He used to look for me when he was alone and I would be waiting, all of me ready to offer him one more bite. For years this went on, this secret friendship that would start with words, lead to sex, and end with abandonment—which he would do as soon as his school friends showed up. For six years, I told myself we would overcome all that because we were soulmates; he just didn't realize it yet. I was sure when he found his true self, he would swoop down and scoop me up—that, in the end, no one could separate us.

I must have read this scenario in a novel. Certainly not in real life.

Whitey had seen Tim and me together over the years, although I was careful to keep our sexual experimentation far from the pier and non-

41

threatening to my father, who was always telling me men were as blind as sharks...and as dangerous.

"Pop, don't you ever think about getting married again?" I asked him once, silently dreading the day he would. I knew better than anyone, he was a man worth loving. I had seen women flirt with him, but he would ignore them, act like they weren't serious. He let his beard grow, almost never spruced up, lived in worn clothes and his pea jacket and ski hat when it got cold. The only passions I could see in his life were books and the sea.

"You're my one and only," he'd say to me then.

Attending his funeral were a few women I didn't know. They were dressed in mourning clothes. I was curious about their relationship with him. I still am, but the message I got from Pop was pretty consistent: he and I were enough for each other. He liked to say things between men and women got messy when they tried to become one, and if they took such a chance, they'd better be of the same cloth. I wondered if his wisdom resulted from his short marriage to my mother. He must have deep wounds to find her so hard to talk about. When I placed a picture of her in his hands before the wake, it was the first time I had ever seen them together.

After Whitey won the vehicular homicide case against my mother's uncle, the trial separated our two families permanently. So I made up my own version of Kirsten Haas, one that I talked to and prayed to—one that showed up in the stars and in the sun behind the clouds. This Kirsten still loved Pop and me. She wanted me to learn everything I could about the world and be a free spirit because she had not had the chance. Perhaps it was Grandma's influence that had me talking to the dead, believing in angels.

No matter what stories I invented about my Finnish mother, I was still more Tesorerio than Haas. How else could I feel? The face in the mirror proved it. I looked like my father's child, an Irish-Italian mixed breed. My love for literature and boats, for the open air—they belonged to Pop, too.

Whitey picked up on the fact that Tim and I were becoming attached to each other early in our relationship. He saw Tim hanging around the dock, asked about us talking late at night, and shook his head when he found out Tim and I went to Penny Loaf Island on the Whaler. He said I was playing with danger, that I should stay away from Tim. If it was boys I needed, he would help me meet some other guys. He said Tim was a lightweight and I deserved better. He even fixed me up with the son of a friend of his from the Keys. He had hair on his earlobes and on his knuckles. He walked erect but he thought horizontally. He was an animal. On our way home from the movies he asked if I'd like to walk on the beach. It took no time at all for him to climb on top of me, hold my arms above my head and pound away on my panties. He left me soaked with semen and told me I was hot. I was furious and scared and disgusted all at once. I couldn't have told Pop or he'd have killed him. So, I just explained I wasn't interested. Truth was, even if I began to like someone, it would never work because we were always moving on, or they were.

Anyway, the only person I wanted was Tim; we felt complete when we were together. And, I guess, like for any other teenager, Pop's disapproval made it all the more exciting. My heart would race thinking about his hands on my breasts, how my tongue in his ear made him burrow into me, soft everywhere but in the magical place between his legs. He taught me how to please him. To hold him in my lips, to wrap my legs around his backside to arch my back as he dove for my deep waters. I loved the secret codes and meeting places we made up. We were free of the clutter of family and friends from the start. I didn't know how Gwen or Nial Townsend would feel about me if they knew about us, but I imagined how far I may have been from the girl of their choice. Tim told me Gwen would occasionally bring girls home for him to meet. He said she worried that he seemed uninterested, but he never suggested I meet his mother, instead he'd say I was his real girl, his only girl, and he didn't want his mother to have anything to do with us.

Whitey and I were on our way back from the Keys shortly after my twenty-second birthday, off the coast of Red Bank, New Jersey, heading to New York Harbor. I always loved those visits we made to the Big Apple on the way north. They were my crash courses in culture. This year, we were headed to Ellis Island to see the Museum of Immigration. Pop had read about it in *Newsweek* and wanted me to see the photography exhibit of the dark side of immigration. He said we should know what the world was like when my grandparents arrived in the land of honey.

But it was not to be.

A mean April wind greeted our approach to the New York Harbor. Whitey was in the hole and I was at the wheel. I realized he'd been gone for a while and I called down to him a couple of times. When he didn't answer, I put the Serena Marie on automatic pilot and went below. I found him sandwiched between the head and the hull in a heap, curled in a fetal position, his fingers cramped like claws, his pants wound around his feet, and vomit soaking his chest.

Amidst the stench of life, I could hardly recognize death. I stretched him out, pulling him by his feet, then his arms, all the time screaming at him, "Breathe, Pop, god dammit, breathe!"

I put my ears to his heart and shook his arms looking for a sign, something to give me hope. His mouth was slack, his eyes wide open staring into a world I couldn't see. I placed my lips on his; they were cold, unresponding. I inhaled, then tried to push air into him. Nothing. I fell on his chest, listening for a sound. Nothing. I thumped on his heart. Pounded it, yelling, "Wake up, wake up." Despite my begging, my banging, I finally had no choice but to realize he was gone. I pulled his heavy head into my arms and rocked him all I could.

Cleaning him up, handling the boat, waiting for the Coast Guard to arrive, I suppose I was in shock. It took all my strength to dignify our space, eliminate the odor, move him out of the doorway into a restful position. I dressed him in a clean shirt, placed a pillow under his head so he'd be more comfortable. Then I closed his eyes and my own, and lay down next to him, my head on his cold shoulder. It was only then I realized my body was as stiff as his.

I couldn't cry then. Not with the commotion of the harbor police, the Coast Guard and the medics. It was later, once I arrived on shore and saw Grandma coming toward me with her arms reaching for mine. Her little feet running, walking toward me in their black tie shoes, her frizzy red hair, streaming like tears around her face.

We took care of each other through the months that followed, but I think a part of Grandma died with Whitey, just as some of her left when her father Jack Ryan went down, and then her husband, Salvatore. There wasn't enough of her left for me, at least not enough to keep her going much longer.

Fisherman's funerals are usually pretty much the same. The men in port will show up whether they know the fisherman or not. In Whitey's case attendance at his funeral was more than perfunctory. He had a lot of friends, many he had known since childhood. Ted Peterson was there, so were the Townsend men, Nial and Tim. I stayed with Grandma, the two of us draped in old-world black. I couldn't help but appreciate that we were surrounded by a town within a town, the fishing community. In the midst of the greatest sadness I'd ever known, love broke through, somehow, and I felt more for them than I had ever felt before. Our sea lives made it possible for us to share the grief and that sharing held me up—so I could lift Pop's funereal wreath and send it out to sea, so I could let Grandma hold on as hard as she needed, so I could avoid Tim and the pain of the distance he chose when I needed him most.

I moved into Grandma's condo and death's gray face ruled my life for days and weeks then months. I saw it on Bridget's pale lips, in her vacant eyes—heard it in every siren's wail. I smelled it in her tired furniture and the heavy air of trapped summer heat. We watched endless television shows, played rummy and gin and I prayed to die. No one and nothing interrupted my misery, as I longed for the face I didn't know well enough, the lost words that went with him--my dead king, my lost captain, my father/mother, friend. I felt horribly alone, with Grandma, with crowds on the pier, wherever I was, it didn't matter. On top of this I punished myself or was punished, (I didn't know which) with Tim's absence. His disappearance finally made me realize I had to accept the fact I could no longer compete with his privileged college friends. He was moving on and I had no fight in me. I was too numb, too tired. We were history.

It was then Nial showed up to secure my independence from his son. It wasn't intentional. I saw him as Tim's father, had never seen him as anything else, until he arrived one afternoon with two bottles of beer and an order for six lobsters. He sat on the pier in a rusted old metal chair like a great preying mantis, his knees as high as his shoulders. It was then he told me Tim was in New Hampshire doing an Outward Bound Program. He said he was not going to be back for the remainder of the summer. I told him that

I hadn't seen him all summer anyway, that my glimpses of him had only been with his college friends.

I wondered why he chose to talk to me. What did he really want to ask me? Where was he going with his conversation?

"I think he's into drugs," he said.

"What makes you think so?" I asked as casually as I could.

"The signs are there, that's all. He can't seem to graduate, for one thing."

"You clean of that stuff, Serena?" he asked directly.

I flared, "I know better, thank you." If he was going to trace the source of his son's problems to the poor fisher folk on the pier, I was going to set him straight.

"You might sit down and talk to some of those clowns from college—try Spiff or Jiff or Chip or Buff, or whatever the hell their names are. I think you'll get more help from them." I stood up and headed for the Serena Marie.

"Hey, hold on. I never meant any..."

I continued to walk away. I couldn't talk for the pain in my chest. Hot pain. He followed me, climbed on board and came into the cabin.

"Serena, I swear I didn't mean a thing by that. I don't think a woman with the tenacity and independence you have would fool around with drugs. Although it would be easy to excuse you if you did—easier than understanding Tim and his antics."

"I don't know what you're talking about," I said, still thinking he was talking about my relationship with Tim as some kind of drug conspiracy.

"I do not do drugs, Mr. Townsend. My father was death on drugs."

"Of course you don't, Serena, I never meant to suggest such a thing. I have just thought from time to time that you and Tim, well...and how terrible it must have been for you out there, when Whitey had his stroke, and now being here where it must be hard not to think about him every day."

"Shit. Don't make me cry, Mr. Townsend. Damn, I am not going to cry, I am as dry as..." I tried, but my eyes gave in to their own water.

He put his arms around me and I felt myself collapse in them. He was Whitey and Tim wrapped up in one. I don't know how it happened, I think he kissed the top of my hair and then my eyes and then I was kissing him with my snot mixed up in his lips and heat kind of rushed up from my legs to my chest to my brain and I was being kissed like no one had ever kissed me before. I blacked out, at least I lost my power. I know I wasn't capable of thought.

If anyone saw us, I didn't care. He didn't care either. His hands took my breasts and then moved all over my body like they were part of it. When we pulled apart, he said, "God Almighty, Serena, you...I...I...I can't say I'm sorry. But, I am way off course, here."

I was really shaken when he left and thought that would be the end of it. And it should have been. It should never have happened again, but he entered my dreams, became my way out of the pain. I would think about his kisses before I closed my eyes at night and before I opened them in the morning. He represented life. Life and wanting and who knows what. I willed him to appear on the deck, on the beach, at my door.

Five in the morning it was, all the fishing boats long gone into the open sea. I heard footsteps, then saw him standing there deciding whether or not to turn and run. I grabbed my blanket around me and went out to greet him like some squaw on the Great Plains. I could hear my heart pounding and my privates screaming. It was hopeless; I had to have him. I opened the blanket and engulfed him, or maybe it was the other way around. We made love over and over again that morning and then for months on top of months, until I could eventually see him without growing weak...and without wondering if each time would be our last.

I wanted him to tell me he loved me but instead he called it lust. He said he loved my brown nipples and my kinky fur. That he loved the smell of my juices. When I tried to say I loved him, he said, "Stop. Love the moment, not me." He said, "We'll have to separate some day. You're just a girl, a beautiful, wonderful, sexy girl, but I'm married." He explained that even though he and Gwen were not in love, their lives were inseparable by time and circumstance. "She must never know about us," he said, and I understood. I did. But the sight of her made my stomach green with envy and my emotions red. I had to find a way out, and yet can fire give up air?

In retrospect, he must have felt helpless, too. He had so much at risk and nothing to gain from being with me.

I didn't go to the Keys that winter. I continued to stay with Grandma instead. She was refusing to eat, to dress. She seemed at critical mass. She began to smell bad, like she was rotting from the inside out, so, I started to take showers with her to make sure she was clean. She would hum a little off-key tune and tremble the whole time. I remembered then, that Pop had told me she was afraid of water. While I washed her armpits and her privates, I tried to convince myself her blue wrinkled skin was not that bad and my old age was a long, long, time away. She was happiest when the baths were over, especially when I'd rub her feet with oil and set her hair and listen to her go on about Mrs. Ruboso next door.

Caring for Grandma was reason enough to stay in the north but those were the noble excuses I gave myself. I really wanted to be near Nial, afraid that, *out of sight out of mind* was not some silly saying. Afraid that, if I left he would forget about me and I would die. He was my obsession while I tried not to think about Pop, or Tim, while I cared for Grandma and watched her slide further and further away from me until she was a just a sliver of herself.

Loving Nial was like loving a dream from which I didn't want to wake, because when I did, I knew a nightmare would be waiting. All winter we found each other's heat and washed away the rest of the world.

Grandma died in April. Her wake was in the O'Malley Funeral Parlor. I had to buy a casket and choose her clothes. I had them dress her in her favorite purple and blue rayon dress, the one she wore for the Feast of St. Peter each year. Her hair still had a little red among the silver, and I wrapped it around my fingers and pinned it in the style she had worn for my entire life. When I brought her black tie-up shoes, (they were the only ones that didn't need to be repaired) Mr. O'Malley said she didn't need shoes. I knew she would not have liked this. "Going barefoot is for peasants, not for Bridget Ryan," she used to say when I would go barefoot around the house. He let me put the shoes on her feet. I also remembered to put the rosary beads in her hands, twining them through her freckled crooked fingers. I even said them one more time for her. This much I did right.

In a trance, I lined up her friends to read Scripture and greet guests at the door. The funeral director asked if I wanted the lid open and I said, yes, but it wasn't her I saw. It was someone who looked like her, a waxen replica on the lilac satin. I knew to expect that. Death was no stranger to me. I could stare it down now.

Three fisherman and Mr. Ruboso served as pall bearers. Nial stood at the back of the parlor. As I followed the casket to the hearse, Nial, stepped out and joined me, holding my elbow and looking as sad as I felt. No one from the Haas family showed up.

Maybe Tim was sleeping on a mountainside.

April, the month of my birth, had also become the month of the deaths of those closest to me. Soon relentless spring rains ended and in came May. I watched the forsythia and lilac bloom but could only see the frailty of life. When the gulls screamed on Penny Loaf Island, nesting and setting up their summer maternity ward, I stayed away in due respect. I kept quietly to myself, waiting for Nial's early morning appearances.

We were a desperate pair, exchanging few words before we got down to business. That would end abruptly after he came in me, groaning like a ship in the harbor. For him, it was an exorcism. For me, a narcotic. I had not known sex could be like this. We were liquid nitrogen—so dangerous we'd almost extinguish ourselves, capable of wiping out anyone too close. We were caught in our own fire. I didn't know how to save myself from this man. I didn't know what could come of us, but a tsunami swept over me whenever he would leave, and I'd be lost until the next time.

By autumn, I realized I was his puppet, waiting for his hands to bring me to life, forgetting that puppets have no lives of their own. Any future to our romance was impossible. I could never be Tim's stepmother (how ludicrous) or hold my head up in town. I couldn't run the household or be Nial's partner socially or in the workplace. I knew I couldn't be Gwen Townsend, and didn't want to be. Hopelessness began to insinuate itself.

The world is never in stasis, but it came as a great surprise when Mr. Peterson came by one day to tell me his insurance company had consolidated all my holdings.

"All my holdings?"

I learned I had money from the settlements of estates I didn't know existed, and my financial circumstances changed abruptly. Whitey had kept secrets from me. The suit that won a lifetime of debt for my Haas uncle had compounded in a trust fund for me for over twenty-one years. Grandma had left me her tiny condo in Granite Shores; Whitey had not only left an insurance policy, but surprised me with a college fund he had never mentioned. I found myself having to deal with financial issues far beyond my imaginings.

Having options helped me decide to go to my southern home port, the one on the Keys. This time, I thought I might experiment with life as a landlubber. I rented a little house in Key West, not too far from Papa Hemingway's place. It was a shotgun cottage, typical of architecture in Key West. The style was so named because a bullet could fly from the front door to the back without obstruction.

I love the renegade character of Key West, the *old South* feel of the place. The cottage lifted my spirits from about six feet under to floor level. Its airy rooms, long and narrow, were cooled by big ceiling fans and a tin cooler on the roof. Palm trees rustled outside the aqua shuttered windows and the porches were replete with rockers, front and back. I stocked the kitchen and bought tableware and kitchen equipment. It felt like playing grown up, making believe I owned the place. But my inclination toward solitary confinement was not good and my withdrawal from the clutches of Mr. Townsend not easy. That's why sleep felt better than consciousness and watching TV upstaged a walk on the beach.

I was hiding. My feelings were hiding. They only came out in the night when I dreamed terrifying dreams of burning in apocalyptic fires or drowning in oceanic whirlpools that sucked me into their vortex.

About two months into this weirdness, I started to read the clippings in supermarkets and on public bulletin boards to see what was happening in and about town. As I was studying an ad for puppies and thinking a dog was what I really needed, a woman who looked like a throw back to the sixties placed a want ad for a roommate on the board. *Only females need respond*, it read. The woman said half to herself and half to me, "I'm leaving this up to the Goddess."

Eight copies of her credentials were splayed on the wall, and when she left, I took one of them and also a slip about the dogs. The dog question proved to be a tough one. Dogs die. I could not love something to lose it again. But, on the other hand, I did not want to live without love.

It felt strange to realize I could choose what or whom I would live with. I called about the dog first.

"Well, it isn't quite a pure-bred Portuguese Water Doag," a female voice said at the other end of the phone, "but it has the same trayits. Really, chile, these heah puppies look like the real thang. They are the damnedest cutest thangs you'll eva see."

"How long do they live?" I asked.

"Oh, they live foreva. You just have to see 'em," she insisted. "To see one is to know what luv is!"

These words proved to be the fatal phrase and I was off to choose my new love.

I arrived at a swampy compound surrounded by wire mesh fences to be greeted by what looked like three dozen dogs. As they all came barking to my feet I wanted to make a fast run for the car, but the lady of the house bounded out her door in a flash. Her frizzed semi-platinum blonde hair stood its own ground while her boobs bounced like beach balls under a sheer hot pink blouse. I couldn't move. It was a sight to behold—that woman and her dogs and the smile on her face. Clearly, my destiny was to make sure she stayed happy.

"Come on in, come in, Hon," she sang. "Yer in foh a treat. Ah keep them in heah away from the otha doags. No problems with fleas or ticks that way."

I wasn't so sure. In we went to the human dog house. It smelled worse than a pound and was littered with papers and dog toys, half-chewed bones and half-dead scamps. "I just love doags you understand. Ah am on the town suckah list. Want to dump youah doag? See Lucinda. Hell, ah don't care because there's just as many people as me need a doag, you see what I mean, chile? Now you look over heah. There they are. Them little pups would cost you a couple of thousand bucks if they was pure, but shit, honey, ya know they's just poor little bastards from Key West, just like the rest of us. Mixed blood makes for a tough breed."

I leaned down to pet them when one little puppy walked right over the heads of the others and licked my face. I picked him up and he buried his head in my neck, his shaggy warm body pressed into mine. His hair was similar to my own. It didn't seem to know where to settle, certainly not flat against his head. His eyes were lit with intelligence and expression.

I had never had a dog. I didn't know what I was supposed to do- what to look for. I took my key chain and shook it for him. He grabbed it with his baby teeth and worried it to my pleasure, then returned it to my hand and thanked me with his little pink tongue.

"That's youah doag, honey, yo' all done here. There's no point in thinkin' twice. He's awl youahs. I see it awl the time, a doag knows its master—it's them that makes the choice not us."

I had to have *the little bastard*. She was right. Reddish brown for the most part, some black spots and golden tipped on his ears and tail. I fell in love. Deeply and undeniably.

"How much?" I asked.

"He's got his baby shots; he's from healthy parents. Ah think a few hundred dollars would do it, Hon."

I knew I was being robbed and didn't care. "Sold," I said.

I might as well have given birth. I couldn't take my eyes or hands off my baby. For days, I examined his fur, his ears, his eyes with a joy that was pure and complete. I kissed his little feet and learned they smelled like popcorn. We learned to play hide and seek, and chase the ball. It was all about discovery.

At the beach one day, a little boy said he looked like a fur ball.

"He *is* a furry," I said. "Do you know what that is?"

The boy shook his head slowly from left to right.

"A furry is a creature that is a little bit human but covered with fur. Mickey Mouse, Big Bird, Bugs Bunny and Mr. No Name, here. They have special talents and the ability to think like people!"

"Well, he just looks like a fur ball to me," the kid said, looking a little dubious.

"You know, that might be a great name for him. Furball. Furble, Furbie. Furbie! What do you think? How about Furbie?"

The kid asked, "You gonna baptize him?"

"You think?" I said, questioningly.

"Ya gotta! Or he'll burn in hell!" the boy warned.

I said, "Well, we can't let that happen- let's do it right away." And so we did. I took the furball into the surf, held him up to the eastern sky, and named him. "From this day forward, you shall be called Furbie," I said, then dunked him in the brine.

"Amen!" the kid yelled, and dunked his own head. Afterward, the three of us performed a goofy dog paddle to shore.

Furbie had no problem recognizing his name and it took no time at all before he trained me to obey his every command.

Weeks after the adoption, I called the woman I'd seen posting her ad in the supermarket. I reminded her of our meeting and said I'd never lived with anyone but my own family before. I didn't know what to expect. Would she be willing to come for a month on an experimental basis? We talked at length and I had a good feeling it would work out. I didn't mention the puppy but I figured I'd take on that issue later.

When Geena moved in, it was as if I had adopted an older sister and Furbie had two moms. She became my alter ego. Femininity exuded from her. She used perfumed soaps, wore splashy jewelry, had an endless wardrobe and even a tiny tattoo on her butt. She took over the entire place. She had to have music around her all the time—albums from blues to rap, from healing preachers to comedians. I wondered how I could have ever known so little about the world.

I became her devotee. So did Furbie. We followed after her like two lovesick hounds. When Geena told me what to wear, I wore it. When she said *let's dance* and then corrected every move I made, I did it. Furbie learned too. He even did calisthenics with us.

He grew fast. Tall and handsome, his fur was as thick as a wolf's in winter. One night, Geena took out all her scarves and we danced our colors. We were a family. Geena was queen, Furbie the prince, and I, the adoring slave. My hair grew longer and wilder, and I gave up my heavy boots and sandals for bare feet and bells. Furbie and I rang our way through the streets of Key West. Geena taught me to wear flowing skirts and jewelry I had never considered before. Before long, the old Serena became Geena-ized.

Meanwhile, Geena was trying to find a job, one that gave her mornings free for meditation and the beach. She loved to be first at the beach, and always dragged Furbie and I along to bring up the sun. I felt like we owned the place at that hour with only the combers and the dogwalkers about. Sometimes we'd have breakfast at the restaurant across the street, Destiny's, and when the owners offered her a job, we proclaimed her, *Destiny's Child*. She was excited, pronouncing this would be her new life. The sales job she left in Phoenix was history.

With both of us working, we unfortunately had to leave Furbie by himself. I conducted the Glass Bottomed Boat Tours five days a week so he was on his own for at least six hours. During those hours, he managed to test the taste and texture of shoes and chairs, soap and toilet water and all the things we would forget to put away or couldn't protect. Soon, it became worth the effort to build a fence in the backyard to make his life less tenuous and our lives easier. He barked so much the first few day, we started anticipating an eviction notice, but then he took to our routine and his territory, and became acceptable.

I easily identified with Furbie. We were both adjusting to a new life. It felt miraculous and, for a while, I was able to avoid the sadness that hovered. I stopped waiting every minute of every day for a call from Nial. I even managed to tell him, when he did call, not to come see me. It wasn't easy for me to say, and the hurt showed. Geena kept saying, *You don't need this guy, you have me.* I did have her, but she didn't seem to understand how much I wanted him, the sound of his voice, the warmth of his lips, the fire that was us.

Time heals. I waited.

By February, the first glow of Geena and Furbie started to fade. I began to doubt my own happiness. I told Geena I was feeling guilty, guilty for wanting to see Nial so much. But she said to put away the guilt. She said real love can't be wrong. It might *go* wrong, but it can't *be* wrong.

I wondered if Nial was missing me. Wondered if he still wanted me as he once had.

Grandma kept showing up in my dreams, her pale translucent skin hanging on her bones, and wild almost-red hair standing on end. I would try to talk to her, but one way or another, she would leave and I couldn't get her to hang around and listen. Geena said that everyone in a person's dream is some aspect of themselves. She said that I was my grandmother, that I wasn't listening to my own authority. Geena had no problem being wise.

Grief isn't easy. Grandma had been too important for me to get over her death as quickly as I thought I had. I was so full of Nial at her funeral, so needing Pop, so crazy inside I had let her go without the proper mourning.

In the middle of all things new with a friend and a dog and sacred mornings, my mourning for her began. Soon I began to grieve for them all: my mother, my father, Grandma, Tim and Nial. I lost weight and was morose a lot of the time. Sometimes I'd get up in the middle of the night and walk the dog around and around the block. Geena became worried, but she gave me what advice she could, "Things will get better because they always do."

Then Furbie got sick.

I was beside myself. He vomited disgusting stuff. What Geena had dismissed as a hairball began to look real serious. It was a Sunday and not a vet in sight. I wouldn't leave his side. Finally Geena said, "Listen, we will have to do a little magic here."

She took the beautiful green glass goblet that sat in the kitchen window and filled it with water. Then she sprinkled salt in it and put it in front of Furbie in full sun. We sat in the sunshine, we three, and absorbed its healing rays. After fifteen minutes, she removed the star-shaped pendant from around her neck and dipped it in the water three times, each time letting a drop fall on the dog's head. Then she stirred the water three times to the right, three times to the left, and said, "Apollo's light surround us, Poseidon's water protect us, Athena's wisdom guide us."

I saw a white light form around the three of us and felt its heat melting us together. Then Geena took the star pendant and put it on Furbie's collar right next to his dog tag. His tail started wagging; he shook his head and made the two metals jingle together. We both hugged and petted him, and soon he was rolling on his back, frisky as ever. I felt just like him. I rolled on my back, too, and so did Geena. We three started laughing and playing and the whole thing seemed like a miracle.

It must have been March when Geena introduced me to the Wicca. With the Wicca, I began to celebrate my grandmother, wearing her jewelry, sprinkling her perfume into the sea at dawn, placing photos of her in the center of our circle, covering them with rose petals to be loved and lifted into the spirit world. But Grandma didn't go. She hung on and watched me and placed fear into my mind. Sometimes she wielded a grotesque crucifix or sometimes she watched me through stained glass. She was almost always angry. Once she stood at a stove stirring babies in a pot and then she gave them to everyone in the dream but me. I decided she was scolding me about Nial, but, no matter, I still wanted to feel his arms around me; that didn't change.

Then he arrived. He flew down to me in his private plane. Like the Red Baron he landed on the small runway, but when he disembarked it was no Lindbergh I saw. He looked pale and tired, his shoulders weighted. Despite the initial rush of heat when we embraced, he seemed silent and dark. Anxiety loomed between us like green skies before a storm.

Bed was still our best meeting ground. I understood that's why he had come, to fuck me. When I asked, he frowned. It was as close as we came to a confrontation. Incredibly, even though we made love for hours and it was as good as ever, I felt relieved when he left for Nicaragua. We had resolved nothing because nothingness was our fate.

After he left, Geena shook her finger at me. "Love is supposed to fill you up, empower you, not make you miserable. Neither of you seem to make the other happy—isn't that what you're looking for, happiness? Either give up the misery or decide what you have is all you'll get, and let it be enough."

Still, Nial and I stayed at ground zero. Our fear came from knowing the disaster that would follow if our relationship was exposed, and knowing we were going to continue to see each other anyway.

I tried to explain to Geena that no one like Nial had been in my life before, and I couldn't believe he chose to be with me—to hell with the reason. I told her he could have had any woman in the world and I couldn't help but be grateful that he chose me, cared for me. He gave me the power to drive him to do things and go places he'd never been before. I said, "He needs me."

"He needs you, Sweetie? He needs a roll in the hay, that's all!" she said. "You don't think you're the only one he's fooled around with?"

"I do. He told me so."

It *was* hard to believe he had no more experience than he claimed. Nial knew how to play with a woman's body. He made love to all of me. His lips on my lower spine made me wild. He aroused the back and the front of me at the same time, the top and the bottom, my feet, the spaces between my toes. He excited me in obvious and surprising ways. He was not self-conscious or apologetic. He was hungry; deft and creative. I couldn't imagine another man who would satisfy my body as he did.

Geena said sex was to enjoy, not exploit. She asked if he wasn't actually using me like some sex toy, and said I was going to get sick if I didn't take care of myself. One night in March, she begged me to go to a coven healing session with her. She said that she had found a comfort with the Wicca she had not found anywhere else, no church or sorority or group of friends.

I began to read about the Wiccan movement. How the Pagan spirit holds all life sacred, believes each living thing has a soul. Beyond that—the rocks and the sky, the water and the moon—all of nature is sacred. This is what appealed to me most about the pagan path.

I know what the absence of reverence has done to the ocean, how ecosystems that took millions of years to evolve are endangered. Over-fishing was one of the differences between Whitey and his friends. They prayed to St. Peter while Pop met with the politicians and used his experience to create fair laws for decent regulations. The Bible says we rule the earth and all its living things, but Pop used to say that was a homo sapien illusion, that the human race was in for a shock. Why should we think we are any more or less than any other living thing? Why can't we be spit off the planet as easily as the dodo bird?

A week after Nial left me to continue his trip to Central America, I remained in a gloom cloud. Geena was getting ready to go to the Wicca Sabbat celebrating the spring solstice and said I should go with her. Their ceremony was consecrated on the beach at midnight. I decided it was a good time for me to participate. We left Furbie and took Geena's Tracker down Magnolia Street through Old Town onto Blythe Street to a cloistered section of Twiggs Beach.

53

Here, in the middle of the night, with the lights of houses and street lamps far behind us, the beach had mysterious, ethereal qualities. No boom boxes interrupted the soft rolling surf, no water sprites to distract us, just the moon and stars dominating the landscape, making the water glow. Land and sky and sea were diffused into a perfect whole.

A group of women wrapped in loose cloth arranged a circle of stones. They enclosed a nine-foot area marked on the north, south, east and west with votive candles in red glass. One used a wand to draw the sign of the pentacle in the center of the circle. It reminded me of the stars I had learned to make without lifting my the pencil from the paper when I was six. I heard about the pentacle's ancient history, all the way back to early Egypt when it was the symbol of the Kore, of fertility and female power.

A bell rang and the women stood in a circle at the edge of the rocks. It rang again; someone read a poem. Then they took off their clothes. I would have felt peculiar if I'd stayed dressed, so I took mine off, too. Stark naked, we held hands and began to chant and sway to our own rhythms that soon became one.

This ritual was dedicated to the parting of ways. Sage was lit and the circle cleansed in a dance in which the pungent smoke was swept over the sacred space. I looked at the women in their nakedness, so different from each other and so beautiful. Big breasts, small ones, long legs and short. Some of us were angled, some were soft. Some were hairy, some relatively bald. I felt like a woman as I had never felt before.

My naked body trembled in the warm air but not from cold. I was moved by the music and thrilled by the trust. All of a sudden I heard deep hiccuping sobs and was shocked when I realized they were coming from me. Later, when I could hear, each of the Wiccan offered me wishes of well-being as they passed me a crystal goblet. I drank what smelled like lavender and tasted like herbal tea. Afterwards, with drums and songs, I whirled and danced as I had never done, like a nymph in the moonlight.

We sat around the sign of the Pentacle and I listened to Wiccan wisdom. They explained that to join the Wicca was to empower your female self—to do good work, to heal others, love the earth and know compassion. They reminded each other to honor and respect the souls inherent in all things, to replace their inhibitions with freedom of expression and take on the cloak of healing; to celebrate every aspect of life as it unfolds; to replace sin with joy and judge goodness in terms of what works, rather than what does not. Above all, be natural.

My reality shifted in that tiny circle of magic that night. I felt my Wiccan heart open and allowed myself to become a new self. I became a member of the coven—a sisterhood—an opportunity that had escaped me until that moment. Geena and I embraced one another and I embraced her world.

We went home before dawn, removing the signs of our meeting from the beach. We even raked our footsteps behind us. I was lighter, happier than I'd been for months, perhaps ever in my life.

In the weeks that followed, Geena and I spent every possible moment together. We saw dance concerts at the Tennessee Williams Center, watched sunsets from Mallory Square swaying to the sweet notes of jazz, took salted meditation walks in the early morning at various beaches. We tuned into each other and shared confidences in a way that made our safe place even safer.

I guess Geena's childhood was normal compared to mine. Maybe that's why she sought out the unconventional. For the six years following her graduation from the University of Arizona, she stayed in the state of Arizona. She had been introduced to the Wicca when she was studying alternative religions, and her curiosity grew as she read about their practices. She heard about a coven in Sedona just north of Phoenix and so, on a field trip of her own, she went there. She fell in love with the *bewitching* Red Rock Country and was drawn to the people it attracted. She described it as a mystical place, where the earth has steeples of rocky spires that burn orange into permanently blue skies. Just about any cult you were looking for found its way there. When she found the Wicca, she was an easy convert. Paganism took her as far away from her roots as possible, which is exactly what she wanted.

She isn't a bit sentimental.

Harold Swicker, Geena's father, still has an auto dealership in Dewey, Ohio, and her mother has Jesus. Not Bridget Ryan's kind of Jesus, no, more the evangelical variety. The Jesus that talks back and puts fire on people's tongues. The kind that lifts up the arms and wriggles the hips. It sounds like more fun than Father Francis' version. Geena says *not*.

Her parents have lived in Dewey since they were born. Geena says they will die there, too, unless the federal government relocates them to a concentration camp for nerds or they all move to Belize and drink Kool-Aid.

She's convinced she's not their child, that they found her in a rest room. Her Christian name was Tisha Swicker, "Tish for tissue," she laughs. Geena thinks it sounds like a toilet bowl cleanser. "Swish with Tish! Swicker is Quicker!" She's number seven of eight siblings, and the only one to leave Dewey. But, "That's good," she says, "there will always be someone there for my folks on the holidays, 'cause it won't be me!"

I love Geena as I've never loved another woman.

April came and with it the time for my return to New England. Flying back on American Airlines, Miami was my first jolt into reality. So many people, so many foreigners, so much energy.

I still think flying is exciting. Whitey and I had traveled by boat and bicycle, car and train but not by plane. I had gone, into the sky with Nial only twice, and seen Key West from on high, but was real happy to land both times. Little planes are similar to little sailboats; the wind is your best friend and your worst enemy. And I knew nothing about the Cessna's controls. I don't like that.

Although I planned to bring Furbie back with me when it came time to leave, I couldn't make myself put him on the plane. He had grown too big to fit under a seat and would have had to go into storage. Geena insisted he was better off on land and flying might be traumatic for our boy; everyone knew how many dogs die from heart attacks that way, she argued. I said she was ridiculous and I was his *true* mother and should decide what's best for him. In the end, I relented because I thought she was right about the trauma part.

I had clarity as the plane lifted off that April 30th. The months of grief seemed behind me and so was my dependency. There would be no Pop, no Grandma, and no Nial waiting for me at the other end. No one to hide behind. I resolved to navigate my New England life for the first time, completely on my own. It wasn't as if I didn't have friends; there are few strangers in the life of the harbor. The time had come for me to reach out and test myself.

When I returned, I stayed at Grandma's condo in downtown Granite Shores. It lacked the sunny simple lines of my cottage in Key West; in fact it smelled stale and sick. To make it mine, or anyone else's, I would have to get rid of Grandma's old furniture, strip the walls of fading paper and throw out her ancient wine-colored rug. It felt too much like I was erasing her, though, and I couldn't bring myself to do it all at once.

Outside, the world was moving on. Warm air encouraged the pale green buds to open; forsythia was spraying bright yellows throughout the neighborhood along with stately stalks of daffodils and jonquils. Down on the wharf you could hear the buzz of spray guns and saws, cranes and drills—the harbor's first signs of spring.

Year round, mornings start early. Draggers leave around three and fleets of fisherman follow from then until dawn. Cargo ships make their entrances and exits by the tides. We lobstermen have an advantage. We choose our schedules according to what suits us.

With the balmy days, I was encouraged to make the trek to the Longhouse Marina to check on the Serena Marie. Her twenty-eight feet were looking needy. It would take weeks to get her in top condition. She's got two engines but they have to be overhauled. Her hull, rounded and sturdy, needs yearly attention with sanding and paint. Pop and I talked about trading wood for plastic but we couldn't bring ourselves to do it. I still can't. The truth is, I like the process—the concentration of hard work and hanging out with the gang in the boatyard.

The Serena Marie was ready for action within three weeks. Working on her, I recognized how much I loved every board and bruise she had. Sanding and painting her sides, tuning her motors, scrubbing down her cabin were satisfying rituals.

Staying away from Townsend Cove proved impossible and regardless of my good intentions, I was not above hoping for a glimpse of Nial. I wanted to make our meeting as painful for him as possible. I rehearsed what I would say, how my hair and teeth would be brushed, how my hands would be clean and soft when he arrived, and how I would turn my brain into ice so that I could leave him wanting. But for weeks the only Townsend I saw was

Gwen: Gwen sweeping winter from her decks; Gwen planting her perennials on the slope to the rocks. Always working at nothing. Why is it some women never seem to get dirty—even with their hands in the soil? I hated her. I hated her for her blindness. I blamed her for Tim's shallowness and I blamed her because I couldn't have her husband. I hated her for not seeing me as a threat or so much as a pebble on her beach. I hated her for not seeing me at all.

Then one morning, as I puttered into the harbor and tied up, I could feel Nial's eyes on me. Despite the quickness of my pulse, I stepped out on deck deliberately, picked up an oil can and began to oil the pot hauler. Then I climbed onto the wharf and began to load my markers and pots. Frankie Haskell came to my side to help. He waited until we'd planted the last pot in the lower right hand corner of the deck before he told me, "The Townsend guys were lookin' for ya, yesterday."

"Really?" I said as casually as I could. "What did they want? You tell 'em I'm not set up yet?"

"Naw. They seemed to want to see ya' for somethin' otha 'n lobstah." He rolled his eyes.

"Ah, I'm sure. Get out!" I said, poking him in the ribs with a marker.

He and the other guys had watched me like a hawk for the past two years trying to take the place of Pop. I wondered how much they knew about Tim and Nial. I figured nothing because they weren't known for discretion and they never said a word.

Tiny Haskell was earnest. "No shit, Serena, they acted like you was workin' for 'em or somethin'. Acted pissed when we said you ain't been around much. We told 'em we could get 'em lobstah's but they just blew us off."

"Who knows what they want?" I shrugged, acting uninterested.

I pulled pails of bait on board. It slopped on my gloves, soiling what was to be my lavender-smelling hands. I checked to see if my gaff hook was in place.

My heart was racing. Evidence that it was not over yet. I was foolish to think a witch's dance on the beach was enough to wipe out ten years of attachment.

Two days later—when I was picking up some tools at the shack, long before light broke—Nial leaned into the door. I jumped a little when I saw him.

"Serena, what's is going on in that red head of yours?"

My hairbrush was in my hand, my head bowed over, frizz falling over my face like a curtain. I flipped my hair back, looked straight at him and took a deep breath.

"Serena, what's the matter with you? Why are you avoiding me?" he asked.

"What do you mean, *what's the matter with me?* What am I supposed to do, go knock on your door? Hello, Gwen, can Nial come out to play?" I plunged my hand in my pocket looking for an elastic to tie my hair back in a pony tail. My hands were shaking so much, I could hardly expand the thing enough to get it on. Then my hair snarled when I tried to pull the damn thing out. "Ouch. Shit!" I cried. My eyes smarting like a ten year old's.

"Serena. Stop. You're angry. I can see that, but nothing's changed. There's no reason for us not to see each other. Don't hide from me."

"Nothing's changed and nothing can ever, should ever, will ever change. I'm not hiding, I'm through."

"What do you want?"

This was the moment. I had to pull it together, right there on the spot. Send him home with his tail between his legs. "I want you to leave me alone. I'm a working girl, for God's sake. Listen, I've faced it—it's over. I know it and you know it! There's no where to go from here. Let's just remember what was good."

I was convincing. He went on the defensive.

"I just wanted to know you were all right. I mean, why should anything change? We can be friends, can't we? You're important to me." He walked over to me, his shoulders doing that hunched thing, one always a little higher than the other. He wore his crooked smile, too, the one that looked like he was coming to get me. Like he was sorry he was so helplessly wanting.

I picked up the straight-back chair like a lion tamer and held it between us. "Don't come near me," I warned.

"Serena, put that chair down. For God's sake. I'm not going to attack you."

"You, go," I told him, as plainly as I knew how.

He grabbed the chair and put it aside then pulled me into him. I meant to fight. He kissed my face my neck, ripped my shirt right off me. With his chest heaving against my breasts, we fell onto the bed in a kind of wrestler's melee. "Stop it!" I begged, at least I think I did.

"Just one more time—one more time and I'll go," he said. "I can't stop thinking about you. I need you. Please." And our fight slowed and turned into sex, too hot and steamy not to stop until its noisy messy end. Of course he didn't have a rubber and, of course, I convinced myself not to care if he did. He took me again, turned me upside down and inside out and came again. I came with him, and my climax could have lasted hours if he hadn't cried like a little boy. I lay there, my own tears mixing with his, all the while his semen running amok.

"I'm screwed up, Serena," he said. "I'm living in a house of cards, and it's about to fall." He held onto me, wrapping himself around me.

"What do you mean?" I asked.

"I mean, nothing is working. I can't do it anymore."

I thought he was going to tell me he couldn't stay with Gwen, that he was going to choose me after all.

"I can't make any sense out of any of it. The last time I was happy was a thousand years ago, when I thought I made a difference."

"But you do make a difference; you *are* making a difference," I protested.

"I don't know. I don't think it's possible."

"Can't you be happy right now, with me?"

"I'm not. I'm sorry. I'm not."

"Well, what made you happy a thousand years ago?" I asked, even though his words stung.

"I believed in something."

"You still believe in your work. Don't you? You make a difference to a lot of people. You make a difference to me. What more do you want?" I asked, wiping my snot on his sleeve. "Look at all the people in Nicaragua that you helped."

"I wanted it to work. Now I'm not sure if they can make it. If I can actually pay for the crop. Business is off. Way off."

Suddenly, it occurred to me that his grief had nothing to do with me. I was his handkerchief, that was all. A receptacle. I untangled myself and pulled away.

He said, "What's the matter?"

"You don't care about anything but yourself. The great Nial Townsend who can fly in for a fuck and come and go as he pleases. You need to go now and for good."

"I thought we understood each other."

"I understand all right. You bastard. Leave, and go back to the people in Nicaragua where you want to make a difference. Forget the real people, the ones in your face."

"Serena, I'm sorry."

"Get out! Go away. Leave me alone! I mean it. Stay away... forever!" I shouted.

He left and I took the Serena Marie over to the big harbor, docked her alongside International Fish and half blind, made my way to Grandma's house. I sat in a tub of scalding water and cried for a half an hour. Then I called Geena. I told her the story and she said, "You're owning your power, girl. You have to own your power. Visualize this guy out of your life. Make choices and then start making up new pictures. You're not a victim and no longer the sex object for Mr. Wonderful."

Easy enough for her to say. I didn't care if I was a sex object or not—at least I mattered for a minute or two; I was something to someone. Throwing Nial to the wind felt like letting go of a lifeline. His was the breath that had breathed life into me after Pop, after Tim, after Grandma.

With a kind of suicidal fervor, I attacked Grandma's apartment. I went about ridding it of junk and history that was just more of the miserable meaninglessness of everything. Taking apart her bedroom shrine was the hardest. It represented the story of all that mattered in her life: pictures of her husband, my grandfather Salvatore, and their son, Sean—Whitey to those who cared—Pop only to me, even one snapshot of my mother before I came along. The photographs had been arranged ceremoniously on the dresser around a plastic figurine of the Blessed Mother. Prayer books and beads lay at Mary's little white feet, testimony to Grandma's primary adoration. Above all this was a boyish portrait of Jesus with last year's palm fronds stuck behind his framed face. Another brass Jesus hung above her bed...this one in mortal misery, being nailed twice, once to a cross and again to her wall.

After having the best photos reframed, I moved them to a wall in the front hall where we looked more like a normal family. Mary's white toes went into a box called *stuff* and so did the crucifix and the print of some artist's vision of Jesus with blue eyes and blond hair.

With my inheritance money growing comfortably in funds I could hardly name, I didn't have to work as hard for my physical survival anymore. If I was tired or it was cold and wet and windy, I stayed home or hung around with the guys. Sometimes it felt good just sharing fish stories with them.

Tiny's boat, a rusted-out dragger as scruffy as one of the wharf cats, was his major concern. He loved to bullshit about the day he'd run some heroin, then sink his boat ten miles out. At least five boats had sunk in the past year. We all agreed it looked suspicious.

Lots of days, we'd have breakfast at Sailor Sam's and load up on pecan pancakes or the sea lubber's specials of fish cakes and eggs. I liked the Eggs Benedict best.

Sailor Sam's is the neighborhood kitchen, a ramshackle little clapboard building with booths built in the '50s and linoleum floors of the same vintage. It's the hub of Rocky Point, providing breakfast and lunch for the old, and easy camaraderie for the lonely. The fishermen sit in a corner by the door. Same seats every morning. No one assigned the seats but they might just as well have our names on them. The artists from Rocky Point sit catty-corner to us.

While artists argue about politics and art, we do the same about regulations and fish. Sometimes I've felt I was at the wrong table. Too often, the guys at my table were lying to themselves.

One rainy Friday morning, Tony Tedesco and Tiny were having another go 'round about a Japanese fish processor in the harbor. They were in a rage. "How the fuck are we supposed to earn a living when the Japs sit right out there processing our fish? The government shuts us off and then lets them foreigners get away with this shit! I'm going to put my lady down soon, I swear to fuckin' Jesus Christ I am. Sink her right in the middle of the harbor!" Tiny threatened, as if it he could make a dent in Washington by sacrificing his own beat-up tub.

I looked up and saw Gayle Desmond, the reclusive artist who lives in an uninsulated loft across the street, come in with her tea cup and a tea bag asking for hot water. Raw cold days must be hard for her. Pam, the waitress, looked my way and threw me a wink. She's a good soul, knows all our stories and makes room for our eccentricities.

When Pam came over to pour our second cups of coffee, she asked, "Didja heah 'bout the Townsend guy?"

"Huh?" I asked.

"That little plane o' his is missin', made Boston news this mornin'."

I made it to the door without focusing and forgot to pay. My car was parked around the corner. I drove straight to The Last Chance Grocery store, grabbed some newspapers and managed to get to the Serena Marie before I opened them.

Thing was, I didn't have to open anything. There it was, a front page headline: **Lost at Sea**.

What did it mean? Did it mean he was missing? Lost forever? Hiding? Had he decided to disappear? Kill himself? What did it mean, **Lost at Sea**?

I had sent him away forever. Told him it was over. Lost at sea? Was he actually gone? Was there no hope of seeing him again? No meeting on the beach—in his boat or on the wharf—ever? No little red plane flying in circles above my head? No lips that made mine his? How could I find out more? Where could I possibly go in order to get the facts? I felt cold and scared. I curled up in a ball and rocked myself. Rocked and rocked. The only person on earth I dared call was Geena.

Geena told me to come home to Key West. I wanted to. In the weeks that followed, I wanted to run and many times planned my exodus. But I couldn't go. I couldn't leave the questions still in the air. I couldn't leave the scene of the crime. It was a local story, so I felt compelled to stay nearby, as close as I could, to keep vigil. I did it by reading the news, listening to gossip and praying to the Goddess. This family, the Townsends, belonged to me and I was hanging on, but I didn't know exactly to what or for whom.

It took at least a month before Tim came to see me. He looked too thin and yet his first words to me were, "You look too thin."

"Sorry about your father," I said. My eyes got watery. He thought it was sympathy. I wanted to say, "It was *your* fault! If you had loved me. If you had been half the man your father was, none of this would have happened."

"Jesus, Serena, I feel guilty about it," he said. "Like I made it happen, somehow. I never wanted the business."

He sat on the edge of the bowsprit facing me. His knees jutted away from each other at sharp angles and his hands held onto the gunnels as though a raw wind was blowing. Nial was present in his brow, his neck, the hair on his hands, his sad voice.

"I couldn't be the kid he needed. It's as if I lost them both, my mother and father."

"It must be hard for her," I said, because that's what I'd be expected to say.

"My mother's a zombie, driving me up the wall. She's locking herself in her room and doing weird things, like answering phones and then hanging up without talking."

I understood. I understood too well.

"...sitting in dark rooms and talking about stuff, I don't know. Stuff that isn't important right now. And the fucking business—I can't fix it. I've always hated it and now what am I supposed to do? Love it?"

"But you liked working and traveling with your dad, didn't you?"

"Yeah. When I went to Central America with him. We had some good times together. Those are the best memories, as a matter of fact."

"I'm sure you have others."

"Dad and the plane. Dad and the villagers in Tequantepe. Him so tall, like a god, and me like a little disciple on his right hand. We could have told those people that pink clouds would come and open at noon, and they would have bowed down and waited. They're beautiful people, beautiful."

I said, "Your father loved them, too. It was the last thing he said to me, that working with them was the best thing he had ever done."

"He said that? He talked to you about it?"

"Yes."

"Well, then, at least he died on his way to doing something he thought was worthwhile. He sure as hell didn't think *I* was. I wonder if I'll ever do anything that's worthwhile, Serena."

"Why are you so convinced he's dead? Maybe you should go back to Nicaragua and visit the town where you and your father worked. Maybe they'll know something."

"If they knew something, they would have done something. We have contact people down there. He's not there. The people will have to harvest their crop without him."

"Why don't you go in his place?"

"I can't. I don't want to be the bearer of sad tidings and I don't know anything about farming. Shit, I just did what my father told me to do."

"Maybe this is not about you."

"Listen, Serena, get this. I am not going anywhere. I'm stuck. Stuck in a nowhere place, with a business that is going under. I don't know what the fuck anything is about!"

Dramatic, at best. I must have forgotten that Tim's world centered on the spot where he stood.

It came as no surprise when I heard three or four weeks later that he had left Granite Shores, the company and his mother's misery, to crisscross the country. I lost hope for him.

Then the face of my own guilt appeared. I began to suspect I was a hex on the people I loved. Too much pain, too many losses in too short a time. I functioned automatically through each day. When I talked to people, I revealed nothing. No sorrow and no joy. I moved in a mist thicker than late summer's fog.

My period was late. Was I pregnant with a dead man's child? Was I going to have to raise this child myself, me, who never had a mother? I experienced terror and joy at the same time. My breasts were tender, my tummy swollen. I tried to picture the baby, then asked myself if I should abort it immediately, because it would ruin my life. A child with an inexplicable conception didn't work for me. Geena said abortions weren't that bad. But Geena also said, "Hey, if we can raise Furbie, we can raise a kid."

It started to appeal to me, having Nial's baby. I saw the four of us walking on the beach, Geena, Furbie, Little Nial and me. He would have straight blonde hair like Kristin Haas and eyes like Nial's, and he would be special because he was raised by women.

Pressure to know increased with time and soon I was a full two months late. I decided I had to do something so I went to Osco Drug and bought a pregnancy kit. As I had unwrapped the box, I realized what knowing would mean. I would have to make a terrible decision.

But the test proved negative. My period arrived two weeks later, and by then, this too, felt like another absolute loss.

Geena understood my mixed emotions. She was as close to me over the phone as when we were together. I knew she listened and cared as I described the guilt and anger weighing on my shoulders. When she told me to "Get rid of it!" I told her I deserved the weight. I had sent him away. Her response? "Get yourself to a coven, woman."

I tried. I went to Salem and found witches there; learned there were at least eight hundred residing in the city. I met a Sabrina, a Sybil and a Desdemona but they were into the lesbian thing and just using Wicca to meet women, as far as I could see. I was turned off by their lack of spirituality and their pretense at witchcraft. It might have been entertaining to a visitor but wasn't genuine to me, not what I needed. I needed something purer, less self-conscious, as in the secretive mantle Wiccan women maintained in the South.

Like a great ox, I hauled my yoke around from June to September until, suddenly, magically, I found my Wiccan wisdom again.

I was walking out near Eastern Light. Dawn was breaking and, as usual, I experienced the significance of that first slice of sun separating the dark of the horizon from the long clouds above. I have my best thoughts at such moments.

It was then I found the monarchs and stood wondering at their innate knowing. It was then I remembered I had innate knowing of my own and decided to meet Gwen Townsend.

Seven

Gwen

Serena keeps playing with my mind. It's been that way since we first met. She's intelligent and courageous, but extremely intense. Perhaps that is why she continues to fascinate me. I have to admire her willingness to map out her life—ask myself if I can do the same.

She's looking for her mother. Aren't we all? I mean, don't we all long for that mythical mother who loves us unconditionally and blesses us for whatever we do? The ideal woman to lead our way? Would Serena have been better off with a mother? I can only hope so.

I realize I have been staying away from the nursing home. I had placed Mother nearby so I could visit her every day. But it has become increasingly difficult for me to walk through the doors of that place; to be reminded of those lost faces sitting in their wheelchairs left to wonder where they are, who they are. Another example of life's chicanery; just when we should know everything, we know nothing.

Perhaps if I prepared her a special luncheon it would stimulate her senses. I decide that tomorrow will be Mother's Day, even though we're in the throes of late autumn.

When I arrive she is sitting in front of the bay window looking blindly out on Spooner's Pond. She can't see the swans gliding regally across the water, their cygnets paddling double-time to keep up; nor the mallard family with their six ducklings near the bank. She doesn't have to worry about the snapping turtles rising from the water's depths to wreak havoc on these young families facing their first winter together. She no longer angsts about the loosestrife crowding out the cattails or the long umber shadows signaling the change in the sun's angle, warning of short dark days and endless cold winds ahead.

I move the little tea table from the wall and prop it in front of her, take her floral placemats and some of her china from my basket, the silver spoons and a butter knife—tools of her past life. Then I remove a chilled bottle of champagne and pop the cork, allowing the fizz to entertain her. She giggles at the noise and looks wide-eyed as I pull two long-stemmed glasses from my basket to fill them with the bubbly. A little alcohol may push some blood to her brain.

I unwrap two lovely rolls from a warm cloth, find the butter patties shaped like butterflies, and place them on the blue and white Danish porcelain I brought from home. In a far less gracious manner, I add two paper bowls of lobster bisque to the plates. After I unfold her well worn napkins and spread them on our laps, I lift my glass.

She doesn't appear at all interested. Even when I place her glass in her hands. It's the napkin on her lap that absorbs her.

"Mother, a toast!" I say. "To the woman who has never been anything but gracious and kind." When I click her tipsy glass, she instinctively raises it, but the champagne spills on her lap as she fails to find her lips.

Now her wet napkin becomes a toy. I watch her curl it through her fingers, smell it, and put it in her mouth—as much as she can—before I stop her.

"No, no, no. Mother. Here, I have brought you some rolls and your favorite soup. Taste this and see if you can tell me what it is! Here, let me help." I feed her the champagne. "It's Dom Perignon."

She looks down at her hands again, her eyes fix on the twisted purple lines and ridged yellowed nails.

"Dumb...don...dumb."

"Mother, do you know who I am?" I ask, trying to force feed her. Her lips purse tightly and she shakes her head, no.

"I am your daughter, Gwen."

"My daughter is dead," she says matter-of-factly, and sticks her spoon in her hair.

"Mother, where are *you*?"

Such a silly question when it's clear she's a ghost. An illusion. Her eyes are the color of pearl, empty. She picks at her hands instead of the food. I want her to tell me one more time that I am all right, that I am a daughter she can be proud of. I remove the spoon from her hair.

Once, she would have died for me. Almost did, in a car accident when I was seven.

Just as I was a city child, my father's Cadillac was a city car. He had to forego his joy of driving fast in the restraints of Manhattan traffic and used a driver to take him to and from his office at Rockefeller Plaza. But he actualized his passion for speed on weekends in the countryside. He drove too fast on the empty roads. I never liked that, nor did Mother.

"Darling..." Mother would say when he got above fifty-five.

"...this isn't Monaco," he'd finish.

One weekend we had traveled all the way to Vermont. On our way out of Putney, he realized there wasn't a sign of traffic, not a house, not a crossroad, just an open road. The S-curves had me swaying from Mother's lap to Father's. I had the premier spot between them. My new baby brother slept in the bassinet behind us. Seatbelts hadn't been invented yet. I had a problem with carsickness when I sat in the backseat, so the front middle seat was Father's way to keep me tucked somewhere. This position shielded my eyes from the edge of the road where cliffs fell into rivers and shards of shale lay like pages of history. He told me, "Just keep your eyes focused on what's ahead and you'll be fine." I never could.

We were on our way back from Aunt Gigi's house and I felt happy to be going home. The woman was as bald as a baked bean and strange to a little girl from New York City who carried an ermine muff and wore jodhpurs and velvet-collared coats. Her house had a musty smell from the wet wood that fed the Franklin stove and clouded up the place. The fire's smoke made my eyes burn. Gigi showed no shame about her bald head and she didn't smile once the whole time we were there; she just kept wiping her hands on her apron.

At one point, though, Aunt Gigi took a coin out of a cigar box and handed it to me. "Go next doah to the stoah and git yerself some taffy," she said. I had never been given money or the permission to go shopping by myself. I was more grateful than the old woman probably could have known. I smiled and thanked her in my best good child voice. Then I skipped outside across the unpainted porch toward the country store a few yards from the house.

Two male clerks sat just inside the door. A thin one on a wooden barrel, a fat man on a huge milk can.

"You musta come up heah in that big boat," the fat man said.

"Must be one of them fellas straight outta Washington," the other man said, grinning real wide so I could see all the teeth he had left.

"My father bought it in New York City," I answered.

"City slikas up heah looking at the hicks, eh?"

"We came to see Aunt Gigi," I answered.

"Auntie Gi? You came heah to see Auntie Gi? We didn't know she had rich flatlandah blood, now, did we, Slim?" said the toothless wonder, winking at his friend.

I scanned the counter for my favorite candy, determined to take care of myself. But I only saw Hershey Bars, Life Savers, Tootsie Rolls, and Chiclets.

"Watcha want, Missy?" the fat man asked, his elbows resting on his stomach, which was resting on his lap.

"I'm looking for Bonamo's Turkish Taffy," I said, thinking everyone in the world knew about Bonamo's Turkish Taffy.

"Don't have none of that!" He turned and pulled some wrapped candies out of a jar on the shelf. "Heah, this is the best taffy you've evah et!"

I took what he offered, gave him my coin and got out of the store as quickly as I could.

Back at the house Gigi never came close to me and forgot to ask us to come and visit her again when we left. I decided she wasn't used to company.

"Father," I asked, as we drove along, "why is Aunt Gigi bald?"

"She had scarlet fever when she was just a girl. Her fever was so high, all of her hair fell out."

"But why doesn't she wear a wig?"

"Probably because she'd just as soon stay herself. I can't answer that one for sure, Princess, but my guess is she doesn't understand vanity."

I considered that for a while. Vanity? What was that? I had always thought it was a table where Mother sat. Going near the *vanity* was a no-no for me for as long as I could remember. But, there were countless times I did trespass, sitting down in front of the great mirror to study her powders and creams and use her soft sticks on my eyebrows and lips. I had blotted my lips on her tissues while I looked for her in my face in the glass, hoping some day I would be just as beautiful.

"I must admit, Stephen, seeing Gigi and that crude place where she lives is a culture shock," Mother had said. "The backwoods mentality is obvious. The people are culturally deprived."

"I'm sure the shock went both ways, Leslie," Father said, laughing. "Looks like the bald-faced truth is that Mother's sister has long since forgotten her roots, if you'll forgive the pun."

"Never!" Mother said.

At that moment, a rickety pick-up truck came around the bend heading straight for us.

"Stephen! Stephen! Watch out!" Mother screamed.

The old man at the wheel veered to the left and then to the right and our Cadillac had nowhere to go but the outside edge of the road."

"Damn!" Father swore as his arms tore at the steering wheel. His sharp turn catapulted us off the road and we flew, still moving ahead until a primordial silver birch halted our flight. Mother's arm flew protectively across my chest and then, in a swan-like motion her head went through the windshield. I heard a metallic crunch, then another and another as the car rolled down the hill, heads down, heads up, me, still held by Mother, but blood now blinding both of us—blood that gushed from Mother's head. A strange silence told us when it was over. We were miraculously upright, the crinkled roof touching our heads.

Little Carleton cried in the back seat. No one moved as Mother's pale yellow cashmere coat turned red.

Two days later, when I woke up in a hospital's high metal bed, I was alone. Images of disaster ran in front of my face. My family was dead. I knew it. I had read enough and heard enough to know some children become orphans. Aunt Gigi's strangeness and the weird men at the store, the swerving old truck and the blood—it all jumbled together like a bad dream.

A crisp looking nurse appeared in the doorway.

"Well now, it looks like we've decided to wake up, now, have we?" She looked all starched and happy, but I recognized the cover-up.

My mouth was as dry as a cotton swab.

"Are you thirsty?" the nurse asked, pouring water from a metal pitcher into a plastic cup and placing a flexible straw in it.

I sipped and waited.

"Let's take your pulse, see how you're doing," she said, wrapping a heavy band around my arm. She was being much too kind. "How old are you, honey?"

"Eight," I lied. I wanted her to know I could take care of myself.

"Same age as my little girl."

I thought, *Maybe she's planning to adopt me.*

"You seem to be all right. I think we should take your temperature now and see if the fever's gone down any."

I burst into tears.

"Oh, don't worry, this won't hurt. You're going to live, I promise," the nurse said.

"I want my mother," I wailed.

"First things first, young lady. We want to get you well. You had quite a fever for a while there."

"But my mother, what about my mother?"

"She's fine. Your family's waiting just for *you.*"

"For me?" I couldn't believe it. I didn't believe it. The sight of the blood spilling from Mother's head was too real.

"I want to see her!" I said.

"I'm sure you do."

It seemed like hours before I was taken to see my parents. There they stood, alive and smiling. My father had broken his arm trying to hold on to the steering wheel. Mother's head was wrapped in bandages. They had shaved off most of her hair. Carleton had only a scratch on his lip. I was the one who was too ill to be moved. A high fever caused by shock, the doctors said.

But I already knew what that was all about.

"I caught it at Aunt Gigi's," I said.

"What's that?" the doctor asked.

"The shock. Right before the accident Mother said we got the culture shock. Is my hair going to fall out, too?"

"No. You'll be just fine," he promised.

The long black limousine that arrived to take us home looked very strange at the front door of the country hospital. Father had a cast and an armrest stretched in front of him, Mother wore some stranger's dark coat. Her head looked exceedingly white in a turban of bandages, and Carleton struggled in her arms, his little face twisted with misery and his hands a splotchy red. I knew what it was to be embarrassed by such a group of city-slikas. I also knew what it meant to be thankful.

That was almost forty years ago. Imagine! Life speeds by. Is this woman who sits in front of me the person *I* will become? She gave me every opportunity to grow and be someone, something. What is she thinking? Is she thinking at all?

Am I thinking? Where did the adventuress go, the one who traveled under New York's streets trying to find the real world, who knew she was kept in a tower? Whose life was so pure, she had to find a way to muss it up?

At Miss Grayson's Day School on the East Side, I sailed through school without any great effort. The only forms of discipline I remember were the weekly check-ups from Father to make sure my lessons were on target, and the occasional pep talks from Mother when she thought my attitude might need improving.

I suppose I wished I had more talent, that I could paint a sky or sea the way Sybil could, or match the witticisms that fell out of Sally's mouth, or match Liz's brilliant metaphors. But I accepted the fact that these were special talents bestowed on only a few. My friendships were evidence that I was okay. They were built into the fabric of my life, in the school, in the church and in the shared social life of my parents.

I want that sense of sensibility now. The fabric I thought was whole is in shreds.

From the day I opened my eyes, my parents surrounded me with art, language, theater and music. Beyond owning the Terwilliger Bank, Father was the Director of Unicord a non-profit agency dedicated to bringing order and compassion to the ever-shrinking world. But even though he was worldly in his vision, he felt obliged to keep us away from the nitty gritty of the streets, conscientiously protecting us from the world's disagreeable elements.

Understanding poverty from a penthouse in Manhattan was questionable. All one had to do was see the expenses the *haves* invested in protecting themselves from the *have nots*. The most valuable apartments were the farthest from the ground. Adding to the distance were grand lobbies, doormen and secured entrances and exits designed to keep the poor at bay. Chauffeured cars, private schools, arranged friendships, and tight schedules reinforced these intentions. The Terwilliger's name was not on any doorbell or in the New York telephone book. Segregation was as real in New York for our family, as it was in George Wallace's Alabama.

My closest friends, Sally Manship and Lizzy Wainwright, were like my sisters. We had grown up together. Sally's parents were lawyers who my parents had known since college. The Manships were high powered and intellectual and Sally, their only child, was expected to follow suit. From what I could tell, the entire world thought she was perfect. With her bouncy blonde pony tail and a smile as wide as her face, her wholesomeness could fool even the most cynical. I thought she was outrageous. She would bite into a lemon just to make me laugh; would say fuck for the fun of it, and stole things from Bergdorf's in order to prove she could.

Lizzy was the most academically curious and serious in our trio. We counted on her hyperactive sponge of a brain and knew she would understand the homework assignments when we didn't. Nothing her parents or teachers said went unchallenged, but her friends could do no wrong.

I, meanwhile, took on the role of follower. In kindergarten when I poured the green tempera paint into the toilet, I only did it because Sally had poured her pot of red into it first. The ecstatic bad deed ended in shame. We had to sit in *time-out* chairs in opposite corners of the classroom for an entire half hour. Long enough for me to discover I did not like being naughty.

When Mother heard about my evil deed, she acted shocked and concerned. She thanked Mrs. MacDonald for taking the appropriate action and never mentioned it again, except to Father when I heard her say I was "experimenting" with the paint.

69

At ages eleven and twelve, we got into telephone tricks. "Hi, is Red there? *Red who?* Red Pepper, ain't that hot?" We never got caught.

At fourteen, dirty books were our fascination. Lizzy contributed *Peyton Place* and her older sister's sex manual by Masters and Johnson. The manual told us more than we could believe. We decided the book was a fake; our parents didn't do such things.

The illusion of newfound freedom came the next year when we discovered the New York subway system. For protected girls who went to and from Miss Grayson's Preparatory School for Young Women in chauffeur-driven cars, the subway became an avenue to reality. We devised excuses for being in places we were not, and began to travel underground. It was our own version of civil disobedience, a way to free ourselves from our tethers.

New York's anonymity encourages extremism; ours took the form of water pistol capers. From spots nearest the subway doors, we shot squirts into crowds of exiting passengers just in time to watch them look up and jump a little as the train pulled away. Lucky for us, it was not an era of travel rage. We counted on people's forbearance as we watched them react to subway rain like it was just one more thing to endure. Our dubious protection must have been our preppy clean-cut looks.

We were a gaggle of girls—Lizzy, Sally and I—attached at the hip; three pale blondes in a gray city. Compared to fifteen year olds I've heard about lately, we were incredibly naive. Of course, we fantasized about sex, but had no takers. At least no young males in our formal social circles seemed to find us desirable. Perhaps we were too foolish or too thin, perhaps too innocent. But more than likely we had no idea how to send out the right signals. We were in love with love, Tab Hunter, Paul Newman and the Beatles, and settled for dreaming and practicing kisses on mirrors.

One June day, when we were supposed to be shopping at Bergdorf's for summer dresses, we hit the BMT lines and took the E train to Coney Island in Brooklyn. The rest of the world seemed to know about Coney Island but we had never been there. To make the trip more interesting, Sally pretended to be insane and kept brushing off imaginary ants. Then Lizzy stamped on them with her penny-loafered feet. I acted like I was afraid of the two of them and moved to a seat at the other end of the car. We were truly dedicated in our efforts to make a wave, but to no avail. No one noticed. No one even smiled, well, except for me, who rolled around in my seat snorting like a laughing hyena.

When the train came to the end of the line, we stepped outside into a subway graveyard where a maze of rails and rusting subway cars were exposed to the unpleasant light of day.

I remember feeling foreign, very white, very fifteen and disoriented as we walked down the streets. We spun in our tracks looking for a sign to Coney Island and saw only the top of a roller coaster arching above a row of warehouses and tenement buildings. Dark people were hanging out on the streets. I wanted not to feel frightened, but I was; so was Sally and even Liz.

When we rounded the corner, we looked up and saw we still had a way to go.

The weather was uncomfortable. Instead of sunshine, a hot haze made the air smell like a foul soup. We knew the beach had to be near, but the familiar scent of salt spray, the kind we knew at the Hamptons, was missing. Instead, the stench of urine rose off the steaming pavement. Underneath the roller coaster's girders were piles of garbage, a picnic ground for rats. Screams rose above in the roar of the tiny cars plummeting from a distant peak above our heads. Two bleary-eyed men surprised us as they emerged from the dark maze of wood and steel beneath. They held their hands out in beggar fashion but neither Sally nor I could make out what they said.

By the time we reached Coney Island Avenue, it looked and sounded a little more like we expected. The cranked music, the hawkers, the cotton candy vendors, the moving lights and neon like a tired carnival.

As we wandered down the main drag toward Steeplechase Park, a hawker begged us to come inside. The building was no circus tent, no colorful canvas to be torn down in a week and taken to some greener place. It was a purple and yellow tenuous structure, a permanent fixture meant to showcase Coney Island's finest freaks. It promised Siamese twins, a fat lady, Tiny Tim, and Donkey Man, who had the body of a man and the head of a donkey.

Of course, we went inside. It was too hard to look at the fat lady whose fat spilled like cream over her shoes, dripped from her inner thighs like putty, lay on her lap like buckets of dough; her swollen face ended in chins shaking like a turkey's waddle. We couldn't look at the midget who spoke through his nose into a huge megaphone and pretended to be funny. We didn't see his little hands gesticulating the meaning of his words. What we saw, what made our hearts stand still, was the extended jaw and gaping mouth of Donkey Man, neighing and whinnying and looking straight at me.

"Ladies and Gentlemen! Ladies and gentlemen, it appears that Donkey Man is very excited. He is restless, and trying to tell us something. What is it Donkey Man?" the man at the mike asked. Donkey Man continued to stare at me. Now he was stomping his foot and braying for all he was worth, a long moaning bray. His weeping wail filled the strange building. People came from the other exhibits to see what was happening. I couldn't move. If a train had been plowing into my back, I couldn't have moved. He had fixed me in the center of the small area amid filthy fake circus straw and sawdust. My feet froze to some unstable earth. Forced me to look into his wide black eyes weighted with eyelashes meant either to catch tears or bat flies.

"Donkey Man, what is it?" the man in the polka-dotted tie asked. His sweat turning an orange shirt brown.

Donkey Man nodded his head vehemently and neighed garbled messages, and the man responded as if he understood.

"Oh! Donkey Man has found the girl of his dreams. It's love at first sight. He wants to tell her, he wants her to know. Sing it, Donkey Man. If you can't say it, sing it!"

And Donkey Man, his eyes never leaving mine, sang, *Let Me Call You Sweetheart, I'm in love with you!*

His words were indistinct due to the grotesque deformation of his mouth, but his tone was clear and his message understood by all.

The crowd that had gathered started to laugh. I could hear them through the redness of my mind. I could feel the shared joke, the sting of me being me, of him being him. I don't know what my face did. I do know it didn't laugh. It didn't move, or weep, or look away. I stood there and took it. I allowed myself to be seen in a blind world.

Can I do that now? Can I stand tall through these hard times? Can I take on the responsibility of finding Nial in a foreign country that has no comfort zones?

Right now, can I face down the terrors of my own old age when I regard Mother's? Of endings that show no justice?

There's nothing larger in my life than Nial or the absence of him. He was, and is, the love of my life. The one who changed the world. I had had crushes before Nial, of course. They were always awarded to *the least likely to succeed.* I loved boys for being boys. All of them and none of them. I loved dancing to seventy-eights, wearing jeans tighter than spandex before spandex existed. I remember how I'd wait breathlessly for Mickey Quinn to ask me to dance, and when he did, try not to think about his brown curly hair and blue eyes. I just let my body join his perfect rhythm. We danced like ribbons in the same wind.

I wonder what happened to Mickey Quinn, with whom I never had a true conversation. Mickey Quinn whose lips were full and pouty, and who smiled with a choir boy's innocence. Who wore plaid ties on blue button-down shirts and blazers and jeans that bulged in the right places. Dream man, Mickey, perfect dance partner, but not the one. I was not in love with the boy.

My first love was Tommy Tuthill. Unfortunately, or fortunately, Tommy Tuthill loved Lizzy. He would talk about her to me, and discuss the problems they had. They were too young, their parents said. He said life didn't promise the right one to come along just because you were twenty-five. He couldn't understand why their folks didn't realize that. He spoke wistfully through long dark eyelashes meant for a poet. I wanted to kiss the overbite on his sensitive, non-smiling lips and touch his long stringy fingers, meant to play piano or paint watercolors-- fingers that held a cigarette like a brush and made points in sexy smoke that crawled out of his nostrils.

If he had told me to remove my clothes and lie down on the road for him, I would have done it. I had no idea whether he was someone with a future or a past; I heard only my primal self screaming *take me.* But he didn't.

He took Lizzy, gave her a zircon, then twin girls, then another and another. By the time she was twenty-three, she was the mother of four. I had sobbed at her wedding, one of my best friends taken, my fantasy man lost forever. Their marriage was the first of many I attended in the following years, but theirs was the only one that lasted.

I saw them on their twenty-fifth wedding anniversary a few years ago. He was getting bald, still thin and sweet as rain. She was harder and tired looking. Perhaps they drink their nights away listening to Frank Sinatra. I saw them in Tampa, with palm trees and pink stucco all around, and a car meant for the recycled metal dump. As I drove away, I caught them in my rearview mirror hugging in the parking lot. I saw her lean into the length of him, like a girl, and knew she was still in love with the boy.

It was my third year at Cornell when I met Nial and my heart tripped. I was twenty and he was all of twenty-three, a veteran, and completely different from the boys I had dated before.

He was not my idea of handsome. His chin was too large and he had dark bushy eyebrows that made the ridge of his brow look somewhat angry. But, he had an intensity that was electric. I first met him in a sociology class where I found myself feeling defensive more times than not because Dr. Seymour Wolfe was turning my world of absolutes into arbitrary social behaviors. Rules I'd always accepted were called elitist standards. Not only was I introduced to a new vocabulary that included terms like white supremacy, social justice, patriarchal power and disenfranchisement, but, it was in his class, I learned how angry my fellow students were with the establishment, the draft, and the war in Vietnam.

I found myself internally disagreeing with Dr. Wolfe on issues, but felt intellectually inadequate and too timid to take him on. When he asked the class who favored capital punishment, I was the only person foolish enough to admit it. It was too late by the time I realized I was alone. Seymour Wolfe's agenda, clearly shared by the class, left me to defend my position.

He proceeded to bring up the case of the tramp who had been burned to death by an eighteen year old in Central Park. Should the boy be executed?

"I think he's beyond help," I said. I had no problem with the basis of my answer. "Why should the public feed and house this homicidal maniac for the rest of his life?"

"You find it that simple, then?" Dr. Wolfe asked, a little smile twisting his face.

"He's admitted he's guilty. He killed for fun. Eighteen is old enough to know the difference between right and wrong," I said, trying to hold on to my confidence.

It was Nial who interrupted me. "What do you know about his motivation? Who are you to describe this kid's idea of fun? He was raised on the streets, and his rules were formed by the streets of the city. He ate out of garbage cans from the time he was eight. Who are you to say what this kid is guilty of? What was his reality? Who taught him right from wrong? Maybe he thought he was doing the guy a favor. Maybe we're the ones who are guilty for not giving either of them a life. They probably had no alternatives but the streets. Why should a kid like that believe there's value in a human life?"

73

"We all know that killing is wrong. I don't care where we grow up," I argued. My cheeks burned and I wished there were buttons on my wrist to make me invisible. Fortunately, the bell rang and I could escape.

When he asked me to join him in the student lounge after class, I was flustered, but agreed because I didn't want to look intimidated. We walked across campus where ivy spilled over the sides of the walls and clambered up steps, softening the hardness of mortar between stones.

"Who do you read?" he asked.

I had never been asked such a question. Cornell boys generally led with, "Do you or don't you?"

I thought for a minute and said, "Well, I just finished *Atlas Shrugged*. Have you read it?"

"Ha," he said. "I knew it. I knew it!"

I listened carefully as he spoke, expounding on his favorite topic, which just happened to be Ayn Rand and her rugged individualism. He told me how flawed Rand's thinking really was. "She's an angry little Cossack," he said, "with a great big axe to grind."

He said her schtick was a belief not in the survival of the fittest but in the survival of the powerful.

I thought to myself that even if Rand's agenda was unpleasant, she had a rational position. As I saw it, some were blessed from birth and those who were, would most likely succeed. Others would fail, no matter what society did. Certain people were damaged goods, irretrievable. For them banishment or death were the practical solutions.

I tried to explain, "It's easy for you to think all your liberal thoughts but I live near Central Park and I don't want this murderer in my neighborhood—ever!"

"Well, I suppose if you have any say over it, he won't be! He'll be fried. Would you be willing to press the switch?"

We maneuvered ourselves through the coffee line and sat down in a corner of the lounge. I couldn't pick up my cup, my hands were shaking so. He pushed his chin at me and looked through his eyebrows into my eyes.

"I suppose you call yourself a Christian?" he asked.

"You could say that," I answered lightly, although I was not altogether sure.

"A Calvinist? Predestination and all that stuff? Seems like you're hell bent on locking people into their places. You should give up Cannes next year and go to India."

"I think you're turning this into a personal argument."

"Just using you as a scapegoat. I like people willing to argue."

I knew other people could hear us. The clock on the wall read that my next class was about to begin, but I was stuck in this awful debate I had already begun to doubt. I had to stay and fight or lose. Lose what? I wasn't sure.

"What proof do you have that society can change a person's soul? It's the individual who has to change," I said. My cheeks burned again.

74

"If their souls can survive long enough to *choose* change! Between street kids, race, and 'Nam, we're losing it. We used to have the God damnedest land of opportunity on earth. There are people making it here who were drinking their own urine a few years ago, and a lot of them are already on the top of the heap. You don't think that having money has changed their souls?"

I knew he was more right than wrong, but I persisted in continuing my hopeless argument. I looked around the room, as if I might find help. Students were leaving, new ones coming in.

He went on. "And now we've got a bunch of GI Joes who want our generation to go their route. The war is bullshit but the black kids will race to it because it's a way out for them; out of poverty, the ghetto, the hopelessness. When war becomes man's best opportunity for change, we've got to figure out another way. The country's in trouble."

I looked at his square shoulders and my eyes followed his long arms to his fist, punctuating his point on the table. I forced myself to look up at his face. I saw a little scar right near his left eye. His lashes were dark for a blonde, heavy, his eyes questionably blue. The hair cut by a lawnmower, messy.

"What is happening here is like a time warp, a black hole of American integrity. The war is a blasphemy against choice and respect for personal destiny—everything we say we stand for."

He reached toward me. I thought he might actually grab me.

"The Cong *want* communism—it's *their* country. We have no business over there. We should stay home and build our own lives in the land made safe for democracy. Is that wrong?"

The bells signaled the start of my next class but I couldn't leave. Not yet. I said, "Well, I thought we began by talking about a murder. And I believe that's wrong, and there's room to question the death penalty, but now you want to take on the Pentagon! Is that what you think we should all be doing?"

"Yes! We should! If killing is wrong, then training kids to kill is wrong, too. The war is training men to murder. Telling them it's honorable, then holding them responsible when it spills over to the streets."

Such passion! I admit I hung on his every word. He obviously cared deeply about things to which I hadn't given much thought. The truth was, I wasn't sure I had any fixed positions on issues that went beyond social correctness. Wasn't Vietnam just a police action meant to stop the spread of communism? Wasn't freedom truly at risk? Why did this man think it was high moral ground not to fight for our way of life? I was impressed but cautious. He assumed he knew more than the president and his cabinet and I refused to appear helpless in the face of his zeal. Inside, I wanted what he had, to believe in something.

"You need me. Meet me in the lounge at seven—what do you say?" he smiled.

"For an argument?" I asked.

"Got a better idea?" he said.

Somewhere over the twenty-five years that followed, we stopped arguing. Somewhere he stopped believing I could be changed, and I didn't care.

"Mother, mother, don't leave. I have so much I want to tell you, there's so much left for you to tell me."

Eight

Serena

It's Halloween and the loonies are out. Gwen and I are just another odd couple as we canvas the shops: The Broom Closet, The Witch's Attic, Tituba's Candles and the like. We're obviously no mother/daughter team, no sister act. We're an unlikely match to anyone who might be observing us; she's decked out like a middle-aged school teacher wearing all things tight—tight hair, tight earrings, tight shoes, probably a girdle. Myself, I'm dressed for the town in a crushed velvet shawl over acres of Indian cottons, hair out of control (as always), beads clacking, earrings swaying, rings in my nose, my ears and on at least four fingers. This place gives everyone permission to wear a costume.

We're in Salem, known as Witch City to those who profit from her dark history. It's a town that's turned itself around by transforming old Victorian houses into colorful painted ladies, one more ornate than the next. The original clapboard witch houses are painted black, distinguished by their pointy gables and leaded glass. On the streets and in the buildings, reenactments remind visitors that Salem was far from a party town in the past. It seems to me all this capitalization of bad history would be offensive to modern witches, but so many live here I must be wrong.

We enter The Wicca Station and Gwen discovers an herbalist who invites her to sit down at a little table decorated with stars and moons. Before you know it, she's confessing something to this self-proclaimed witch who, in turn, promises her she has healthy brews for sleeping and waking. The woman explains that if she's waking up tired each day, it's because she's not truly resting at night, not getting to REM, the deepest consciousness. She warns her that she must be sure to go there because that is where our needs are fulfilled—where we take care of our fears and wishes—where we learn things we can't face in the light of day. I hear her mention the familiar sleepytime ingredients of sage, chamomile, valerian and hops. Now, Gwen is sniffing a sachet of lavender. What a kick!

I don't know when it started, this friendship thing with Gwen Townsend. I'm not sure I even believe it. She shocked me by knocking on my door a couple of weeks ago. We talked about a lot of stuff that night. It was like she wanted to talk to me, but I don't think she ever said what she wanted to say.

Then she invited me to the house one night the following week for supper. That was totally weird. We looked at family heirlooms and she took me into Nial's den with its homage to rope; rope between the floorboards, rope embedded in walnut picture frames, rope beneath the glass surface of his desk, rope defining the edges of his furniture. Even the rug was made of sisal. I tried not to touch anything, understanding his room was a shrine, but I wanted to. I wanted to run my hands over the chair where he sat, the books he read, his pipe. I wanted to examine the face of Nial the boy, then Nial the student, and later Nial the navigator, the father, the businessman. He looked so much like Tim but more intense. His charisma was there from the beginning. I didn't look at their wedding pictures. Not that.

She also wanted to share her son with me. Took me into Tim's bedroom, a perfect space for a boy-man who, at twenty-five, was still looking at school flags and photos of himself from the cradle on. He'd been living at home since college but hadn't changed a thing. He must have felt like he was caught in a time capsule.

"Did you know him, Serena?" she asked me again.

"A little."

If I'd had more courage, I would have told her the truth right then. That I knew him as I had never known anyone else. That he was sick, lost and miserable. But I couldn't. I thought she didn't need to hear that. What she wanted, what she needed to do, was brag to me about his rowing medals at Endfield and his science degree from Cornell. She went on about his love of nature and concern for the environment. I knew all these things to be true. I didn't mind listening.

What she didn't say, because she probably doesn't know, was that she had placed him in a box so tight, even Houdini couldn't have escaped. Its floor was made of family history and its walls were made of rules that weren't his choosing. Above the walls was a ceiling that no light or fresh air could penetrate. It was the ceiling that did Tim in; the ceiling said, *This is it— you have all you need and can't go beyond this space.*

For me, it was hard to imagine why he let himself be trapped. He'd seen more of the world than I ever hope to, before he was twenty. He'd traveled to Central America with Nial, been to Europe skiing, spent a Semester at Sea sailing halfway around the globe in his junior year of college—he had every reason to choose to live outside the box. But he didn't. He hung around for three years in the place he claimed suffocated him. Poor Tim. Bad Tim. Messed up Tim. My Tim. No one's Tim.

I knew about his sister. *Sabrina the Perfect,* he called her. Even though he'd never known her, he resented her because his mother became so overly protective when he came along. Gwen wouldn't let him out of her sight, kept him out of sandboxes, off jungle gyms, away from swings, out of nursery schools. He slept in his parents' room until he was four and watched his toys whirl in the washing machine or soaked in detergents every other day. He said his mom should have called herself Auntie Septic. He actually thought toys were *supposed* to smell like Clorox. Not trusting God to protect her boy, she made him sit with her in church services rather than expose him to runny-nosed Sunday School kids. She carried her own brand of Handi-wipes with her and scrubbed his hands and face constantly. Maybe that explains why he still loves the smell of alcohol. Live animals of any kind were a no-no.

It was his Grandmother Terwilliger who finally said something like, "Gwen, you might as well put that child in a bubble. He will not be any healthier for all your protectiveness. He needs children around him and germs to build his immune system."

Tim overheard "build" as in erector set, and decided an immune system was a toy, something to put together. He asked his mother where they could get one. She and Grandma Terwilliger had laughed at that...at least hard enough for him to remember. Anyway, not long after, he went to a private kindergarten in the Presbyterian Church. The students were from the best houses in town and that helped Gwen feel safer. She must have believed Presbyterians didn't get head lice.

According to Tim, his father tried to contradict the messages his mother sent his way. Nial had him scaling mountains, ice fishing, skiing on Terrible Mountain from the time he could wrest him from Gwen's sight. Tim's speed demon tendencies on the Whaler, stunts on water skis and abandon with pot and booze all proved he was beyond her control. So far beyond that she didn't seem to notice. Not so far that he left her house.

"The Wicca are healers. We're naturalists who integrate our spirits with the spirit world," I hear Gwen's bangled advisor say.

"Pagans, then?" Gwen asks.

"Proud Pagans, yes."

"I see. Do you actually have covens?"

Gwen is a surprise. I like her curiosity.

"We do. There are at least eight hundred Wicca living here in Salem."

"Do you meet regularly, like church-going people?"

"A large number of coven members are also churchgoers."

"Indeed?"

We stay for a few more minutes and Gwen buys a brew for more restful sleep. I smile at her receptivity. She has never heard of the Wiccan Movement. But then, neither had I until I met Geena. I had thought to be a religious Pagan was an oxymoron, but after meeting Geena's friends, I decided they were more spiritual than Grandma's Catholics who broke every rule during the week, confessed, were clean by Sunday Mass and started to sin again before the day was out.

Pagans in the kooky town of Key West made no bones about pleasure. They danced and banged drums to their own rhythms, sang and conjured up their animal spirits. I joined them in the celebration of life. I understood their relationship with Mother Nature better than I did the God who killed his own son so I could be forgiven. Isn't everything in God's creation coming and going? Good and bad depending on your perspective? I've watched the sea, where all things feed on each other and operate in balance. Out there in the wet blue world believing in a sun goddess or a rain goddess or the phases of the moon isn't hard. That's when you know you're just one small piece of the scheme of things.

"Where shall we do lunch?" Gwen asks.

I have never *done* lunch. I have eaten lunch, ordered lunch, finished lunch, but never *done* lunch before. Can this woman possibly understand how different we are? Does she have a clue?

"Let's try Witch Hazel's," I suggest.

We walk down the busy streets where women were once tortured, perhaps not as many as one might have heard, but enough to keep the stories alive. For those found guilty of witchcraft, their punishment was horrific. When they weren't hanged, they were publicly pressed to death under the weight of great stone mill wheels meant to grind corn. Their guilt? Herbal cures, acts of midwifery, superstition and hexes. Not so well known were the men wanting to rid the town of independent women who spoke as healers and owned their own parcels of land—just as much chauvinism and politics as witch hunting. Not so different from the way things seem to go today: the *whores* who seduce otherwise upstanding men, the *bitches* who seek power, the *witches* who speak their truths, the *heathens* who are pro-choice. It hasn't changed that much: the name calling attached to autonomous women, women who love sex, who name their own rules. Of course, there are no public pressings anymore. Just bad press.

I say all this to Gwen over green tea and stuffed avocados. The room is pungent with incense. I've never liked the smell.

"There's a witch doing a Tarot Card reading over in the corner," Gwen says. "Have you ever had it done?"

"Nope. I'm afraid of that stuff because I would believe in it even though I'd try not to."

She smiles and folds her napkin perfectly, placing it near her empty plate.

"Why? Do *you* want your cards read?" I ask.

"Well, it might be fun. Of course, I know it's nonsense. There isn't a bit of evidence that these things are credible. But wouldn't it be fun to do anyway?"

Gwen is saying *fun*. I'm sure "fun" has been out of her vocabulary for a while. She's smiling, her face is softer, her eyes not as dark as usual.

"I guess so."

"Come on. It'll be my treat."

If the Tarot reader wasn't wearing all that makeup and if her lips weren't painted quite that red, I might think she had more legitimacy to her act, but she's actually a Hollywood version of a witch. It doesn't matter in the end. I'm mesmerized as she spreads the cards for Gwen. Gwen sits, poised, her back very straight, her feet tucked beneath her side by side, black pumps polished and slim, hands folded correctly on her lap. Her whole person is incongruous with the veils and Indian Madras patterns behind her, the Himalayan music, the wickers and beads everywhere.

She folds the cards three times and waits.

I see her past in the reversed strength card.

"Too much control," says the gilded lady. "Your life has been about that, but things are about to change. Go slowly, not too much at a time, not too fast or you will have trouble holding on your course. Here we see a reversed Tower Card. You are not seeing the truth of the situation. Are you listening, dear? You must first get to the truth of your situation before you ride the chariot that is waiting in your future. If you stay calm and patient, that chariot promises you a transformation, a life evolvement that will advance your spirit to a new place."

Gwen turns to me and raises her eyebrows. She's humoring the reader.

I look at the chariot with its sphinx-like critters at the base and the chariot driver, androgynous, like most of the cards, bearing a wand and looking straight ahead. The sign of Cancer is on the chariot driver's head, representing diligence and perseverance.

"You will need to sort out the past before you let the stallions stomping at the gates take you where you must go. When your will is empowered and your house is in order, renewal will be yours."

Something is pushing against my windpipe. I realize it's air. I've forgotten to breathe.

The reader continues, "Ah, now look here, you have a challenge. You are blessed with a Sun Card, but it is also reversed. You are capable of great energy and talents, but your light has been lost in a shadow. You must step out and reverse this situation on your own, move into the light, carefully, deliberately. Remember, *you* design your fate. It is up to you."

The reading is too close, too good. I don't want to hear my own.

Gwen smiles, I guess the message hasn't sunk in. "Now, you, Serena. Let's hear it for you. It's my treat!"

Shit. I know better than to do this but I say yes, anyway, and trade places with her. The woman stares into my eyes. I stare into hers. They're sad, lonely. I look at her loose lips painted hard red, then I notice the stubble on her chin, the masculinity of the cheekbones, the Adam's apple in her throat. My God, she's a fucking *he*.

"We are going to shuffle the cards and wait for your energy to fill them," he says, handing me the deck.

I'm uncomfortable.

"You are uncomfortable," he says.

"No, I'm fine."

"Have you done the cards before?" he asks.

"Once or twice," I lie.

He winks and smiles, which says more than words.

Damn it, I'm blushing. I cut the cards three times. He begins to turn them over like pages in a journal.

I see them fall and wait.

"Behind you is the Fool, the one who took a calculated risk. You know that now. You are ready to move on, but wait...here in the present is the Magician. Ah, the Magician reversed! He looks away, embarrassed because you have used your magical powers to deceive. And yet...look. Here we are in the future and the Devil is leaving the scene. You will experience a release from self entrapment, from your obsessions, your guilt. You will master the Devil within. This is a good sign."

Gwen is leaning toward me, more interested in my reading than her own. She crosses her arms and scrutinizes the cards.

The cards look sinister, ominous and condemning. I don't care what the reader says; they don't feel like a good sign. I know now why I didn't want them read.

I don't like this man, posing as a woman, telling me I'm a con artist. There is only one imposter in the room. Then again maybe not. But I'm only temporarily guilty as charged; I'm going to find a way to talk to Gwen and it will be soon.

She calls the readings *shrewd*, suggests the information offered is *moot*, put into words a person can make relevant or not, depending on their willingness to believe. I'm noncommittal. My day has changed its color from orange to black. The masks and music, the teeming streets with their stupid knick-knack stands and costumed Draculas selling bloody eyeballs and fake puke—it makes me angry. She seems to know that and suggests we take in the waterfront before we leave. But even the waterfront is disappointing. It's yuppified now. The fishing boats have been replaced with yachts. Oh, a few rust buckets remain, but the harbor is dominated by play boats, even at this time of year.

There are some rowdy kids on the pier who should be in school, but they're drinking wine and smoking grass instead. Looking up at a vee of migrators in the sky, they hold their privates as they scream "Honk if you love Jesus!". Like a bunch of misplaced ducks, the boys waddle around in circles honking. I laugh despite myself. They're as stoned as they can be. Knapsacks and dogs keep them company while the rest of the world, including us, steers clear of their stage.

Tim wasn't much different than these kids when he was eighteen, only doing his drugs with style, on sailing ships and in college dorms, at Aspen and St. Martin.

It still hurts to remember the day I ran into one of his little parties. Buff Harriman, Chip Mortimer, some fair-haired prima donna named Gillian and he made a blissful foursome when I showed up at Penny Loaf Island. I didn't recognize the sloop anchored yards from the beach, but the scent of marijuana seemed familiar enough. Pop's friends were bonked out on it more often than not. He called it the Devil's Weed. Hated the stuff; said it was Vietnam's curse, the highway to heroin. He'd watched too many of his friends get hooked.

I realized, after the fact, I was intruding on a scene I cared desperately not to see.

Tim's eyes were red and squinting as he looked into mine, "Hi, Mermaid, what's new in the fish business?"

He was a mean stupid bastard. Was his intention to humiliate me or teach me to hate? Heat boiled through every pore of my skin, burning so badly I could hardly speak.

"I'm outta here," I answered, blinding myself to the girls' bare breasts, to the garland of leaves on his head.

"Hey. Don't go. This is Buff in the rough, you might say," Tim laughed, introducing his naked friend. "Buff, my boy, this is Serena."

"*The* Serena?" he said. "Man, it is making sense to me now."

It was bizarre, his introducing me to people from whom I had been ostracized, and at the same time, pointing to Buff's private parts flapping in the wind.

Buff held his penis up for a salute. "Pleased to meet you, Serena!" he said.

They all thought this was hilarious.

What had drawn me there in the first place was the red and green handle of one of my pot markers sticking out of the sea grass. It *had* marked the spot. Nature's pun. I walked to it, grabbed it and yanked it free.

"Here, I've got the anchor," I heard Tim say, helping out as I clamored back onto my boat. He lifted it onboard and I revved the motor to move away to safe harbor. I saw him standing knee deep in the water for long time, watching me as I made my way across to the cut. I couldn't know what he was thinking.

When my childhood friend Teresa moved away, I lost my one real connection to the land. I had tried to replace her with Tim, but soon he managed to hurt me more than not. I didn't understand what came between us. We lived in different worlds, that was true, but when we spent time together the rest of the world didn't exist. I don't think it was meanness that messed us up. No. It might have been my needing him too much. I would try to let him go, stop waiting for him and thinking about him. But, no matter how hard I tried, no matter how cruelly he pushed me away, I chose him again and again rather than have no choice at all. And he did the same. Just when I would think I was done with him, he'd bestow some little act of kindness on me, and then I'd remember he was my first and only love and I'd be hooked all over again. Like the day he showed up with a book named *Lives of a Cell* under his arm and handed it to me. He said, "This guy has got the whole idea." Inside the book, I found a note that read,

> Mermaid - Lewis Thomas says, *a steady flow*
> of energy from the inexhaustible source of the sun to the
> unfillable sink of outer space...is mathematically destined to
> cause the organization of matter into an increasingly
> ordered state...
>
> I'll be getting my act together—soon.
>
> I love you, Tim

I took this as a promissory note to our future. He had just graduated from Cornell and I figured I'd continue to lobster until we walked off into the sunset together.

Gwen interrupts my thoughts. "I do not understand what is happening these days. So many young people are lost."

"They aren't like you. That's all."

"I think my generation produced a lost generation. We made some terrible mistakes. I don't know what's to become of them. Of course, I don't

83

mean you. You're exceptional...but I can't help but think of Tim. How well did you say you knew Tim?"

"A little."

"He's lost. He sees no reason for anything. I just can't understand that, can you?"

Here it comes. Where will I go now? What was I going to say? She's opening the door I wanted opened and I can't go through it.

"I think he's probably like most kids, Mrs. Townsend."

"Please, call me Gwen, dear."

"Gwen. He needs to make up his own world."

"He's not a *kid*. He's twenty-five years old. What makes you so wise, Serena? You're just a girl yourself. You're probably half my age. How old *are* you?"

"I'm twenty-four. The thing is, I've had to figure it all out for myself. My father gave me what he could, Grandma, too, but I never had to be anything other than what I am. It hurts, it's scary, it's lonely sometimes, but I've learned things no one can take away from me."

"I must say it amazes me to see how strong you are. You're an exception to the products of this Generation X, as they call it."

"But don't you see? I'm not a *product*. I'm my own person. I've been choosing for myself since I was old enough to choose."

I hear myself and think it sounds true. It *is* true if I compare myself to Tim. It *is* true if I look at the kids waddling on the wharf, compromising themselves for each other. But it isn't proof that my life works any better than theirs.

She pats my arm. "None of us can help but be affected by the people we know and the ones we love. I think choosing is a luxury granted to only a few."

Truth is, my whole world has been undone in three years. One by one, the people I loved most were taken from me. I'm the walking wounded. I look at Gwen. She holds her head up in that regal way and lets the wind pull free some of her hair.

We're both the walking wounded. We have this much in common.

Nine

Gwen

We had a lovely day. Really. I actually had fun doing Salem with my own pet witch. Serena would probably steer clear of me if she thought I perceived her this way, but there *is* something witchy about her. Perhaps it's associated with how she appeared to me in the first place, her tall dark shape backlit with fire, acting familiar and mysterious at the same time. It's obvious how she uses the physical to explore the metaphysical. She's charmingly intriguing. Her youthful directness is good for me. I prefer to be with someone who says what she thinks and doesn't expect me to be grieving or try to get me to talk about *it*...someone who doesn't want me to be my old self. It's the pretense I find exhausting. Trying to give one hoot about the church's fund drive is enough to make my eyes bleed. I may never be as self-sufficient as Serena has learned to be, but right now, I'd prefer to be alone than face the Bridge Club or the Guild.

No matter how remote the possibility, I need to believe that it's just a matter of time until I see Nial again. Meanwhile, I'm doing my best to understand the cordage industry so I can handle whatever comes along. Plenty of documentation about the company's history has turned up and I am still gathering all the information I can about cordage—from the varieties and competition to the specific plants that yield the best fibers for rope production. I know now that Nial's plantings of abaca in Central America reaped large crops—and it should have. He started planting four years ago, right after the Sandinista revolution, knowing the area's climate was perfect and its soil right for the plants. He predicted it would not only benefit the people in the collectivos, but also create a low-cost resource for his company.

I had laughed at him when he kept referring to his plants as *little suckers*. But I have discovered that is exactly what rhizomes are called, suckers—if they're the underground variety. He took his "little suckers" down to Managua and found groups of liberated workers. Then he encouraged them to farm for the future. Of course, the American embargo on goods at the time made it a terrible gamble. But Nial knew politics had to change by the time his crops were ready, and he was right. Unfortunately, he didn't anticipate how much his own cordage business would slip at home.

I found many letters that revealed Nial's anxiety about the survival of his company as well as how he would pay his *farmworkers*. He had offered them a considerable financial reward at the end of three years if they would put up with subsistence funding to get started. When Nicaraguan politics started to move from far left to center, he had concerns about whether the collectives could hang onto the land they'd acquired from the former patrones. He had heard charges that the land had been stolen and the exiled owners were putting pressure on the new government for their return.

Meanwhile, the workers' childlike belief in Nial's wisdom became a personal burden. He kept assuring them it would work out, that the crop would move them beyond what had once been slavery and past their present dependence on government rations. He even wrote to the U.S. Embassy, to a man named Trainor Steele, to protect his project. Trainor Steele's response may have been the reason Nial was on his way to Nicaragua when his plane crashed.

I keep fantasizing he is living somewhere among them, but it isn't rational. We would have heard.

And the litigation goes on. It is abhorrent. Ted showed up, as promised, at the last meeting in the lawyer's office. He's convinced the lawyers were purposely complicating the language to force me out of the loop when it came to decision making. Evidently, Cordage & Rope International has made an offer to buy out the company. The banks want the resolution to go in this direction. They see the buyout as a solution to our outstanding debts, but I know that buyouts often lead to depersonalization of a company and this company is part of the town's identity. The fact that I am a major stockholder does not seem to worry anyone, as I have never voted before. They assume I will do what I am told. Ted, evidently, has a considerable investment in the company, too. I was not aware of this fact. He didn't pull out his money when he heard about our difficulties, but he doesn't seem opposed to the buyout either. Clearly, I need to think for myself and the company's best interests.

It is difficult for me to become this circumspect; it's a real deviation from my life as Nial's wife. But only one person can make decisions for me now, and that is me. I force myself to read the papers stacked in front of me; sort them into piles. Bank loans, private expenses, tax statements, business reports, insurance papers, paper ad infinitum. Eating ice cream, French vanilla smothered with hot fudge topping, is what I'd prefer to be doing. I give myself two hours of focusing before I indulge in a treat. It's as easy as that; at least it helps me launch into the business world.

It doesn't take long before I discover Nial has been borrowing from one bank to pay another. He has seen no profit for three years; his debts building to well over a million dollars and compounding each quarter. He has gone as far as putting our house, his family's trophy, up for collateral. He must have felt like he was drowning.

I am engulfed in the darkness of his despair, unnerved and ashamed that he was unable to confide in me. Was he still competing with the Terwilliger image? Did Father have that impact on him? Was it impossible for him to understand how little my inheritance meant to me compared to his happiness? How proud Father was of our family and our well-being?

If the company is bought out by Cordage & Rope International, that will keep it alive until Nial returns. I am going to have to negotiate what will happen to him then, see to it that he has a place on the Board, or a role as director. Yes, I could make that a condition. On the other hand, if he is truly lost, I can clear up the debts by selling the house, which has to be worth well over a million.

It would free me to create a new life for myself if the business is in someone else's hands. Nial's legacy won't be completely annihilated. No one needs to know how terrible things actually became. Of course, these huge firms that eat up little companies like ours don't give a hoot who works for them or how many years they have left to retirement. And I must take into consideration. A major industry folding in a town this size would hurt many, many people.

Ted Peterson and I discuss some of the alternatives for handling the future of the company. I could shut it down, but this is too easy and too cruel. Instead, I commit to a briefing with the entire staff.

On a Saturday morning, with attendance optional, we meet in the cafeteria where there's coffee and doughnuts in abundance. The employees are quiet and distanced from me. I realize I don't know these people. They are Nial's people, not mine. Despite that, they wear name tags I recognize, because I have spent hours reading the data about their years on the job. In fact, I have read every active personnel file. Our one hundred and two employees represent five hundred and thirty-five people from the Granite Shores community, in one way or another. What I say will be gravely important to them; and I can't help but wonder how much gossip has gone on before I explain the precariousness of the situation.

My carefully written speech is clattering in my hands as I begin.

"I am not used to speaking in front of people so I ask you to forgive me for trembling."

The tension in the room is palpable. I look at the sea of faces and realize my fears are nothing compared to theirs. Nial must have known these fears, had to think about them every day.

My paper stops shaking, and I proceed. "I have put together some information I would like to share with you this morning. For the past few days I have familiarized myself with your names and positions with the Townsend Rope and Cordage Company. I counted how many of you showed up for this meeting and all but two of you are here. What an amazing show of concern. At least, I assume it means you are expecting me to say something important, and I will try.

"For years, the rope and cordage industry has been undergoing a sort of revolution, as you know. It has turned from organic materials to plastics and been absorbed by large international businesses who have destabilized our long-term steady market. My husband decided to build a bridge between the future and the past by importing forty percent of his raw materials from Nicaragua. He is, and always has been, convinced that natural products are superior to synthetics. He believes the company has been on environmental high ground from the beginning.

"But, this is our challenge. We must sell our company's product in a fiercely competitive marketplace, a market without a conscience, and that will take time and effort. We will have to educate the public to the virtue of our products and appeal to common decency. We must take our losses until the cordage world becomes responsible for itself and supports us. I'm sure some of you have wondered what all this means to you and your job security. I am sure you know Mr. Townsend was a responsible employer and cared very much about *your* future as well as his own. That's why he fought the tide and continued the production of cord here at the plant. He hoped he could reach a compromise within the industry. You also may know it was not working as well as he had hoped. Townsend Rope and Cordage is like David facing a world of Goliaths."

I see their heads nodding. Mac Huff strokes his beard. He wipes his nose on his sleeve. He, no doubt, knows more than I thought. He was the foreman of production, after all...Nial's right-hand man. I know he is worried about his health insurance; his wife, Florence, has to have her breast removed, he told me so the other day.

Now for the big news. "We have been approached by Cordage & Rope International with a buyout offer. It is a lean offer. A few years ago, it would have been much larger, but I want to bring this before you now, before I take it to the stockholders and before I speak to CRI.

"I want you to think of pooling your efforts and taking over the company yourselves. It has been done by Reproductions, Inc. and Rockville Ale and most recently, Satellite Airlines. Why not consider it here, and become another employee-owned hometown industry?"

Someone starts to clap, then another and another. I am not sure what it means, but I surmise they are thanking me for the opportunity to choose.

"Thank you, thank you," I tell them. "I know that Nial would have wanted you to have a choice before he made such a decision. Selling the company will only provide a minimal guarantee for all of you, you understand this, don't you? We can negotiate your positions here at the plant for a few years but changes will follow; they always do.

"Our faltering business incurred debts that will have to be addressed should you choose to buy out the company. These are negotiable with the debtors and not insurmountable, if you pull together and include them in your projections for costs and considerations. I am speaking as my husband would have wanted me to speak. You must know how much he respected and cared for you all. He always understood that you were at the heart of his success." (Did Nial put these words in my mouth? They aren't on the paper in my hands.)

"I have provided an attorney for you to meet with this morning. He will answer your questions and provide you with information about how you might go about buying the company and become a profit-sharing organization should you so choose. Thank you so much for coming and for all you have done to make Townsend Rope and Cordage a viable company for so many years. Thank you from Nial and from our son, Timothy."

I leave with everyone on their feet applauding and my heart pounding in my ears for the shear madness of what I have done. I've stood in front of

Nial's people and worn his shoes for fifteen minutes or more. I have forgotten I am as afraid of public speaking as I am of my own death.

Holding myself rigidly, I move brusquely to the car. My keys jangle as I try to start the ignition. I grip the wheel tightly and take off. What do I feel? Is it exhilaration? I am alive. That is what I feel, alive.

As I turn down my driveway I see Serena on the pier. She is dressed in her fishing clothes, her red hair flying beyond the bandana she has tied around it. A woman of the wharf. It comes home to me again that she was invisible until a little more than a month ago.

We wave. I am too excited with myself to go into the empty house so I walk toward her. The air is cold. December casts her gray shadows on the water, turning it to a slate blue. I realize Serena will be leaving soon. I don't want to see her go.

She comes toward me simultaneously. Her yellow slicker brightens the horizon. Her high rubber boots look like a fashion statement.

"Hi, Gwen," she says. "What's happening?"

"Had a big day today," I tell her. I want to confide in her, but it might sound like boasting and I don't imagine she would be interested. I confess my excitement over the fact that I have spoken to Nial's employees and told them they could buy the company if they so choose.

"I'm beginning to think like you do. I think he told me what to say. By channeling or ESP—he was giving me the tools to take care of the business."

She nods. "Mental telepathy."

"Could be. It's hard to accept that Nial may be dead when I can hear his words inside my head. And, Serena, hope is the anchor of the soul. It keeps me going, you know."

She nods. A shadow of sadness falls across her face. The dear. Then she blurts out, "Why don't you go to Nicaragua and find some more facts for yourself? Maybe that would help."

I am taken aback. I can't imagine myself as an investigator in a land I hardly know, where people speak in a language that doesn't even resemble the few years of Spanish I studied. And Nial went down six months ago, along a coast where almost no white man visits, where only indigenous people live. There are no hotels, no paved roads. It's inhabited by primitive bands of Indians with their own sets of rules. They don't even consider themselves Nicaraguan.

"I think not, Serena. If the U.S. Embassy and the Coast Guard couldn't find him, how in the world could I? I wouldn't know where to begin."

"I would go, if I were you. What if he's alive and can't reach you?" she asks. "I would go in a minute if I were you."

It is easy for her to say what she would do; she doesn't have to do it. "What makes you say such a thing?" I inquire.

"Because I would need to be sure, surer than you are now. What have you got to lose?"

What indeed? I am afraid and inept, and that's the short sad truth.

89

"I just wouldn't know where to begin," I admit.

Serena looks at me. She is thinking; I can almost hear her brain whirring.

"It may be that you have to go just for your own good. Let's say Mr. Townsend was running from some kind of a problem. Maybe he needs you to help him face it. Maybe he's wounded and can't get help."

She suspects he's alive too! Then again, why wouldn't she? The papers have insinuated it all along by implying Nial ran from his financial obligations. But I must ask myself if I've lost my mind to even engage in this conversation, as if I can take seriously the nonchalant challenge of a twenty-four-year-old woman who can only pretend to know so much.

"I can't imagine Nial running from a problem; that's not his style. He's a fighter. Mr. Fix-It," I say. Certainly, that's what I used to think.

"Some things can't be fixed," Serena says, "and people who think they can fix everything can get thrown off course."

"I suppose that's possible, but if I know Nial, and of course I do, running from problems would not be his way."

"People change."

"Yes, Serena, that's true, people change."

"People get lost, too."

"Yes. Yes, of course, you're right," I agree.

I spend two days mulling over this conversation. Then a toothache arises to dominate my thoughts. The dentist tells me I need to have scaling and root planing. He scolds me for neglect. Little does he know flossing is the least of my problems.

I take the car in for an oil change, get my nails and hair done, put the storm windows up and take the screens down. In spite of a backache, a throbbing jaw and fitful sleep, I make myself function as the days move forward.

December arrives and I have not thought of Christmas. Thor and I are walking the beach when I see Serena emptying supplies from the boat to the shack. Remembering her imminent departure, I'm jarred into urgency. Thor races down to the pier and I follow. The road feels longer than usual. I've become at home on the old wharf built with Townsend granite and studded with shacks that have one foot on land and the rest on pilings.

Thor is licking Serena's face by the time I reach the boat. His tail ecstatically waves in the smelly air rich with salt and fish. I climb on board the Serena Marie. Its captain pulls her head out of a trap and smiles.

"Are you here to say good-bye?" she asks.

I'm panting. So out of shape. "Not quite. Serena, I...I have an idea...I want...I want you to come with me."

"Where?"

"Nicaragua."

She turns away. "I can't. I really can't."

She starts yanking pieces of orange twine from the turquoise pots. It's weave casts squares across the dark green planks of the deck.

"But, I beg you to do this one thing for me. I will pay your way and reimburse you for anything you might have made fishing. More than that!"

"I don't fish in the winter; I lecture on the glass bottom boat tours out of Key West."

"Whatever. I'll compensate you. I don't even speak Spanish, Serena. Actually my French is dreadful, too. I would be helpless."

"I don't know Spanish any better than you do, and I don't know *Nicaraguan* at all." She points her long index finger at me. "This is your mission. You can do it. You need to go! You will find people there who can interpret for you. You'll be taken care of."

"We both saw the whale," I say, forcing a smile. "Please consider it. I'm convinced you bring me luck."

She screws up her face and turns away again. I realize I'm humiliating myself. She must think I'm pathetic.

"Please, it wouldn't work," she says, her whole self now engaged in hauling a huge barrel toward the pier. A barrel too big for an average man to lift.

I try to determine how absolute the *no* is in her voice.

Two hours later, I hear a knock on the back door.

I open it and before I can speak, Serena says, "I'll tell you what. I can't go with you to Nicaragua--but, I *will* go as far as Florida."

"Come to Salem with me tomorrow; we'll pick up a passport for you just in case you change your mind," I say, feeling doors opening ever so slightly.

"No. No. I don't need a passport because there is no way I can go to Nicaragua. But *you* must go, and this much I can do. I'll fly down with you, to Miami, and stay with you until you make some contacts in Managua. Would that help?"

"It would be even better if you would get on the plane with me," I persist.

"I have to start the boat tours by December 15th. I have a life in Florida, you know. There's my roommate and Furbie. I miss Furbie."

"Oh, is that a someone special?" I ask.

"You could say. He's my dog. But, listen, you give me more credit than I deserve. I wouldn't be any help to you in Nicaragua. You're going to be fine on your own."

I give in. "You will come to Miami with me then? That's wonderful. I will settle for that if I have to." Then I remember the press and all things ugly that rumor can do. "And Serena, please, would you not speak of this trip to anyone? This has to be our little secret. The last thing I want is the newspapers getting involved, especially with the company about to become a cooperative. We don't want to infer there are ghosts in the closet or any other reasons for this company not to go forward."

"Of course," she promises. Depending on an instinct beyond my ken, I trust her.

Parka in hand, we walk together as far as the beach. There's a cold bite to the wind. It's bittersweet. Pine smoke travels sideways out of Ted's chimney, some rotten apples still lie waiting in the yard for something to nourish, the squirrels haven't tucked themselves in yet.

While the water is dark and wintry, Serena seems light and buoyant. I realize how much she wants me to take the trip. Sweet girl. Young enough to believe in miracles.

At least I've crossed over from the plains of shock to the hillsides of possibility. I'm doing something I need to do and for reasons of her own, this young woman has helped me get started. I feel a wave of hope for the first time in a long time, and it is because of her...this Serena Tesorerio and her genuine enthusiasm.

Church bells filter across the harbor. It must be noon.

Nial's mid-day visits sometimes turned into our best sexual play, a touch of lust to break up his work day. We'd have our sex after lunch, coffee hot on his breath, his appetite whetted by the shortage of time and my hands in dishwater or string beans while his hands teased me, toyed with my breasts, his front against my back. The bells go on and on; if they reach thirteen I might fall down. I walk faster and faster, the sound chasing me. I never said no to him, never once. Not once.

Ten

Serena

"You just don't make sense, girl!" she scolds, when I try to tell her how I feel. "I keep telling you, what you need to do is move on."

It's next to impossible to explain to Geena why I'm so tied up with Gwen. I never meant to be. It's like I can't decide whether to love her or hate her. Truth is, I don't want to think about her at all, but I can't seem to help it. She thinks I'm a friend. I don't know what to do with that. It's pointless. She actually wanted me to go to Managua with her! Imagine what a happy threesome we would have made if we found Nial living in some tree house waiting to be rescued? That would've been cute.

I stayed with Gwen as far as I could, helped her make the phone calls to the embassy, even stayed with her at a fancy hotel overnight in Miami. It was one of those museums of excess. Too much of everything. Too many fountains, too many flowers, too many limousines. My closet had a terry cloth robe and little scuffy slippers for after bathing or the pool or something. At first I thought someone had left them behind. Then I discovered the refrigerator was stocked with goodies and tiny bottles of wine and whisky and gin. When we came back after dinner I found my covers turned down and a chocolate mint on the pillow. A single rose appeared on my nightstand. I knocked on Gwen's adjacent suite. I said, "How many roses did you get?"

She said, "Only one!"

I asked her, "Where's the Bible?"

"The what?"

"The Bible. That's all I've ever seen in a hotel room!"

"Your international hotels lean over backwards not to offend. What with guests who are Buddhists and Muslims and Jews," she explained.

At the airport, she kept asking me to get on the plane with her. I wanted to get away from her so much, I almost bolted from the ladies room, but I stuck it out; went with her right up to Customs and, for no reason I understand, hugged her as she left. Her body was shaking. I hung around to watch her plane taxi down the runway; it was an old DC7. I waved in case I never saw her again.

Find him for me; no, find him for you, I thought. Shit, I must be nuts; I don't even know my own motives. There's no way I can make it up her— what I've done. She would never understand. It's better this way, her not knowing. Her believing that she has a marriage worth saving.

It's not as if I'd want him back. I just want him to be alive, his living breathing self, and if he's not alive, I want to know that, too—that he's dead.

Gwen and I are a mess of contradictions. On my part, it's about liking her and resenting her; seeing her up close but wanting her far away. Having to lie on the way to the truth. I pushed Nial out of my life and would give anything to pull him back. And Tim, once my closest friend, so far away now. Maybe, when they're all gone, I will be able to start over. I might remember the someone I once was; someone who never knew Nial Townsend, someone who had never let his hands find my secret places, who had never kissed his scars, tasted the insides of his ears and all the rest. I will forget how he felt inside me, forget the way he smelled and the way I *became* him when we made love—his fierceness, his tenderness. How he made me want the pain. Could she have ever felt the same?

What is it with that woman? Why should I mean anything to her? I'm an oddity, a hired friend—a diversion. She's just curious about me, that's all. Like that time when she and I went to the Museum of Fine Arts so she could teach me all she thought I didn't know about art.

We walked down the white marble halls to the rooms filled with American Paintings. Kids were sitting crosslegged in front of a very abstract watercolor. Their teacher had them copying Marin's work. I asked Gwen, "What's the point of copying someone else's design?" She smiled and said, "That's how we learn."

"I don't buy that," I said. "Art should describe a person's own way of seeing." I gravitated to Homer's painting of Norman's Woe and pointed out some of my favorite Hopper paintings of Cape Ann. She was surprised that I knew anything at all about art.

But not as surprised as I was seeing myself in the glass of the restaurant windows above the Japanese garden. I thought how Tiny would have laughed at me surrounded by a bunch of prissy ladies who never let their elbows hit the table. I got over it, though, when Gwen started to tell me about her father and how she had almost lost him when she decided to marry Nial.

"It seems to me your father should have loved Mr. Townsend for being wonderful and important," I said.

"Oh," she said. "He was all that to me, and yet Father would have preferred I marry the king of Spain."

"And you *only* married the king of Granite Shores."

She laughed. "I suppose *you* would see it that way."

"Pop used to say everything is relative."

"He would have wanted you to marry the king of Spain, too."

"I don't think so," I said. "I don't think he would have wanted me to marry any one at all."

We sat quietly a minute, both of us looking down at the sculpture garden where photographers were doing a shoot of long skinny girls draped on the bulky bronze of a Rodin. When my eyes returned to hers, she was all teary and I was scared I might get teary-eyed, too.

We rented tape machines after lunch and tuned into the Matisse Exhibit. I liked his bold sloppy strokes with pattern and clashing color. She liked his last works, his cutouts best. "He simplified," she said.

Looking back, it was a day like no other; I was glad I'd gone with her and felt good that we'd been able to talk for a while, to just be together. It's all it can be—kind of touch and go. The last thing I need is one more Townsend on my mind!

I've made a promise to the goddesses of the sea, in heaven and on earth, that if Nial is alive, I will be happy for Gwen, for them. And then, maybe, I'll be liberated from the whole thing. If Gwen and Nial could put their worlds back together, I think mine might have a chance.

Eleven

Gwen

I have to keep telling myself this is real. I am in my seat, in a sea of Spanish voices, flying to a country I have never cared to visit.

As we pass over Cuba, I look down at the lush length and breadth of it, and contemplate its modest size. I remember how close the United States came to disaster with its feisty leader. During the thirteen day face-off with Kruschev and the Kennedy brothers, I woke up each morning to the World News Report thinking it was all going to end then and there, that I would never see my teenage years.

It's seven months since Nial's plane went down and I'm still resisting closure. At least I am over the inertia. Flying to Nicaragua is helping with that. If it hadn't been for Serena, I don't know if I would have bought the tickets when I did, but it seemed to be her personal mission to get me on this plane. I wish she had agreed to come. I didn't stop trying to persuade her until the last minute. She stood with me at Customs, hugged me briefly and said good-bye.

My guess is, there's a soft person in there, no matter how brusque her nature. I trust what she says, more than the empty words I've heard lately from friends with the life bred out of them. I can only assume it's a lack of programming that explains Serena's peculiarly direct, unaffected personality.

Nicaragua, lying seven hundred and fifty miles from Miami, has been no more than an abstraction to me. I have not been particularly interested in this part of the world despite Nial's mordant preoccupation with its plight. His sympathy for the underdog never wavered over the years. Between Cuba, Haiti, Honduras and El Salvador the problems loomed too vast and sinister for me to get enrolled. I just nodded in agreement to his bouts of anger when he called the positions of the United States self-serving. I wish now I'd paid closer attention.

I close my eyes and try to picture his face. Are you alive Nial? Can you speak to me? Tell me what to do next. I am counting on you.

The descent into Managua begins less than a few hours after our departure from Miami Airport where the toilets flush themselves. It is only eleven in the morning; I have half a day to fill.

The tiny airport is teeming with small brown-skinned people pressing against the windows of the airport's reception room. They wave, smiling, curious, looking for friends and family. I am immediately struck by the differences in decorum from other airports I've seen. The crowds are noisy and excited. There are no chairs or amenities, no food or magazine stands to preoccupy the people. No chauffeurs or taxi drivers holding signs of people's names. I may be a few hours from Miami but I'm light years away in reality.

Militia guard the doors, but there are no other signs of control beyond Customs. Ahead of me, a military guard escorts a young American who looks like a recruitment model for the Army. Is that a machine gun he's carrying? I wonder how it got on the plane.

I navigate from the Customs line into the crush of the crowd, doubting I will find the person who is supposed to be waiting for me on the other side of the door. Some American students and two nuns stand in front of me. The nuns walk out of the doors first and are embraced by many arms. The students look anxiously around for their contact people. Two young men wave; they concurrently become attached to whatever mission they're pursuing. Gratefully, I see a U.S. soldier and he's coming my way.

"Mrs. Townsend?" he asks. "Officer Cole, at your service. Welcome to Managua."

He takes my bags and we climb into a military jeep that will take me to the American Embassy. The streets are cracked and filled with rubble from the earthquake of 1972. One could believe it happened only months ago instead of twenty years ago. There's no landscaping in sight. Huge buildings stand as skeletal reminders of what was once a viable capital city. Old busses spew black smoke and grumble down the streets; people hang on or leap off their sides when they slow down. We wind around the paths of bicycles, oxen and donkeys. There are few cars.

Legless young men are pushed in makeshift wheelchairs by their women. Unattended children splash in filthy puddles. Cardboard shacks crowd what should be parks. No houses sparkle with beauty or pride, they are in recovery. The war, the earthquake and poverty still rule this place.

I see an immense, intimidating statue, a polished black warrior holding a gun above his head. On a hillside, beyond the threatening figure, is a silhouette of the father of the revolution, Sandino. Its simple shape reappears around the city, stenciled on walls and doorways. The words FSLN (Frente Sandinista de Liberacion Nacional) are everywhere. But I know they have elected Violeta Chamarro president, chosen the middle ground instead of their hero.

At the U.S. Embassy where I am supposed to feel safe, I actually feel frightened. The wire mesh around it makes it look like a high security prison. Armed military stand every six feet; I do not believe they are taking their jobs lightly. I have seen no other such display of military might in my trips around the world, although, admittedly, I avoid countries where overt political or military tensions exist.

When I see the sign **Damas** above a door, I am grateful, and excuse myself for a moment. It is tiled and clean, but only a gasp of water emerges from the faucet. I refresh my gritty face and thirst with water from a bubbler. Its tepid water is better than no water at all.

Officer Cole escorts me to the offices for American visitors and I am greeted by a Linda Perry who tries to put me at ease. Then I'm taken inside to meet two officials, one from Nicaragua, the other from the United States. We make our introductions.

The Nicaraguan man wears an excess of gold. Even his teeth shine with gold. His hair has a high sheen like his officious black suit, white crisp shirt, and dark tie. The American is with the State Department and must be all of thirty; he's dressed in a pale gray silk suit and tropical tie. They both beam at me as if I'm on a pleasure trip. I remind them of my intentions.

"As you must know from my inquiries, I am looking for more evidence of what happened to my husband."

"Yes. We know," says the American, who introduces himself as Trainor Steele.

"I believe you are the same man with whom my husband, Nial, corresponded. Am I right?" I don't say I hope he isn't trying to live up to his name.

"That's correct. And I am the man who also communicated with *you*. As you must remember my telling you, we combed the waters for days; the U.S. Coast Guard did what they could. It is a very remote and relatively uninhabited region."

"It is filled with renegades and hostile indigenous tribes," adds the Nicaraguan. "Your husband's plane was not seen by anyone and only small pieces of the wreckage were found. But of course you know all this. I'm sure those scraps were sent back to the States."

"I want to go to the coast and see for myself where the wreckage was found," I reply.

The gold-toothed man moves closer. He smiles sympathetically, "You should not do this. We don't think it wise. Because of military actions and subversive activities, we are asking U.S. citizens to stay out of the eastern region all together. These areas are the most dangerous, filled with bands of renegades and guerillas to challenge an army—any of us. Of course, you have heard about the nuns, their intestines placed on sticks? We cannot permit you to take such risks. They were harmless women doing God's work. They were warned, but would not take our advice."

My own intestines shake.

He is not done with me yet. He adds, "There is a great deal of misunderstanding that rules the people of the east coast. They are angry and strike out in ignorance at strangers. The central government tries to placate them but they are products of history. Bad history. The nuns knew this but believed that God would protect them. He did not."

I wonder if the gilded man in front of me is capable of ordering executions? I find him intimidating. Is it the patronizing smile or the diamond-studded fingers that make me so uncomfortable? I wouldn't be surprised if I found the Bluefield Indians, who he refers to, less frightening than this self-important man.

I endure many words as both men tell me about the hopelessness and folly of my journey. Mr. Gold Teeth does manage to say he hopes I will take advantage of the "resort" and enjoy what I can during my stay in Managua. His closing political tone is meant to terminate any further discussion. "You must remember, the Bluefield Indians are unpredictable. We don't encourage anyone to go near their region and cannot assume responsibility if you insist."

I am not sure if he is shutting the door or threatening my life. I reply, "But I am the wife of a man who may have been swept ashore. He may even be alive. How can anyone ask me not to go?"

Trainor Steele says firmly, "Mrs. Townsend, we understand your situation and how difficult this must be for you, but we can't take responsibility at this point for such a search. If you go, you go at your own risk. We have done all we could and we must tell you there is nothing further *you* can do. If the crash took place in the area we assume it did, along one of the world's most impenetrable coasts, in shark-infested waters and high seas, we find any possibility of survival implausible.

"The plane's debris is evidence of a hard landing. The coastline is inaccessible, virtually cut off in many areas due to the density of the jungles and rocky cliffs. Add to that the coral reefs."

"He may have survived, nonetheless," I insist.

"Ma'am, if your husband survived, and we deeply hope he has, he has a far greater chance of finding you, than you have of finding him."

Mr. Steele is a well-oiled talking machine whose intentions I don't fully understand. I look around the room for clues and find only sterility. The walls are white. except for a map of Nicaragua which stretches six feet across one of them. The table, a laminated brown, is surrounded by chairs of nondescript steel and plastic. The State Department obviously shows no aesthetic regard for this place; the only real investment they made was in the coils of electrified barbed wire surrounding its high walls. The message is, go away, no one is welcome here.

Through the window I see that a brave branch of jasmine has climbed the wall. Its yellow flowers reflect the sun. Delicate new shoots reach into the pale blue of the sky. Thank God for small favors.

The Nicaraguan official, Manuelo Lopez, must feel he should take one more opportunity to impress me with his authority. He tells me he is a pre-revolutionary representative, chosen democratically in his region to work with the new government. He says he broke his ties with Somoza when he realized how corrupt the dictator was. He brags that his career survived the Sandinista's revolution because his people love him. "But please," he asks, "please understand the revolution is not over. Now we must battle the communists. And the resistance in Bluefields."

After this little speech, he bows deeply and makes his exit.

As I leave, I ask Trainor Steele if there is anyone else with whom I might possibly speak. He rubs his chin, looks left and right, and says softly, "You could go to the Ben Linder House and talk to the internationals there; they work with people in the remote areas." Then he grandly finds my uniformed escort while he explains to me there are no taxis available in Managua. No car rentals either.

As Officer Cole and I ride through the streets, I notice that the black and red flags of the Sandinista hang on many houses. Graffiti brightens the peeling plaster walls. "Viva la the revolucion," it says, over here, over there and again. In the park, I see families and hear music. The families are singing. I ask my driver who these people are; their partying is not analogous to the rest of what I see.

"It's a Sandinista picnic. They do their propaganda through food and song."

"They look happy enough to me."

"They get pumped up and believe they won something. These people paid a big price for the little happiness they got," my driver says. "I would lay odds there isn't a family who hasn't lost someone or something in the revolution. Now they don't know what to do next. The biggest business in town is prosthetics. See that line over there? Now, there's a true capitalist in the making. The guy has a battery charger. They go to him to recharge batteries for their flashlights and radios. It's one of the only chargers in the city. Lines form at seven in the morning and go on all day. So much for communism."

I remember reading a *New York Times* article only days ago that spoke about the unfulfilled U.S. promises of dollars to Nicaragua. Looking around it seems that a little help would go a long way. I wonder why we would place an embargo on people who have nothing to begin with.

"Why do you call the Sandinista *communists*?"

"Ma'am, if you don't think the Sandinista are commies, I suppose you don't think that Castro is right there by their sides, and you probably don't think we should support the Freedom Fighters. Ma'am, you probably believe in the tooth fairy, too."

"I've read that the Sandinista Party is the Nicaraguan revolutionary party, not necessarily a communist party."

"Ma'am, you've been duped by the liberal press."

I don't think so. I surmise it is *he* who has been duped, by the military.

"Isn't it possible that both sides are fighting for freedom?" I ask. "Look, I am not here on a political mission. My husband has been missing for seven months and I am here to try to find out what happened."

"He a political man?"

"Not in the least. He was involved in business."

"Then he was a political man, Ma'am. Everything here is about politics."

I have lied about Nial. Of course he's a political man. This must be the way repression works; opinions go underground. He came here on business, that was true enough, but it was because he was sympathetic to the revolution, astounded that the peasants were able to unite and overthrow a despot like Somoza.

We arrive at the Intercontinental Hotel, which I am told has a telephone and running water—sometimes. The beds are decent and the sheets seem clean enough, though thin. My stained mattress is old and lumpy. There's a notice in the bathroom not to flush the toilet more than once a day and that guests must shower only between five and seven in the afternoon. This is the city's luxury hotel! Still, I feel grateful to be off the broken streets and staying in a semblance of comfort.

I make a call to the Ben Linder House as soon as I have settled in. An American, who introduces himself as Paul, answers the phone and I explain my dilemma. He says I should come over for the evening's activities. Perhaps I will meet someone who can help me further. Positive words make my heart race with hope. He tells me I may have trouble getting transportation, but he offers a solution. "I'll bring *Irene* over in about an hour. Can you be ready by then?"

I had already lived three days in one. "Of course," I said.

I wait in the lobby and see a yellow pick-up truck pull up to the door. This, I realize, is Irene. She does not shine, but she runs. A tall man with a pony tail and an easy smile comes to get me. We make our salutations and, with no choice but to trust, I let him give me a boost into the cab.

The window is open and the dust on the street is kicking up so I reach for the handle to close it. "Sorry," he explains, "the pane is gone. We have to use that piece of plywood behind the seat there for emergencies."

"But how can you see?" I ask.

"Through the other two," he answers, as if this makes perfect sense. "Hey, the old girl runs, doesn't she?" He pats her dashboard like she's a fine horse.

"Precisely," I agree.

"There are only thirty-two thousand vehicles in the country that perform the miracle of locomotion and we have one of them, so, we can't complain, can we?"

"I should say not."

"Now, you won't mind my picking up those men over there who are waving their hands at us?"

How could I possibly explain how much I *would* mind. I would never do such a thing in the States not even in Granite Shores, and here we are in a revolutionary country where the State Department is barricaded and guarded every six feet. And now we are going to pick up hitchhikers!

At least seven men and one woman scramble onto the sides and rear of the old truck. Paul gets out and asks them in Spanish where they are going. He tells me we are making a short detour, not to worry.

I am not so sure it will be short. No, I think we may very well be heading toward eternity.

As we travel toward the edge of the city, around a corner and into the rubble of a side street, I see a village of refugees in a field of tents which are actually black plastic sheets draped on sticks, like tarps in a boatyard; they are no heavier than a common garbage bag's plastic. We slow down and the men hop off. They turn and, firemen style, form a chair wrapping their hands on each other's wrists and lift the old woman down. Kids run to greet their papacitos; dogs bark and chickens scramble to get out of the way. "Mi truck es su truck! Hasta manana," Paul grins.

"Mucho gracias!" they call, and one of them gives him a whistle and a V sign with his fingers.

I think of the breaching whale's tail in the harbor that evening in Granite Shores, the night when I met Serena, and I remember the victory sign of its shape against the sky. *Maybe you have to go somewhere that scares you shitless,* she had said.

We arrive at the Ben Linder compound and Paul parks on the street because there is no room within the walls of the parking lot. *Happy Birthday to you, Happy Birthday to you,* is blasting from the yard across the way as if it is an American pop song. I smile at the sound, believing there's a greeting attached to it. The child who is operating the turntable looks at me with his great brown eyes and sad smile. His little sister comes over to the twisted iron gate and calls, "Hello, Lady!" I find her tousled hair, the little pink pinafore with its dangling sash, and her bare dirty toes a touching sight. I reach in my purse for a dollar bill and her brother upstages her with his hand out, "Thank you, Lady!" Within seconds six more children appear—all with their hands out. I clutch my purse tightly and back away to cross the street.

The Linder House proves to be my escape hatch. I enter the gates and walk into a room filled with young people and animated voices. Pamphlets and newsletters cover tables and shelves. Paul is immediately engaged by a young woman who has a sheaf of papers in her hands. I look for a place to be. A crowd stands around the coffee machine laughing and engrossed in conversation. Their excitement permeates the air; my nervousness doesn't know where to settle or whom to find. Camaraderie seems easy for the two college students I had seen on the plane. They are standing in a corner with some European versions of themselves, obviously experiencing a mutual fervor of intention. I decide it would be inappropriate for me to interrupt with a "Weren't we on the same plane?"

A group is putting up Christmas decorations in a large room to the right. I enter the room and walk around. It appears to be a lecture room, yet, right now, the tables and chairs are being used for decorating. Someone sticks some paper strips and a stapler in my hands.

"We're going to make this place look as festive as possible," a woman says cheerfully.

She must think I am part of something. I decide to go along with her and begin to construct paper chains. They aren't the typical red and green, but a more festive version in bright yellows and pinks, purples and reds. I feel less uncomfortable, glad to be doing something.

A small woman comes to my side. She looks about fifty something. With a knowing ease, she introduces herself. "I'm Penny Ruiz. Is this your first time here at the Linder House? I don't recall having met you before."

She has that look of too many women near my age. Gray hair, wide waist, skinny legs, and glasses. Non-descript at best. "Yes. I was at the embassy this afternoon and they suggested I come here."

"The United States Embassy?" she asks.

"Yes," I answer simply.

"Did you ask for us?"

"No. They suggested I come here."

"Who is *they*?" she asks, incredulously.

"Trainor Steele."

"You have to be kidding!" she says, "This sets a precedent, as far as I know—you're not CIA?"

She is smiling, so I assume she's kidding about the CIA. But I do find her surprise at Trainor's suggestion a bit disconcerting.

"No, hardly. I am looking for my husband. He's been missing for seven months."

"Oh, my dear! I came for the same reason. My husband is missing, also. For three years now. He worked with Ben Linder up in the north and shortly after Ben was assassinated, my Manny disappeared as well."

"How dreadful for you," I say. "My husband went down in a plane off the east coast. There's no evidence he is alive or dead, just some non-descript scraps of metal."

"I see. Was he working with the people or the State Department?"

I was glad to say the people.

"Are these other people here because they are also missing loved ones?"

"Oh my goodness, no. They are here to help rebuild Nicaragua. You can see how desperately help is needed. They come from all over the world."

"But you, your husband, are you still looking for him?"

"Yes. But you might say I've settled in." She laughs. I can't imagine what causes her humor.

"I don't know what to do next," I explain.

"Of course. That's why they delivered you to us. I am still surprised. You must have seen our group protesting there this morning? Sister Ann is our organizer. We demonstrate every morning."

"No. I arrived this afternoon. What are you protesting?"

"We protest the way the U.S. government is aborting the results of the revolution. They don't know what this country is all about. They're only interested in the three c's: communism, coffee and control."

"I feel fairly uninformed, myself. The papers in the States carry very little news."

"Of course not. It's hard to get the truth through the system. Our government acts as if Nicaragua is about to invade our borders. These people don't have legs, never mind ammunition. Few people in the government seem to have a clue about what's going on here. It's discouraging."

She's obviously not worried about my political leanings.

"So how are you going about looking for your husband?" she asks.

"I don't know what in the world to do. What do *you* do?"

"I don't know what in the world I am going to do, either." She says, and pats my arm as if recognizing I am going to be facing years of frustration.

"I am hoping to connect with some of the people on the east coast."

"There aren't that many, I'm sad to say. Do you have a room here in Managua?"

"I am staying at the Intercontinental. I was told at least they have running water and some amenities, like clean sheets."

Penny smiles. "Occasionally. But why did Trainor send you to us? He knows we're against everything the embassy stands for— that The Ben Linder House considers itself the antithesis of the US Embassy. I'm sure Trainor Steele must have had an ulterior motive."

"Well, I confess, I know nothing. Ignorance brought me here and my worst fear is that I may go home no better for my efforts."

"They would like that. They want you to hear our stories, get frightened and leave. I have to give them credit—it's a very sophisticated form of intimidation. You will hear that the Linder boy was murdered, that this house stands as a testimony to his work. You will hear other stories and realize you aren't the only one who has lost a husband or a friend or a relative. Then you will want to go home and forget this godforsaken place. That's what they want you to do. But I came here five years ago and I'm still here."

I don't hear rancor in her words, just a matter-of-factness. She picks up the end of my garland and attaches it to hers. "Here, let's hang these chains from that light where Timmy is putting up the piñata. We can make this place beautiful," she says cheerfully.

I wonder how I could have met this pleasant woman, with whom I feel completely at home, after less than five hours in the most miserable place I have ever been.

As I lift my paper chain to the man on the ladder, I look up and see a person that reminds me of my son. Actually, I think it *is* him. But, surely, it cannot be. Have I lost my mind entirely?

"Tim?" I ask. He is tanned and hairy; his face covered with soft brown fur. I must not have noticed he had the potential for such a thick beard. Did I even remember he shaved? I have been thinking of him as my boy all these months, perhaps all his life.

"Mother! I don't believe it! Who...what?"

Like an angel he floats down the ladder, and before I can be sure of the sight of him, his arms are around me.

"How did you know I was here?" he asks. He is open mouthed, then laughing and holding me off the ground, whirling me around.

"I didn't!" I am laughing, too, or crying, I don't know which. "I thought you were in New Mexico or Arizona or somewhere else. Your letters stopped. No phone calls."

"But how did you know I was *here*?"

"I didn't."

"Then what are you doing here?" he said.

"Probably the same thing you are. I've come to find your father."

"Oh my God, I can't believe this. How long have you been here?"

"Hours."

"You're kidding! Who's with you?"

"I came alone."

"You're bullshitting me!"

"I'm not."

"Well, Jesus, this is pretty amazing, isn't it?"

I look around the room, at Penny, then at the decorations still in my hands and, damn it, when it's the last thing I want to do, my lips quiver and I start to cry. I would prefer he learn I am stronger than he suspected.

He pulls out a handkerchief for me and I blow my nose. "Sorry," I say.

"It's okay. Everyone cries around here now and then. You get used to it."

There are so many words and so few to say. We attempt to talk but are both so stunned by the presence of the other, we have to let our minds come to grips with the moment.

"Why don't we get this decorating done?" he says, finally, as if the world makes sense and the task we agreed to do must be completed.

"Why didn't you tell me where you were going?" I ask.

"I didn't want you to worry."

"Some news is always better than no news at all, Tim."

The music of the street filters through the windows, *"Happy Birthday to you...Happy Birthday to you,* and I smile at him. "Seems like they like that tune a lot."

"They're playing it for Jesus," he says. It's their Christmas song. They remember that the season is all about his birthday.

That had never occurred to me. "Of course," I say.

Penny and Tim are staying at a pension only two blocks from the Linder House. The barrio is protected faithfully by the Sandinista police. Nevertheless, on the day after I arrive, a Father Thomas is senselessly murdered just around the corner by a neighborhood youth. The internationals respond with a curious blend of outrage and sorrow. Father Tom had lived here for seven years. He was with the people through the revolution, then became too radicalized for the local priests and his Roman superiors. He defied the church and maintained a messianic ministry despite warnings not to allow politics to be confused with God's work. Father Tom's response was to continue his outreach declaring politics *was* God's work. Two years ago, when he was ex-communicated by the high church, he chose to remain in Managua, living and working in the rural villages around its parameters. He married the poor, baptized their young, and taught reading as if his dismissal had not happened. He was loved.

Tim is visibly shaken by Father Tom's death, but insists it is no reason for us to be afraid. He says I would be in more danger on the streets of Boston. I think, maybe so, but at least I would be closer to all things familiar.

I am an anachronism here. The internationals are zealous in their work, the Nicaraguans so poor and foreign I cannot possibly relate. The smells, the foods, the poverty and destruction challenge every minute of my stay. I imagine the natives must hate us for the disparity between our worlds, and feel ashamed for missing my creature comforts.

Penny and Tim insist I go to the mass for Father Tom. Paul Pearce drives a group of us in Irene. I find myself sitting on a crate in the back like the peasants did three days ago. Penny Ruiz sits on Tim's lap; there are an assortment of others including two pale blond Danish men who had met Father Tom when he first arrived in Nicaragua.

We debark in front of what was once a real church. Now it is another semi-destroyed remnant of better times in downtown Managua. It has doors and a partial roof. Rough-hewn benches create rows of seating for the parishoners. Empty niches are reminders of walls that once held saints and candles. The front of the sanctuary has no prayer rail, no pulpit. Behind me light pours in through a glassless hole in the wall where a rose window may once have been. I notice holy water at the door in an earthen bowl.

The people start to arrive. Hundreds, maybe three hundred in all. Inside and outside the little church they line the walls and doorways, reverently bowing their heads, some going up to the casket some hanging back. The parade goes on and on and we have seats for the whole thing. The peasants seem to defer to the internationals who gravitate toward one another. I feel wrong taking a space from someone who knew the man. At least we are seated in the far back. I can see by the flowing emotions that many knew him well.

A few sprays of paper flowers have been placed around the simple pine casket. Large candles burn at his feet and his head. A crucifix on the wall looks down on him. Mariachi musicians, dressed in their finest, create their music and a Father Joseph lights sage and murmurs indecipherable prayers.

When he looks up, I see the bluest eyes I have ever seen. His denim workshirt's cuffs are sticking out of the sleeves of his vestment robe. Thick gray hair defines his temples but the hair above his brows is dark. His lips are full and his cheeks thin. He is a handsome man. I am attracted to his magnetism before he has even begun to speak.

The funeral service may be a traditional one but the eulogy is not. Father Joseph holds his hands out to the people and at this point I am thoroughly present. He calls on Penny to translate beside him, to put his words into English. She goes to the front of the sanctuary.

In a gentle, fatherly way, he explains who Father Tom was, explaining his life in the musical Nicaraguan dialect. "Many of you have a family and you take responsibility for that family. You have fought a war for that family, for those children of yours, the muchachos. They are what this whole thing is about, isn't it?"

Heads nod.

"It is not work for you to love and provide for your family; it is what you know you must do. Some of us have large families, some small. Each of us gets what we can handle best. When our families are well, some of us begin to worry about our sister's family or our brother's. Some of us then worry about our neighborhoods, our cities, our countries."

I look at Penny's feet planted securely on the ground, her no frills selfhood clearly established. She understands every word from his mouth and I envy her ability to do this spontaneous translation with ease.

"Father Tom worried about the whole world. He saw the *world* as his family. He lived here, in Managua, because he thought of us as family, too. Many of the people who are in the back of our church right now, and many, many other people, have come from far away to help the people of Nicaragua because they love you and what you are trying to do. They see *you* as a part of their family, the *human* family, and they support your effort and want you to know freedom. They came here from all over the world to be with you...like our brother, Father Tom, who came from New Jersey, in the United States, to make your world—and therefore his—a better place. Stand up Karen and Trina, and Paul and Henry. Stand up Emile and Sven...stand up all of you in the back, everyone who has come from a distant place."

I find myself rising with Tim and Paul to stand there among the volunteers, an accidental hero of the people. From the middle and the sides, people rush down the aisles toward us with wet faces and arms outstretched. Into my arms comes a tiny old Indian woman who embraces me without consideration or question. I have no choice but to hug her as well. My height and whiteness are no longer relevant and I am moved beyond my own understanding. Then the music starts and, still holding onto one another, the group beings to sing—

Solo le pido a Dios, (I only ask God)

Que el dolor nome sea indiferente (that I should not be indifferent to pain)

Que la reseca muerte no me encuentre (That shriveled death does not find me)

Vacio yo solo sin hber hecho lo suficente (Empty and alone, without having done enough.)

My white spoiled hand melts into her hot brown leathery one. We are connected in spirit with something much larger than ourselves.

The sunlight pours through the empty window and shines on the face of the holy man in the front, who reflects his light back onto the people. I am wanting to be his, to be theirs, to be much more than Gwen Townsend.

Twelve

Serena

It's as if I am speaking to someone on Uranus when Gwen calls. She asks me not to worry about her. God, like I am thinking about her every day? Damn it all! How does she do it? She has a talent for making guilt guiltier.

I'm astonished as she tells me about Tim. No, not quite true. Actually, I take a strange kind of credit for it. Maybe he heard me, knew what to do and did it—must be he's more of a man than he was five months ago. It's pretty amazing; they're both in a foreign country and they find each other.

It's the Goddess at work.

"In Managua, the international community is closely knit. They depend on each other," Gwen says. "I was certain to find him."

"So you found him easily?"

"Yes, but not deliberately. You know, I didn't know he was here, and no one knew we were related. We just ended up at the same party. It was serendipity."

"You're going to parties in Nicaragua?"

"There's so little help and so much need. The volunteers keep their spirits up by getting together regularly. The poor people in the countryside are thrilled with a plastic cup, a piece of fabric—anything that's manufactured."

"So, what about Tim?" I ask, thinking, *Have you mentioned my name? Don't mention my name.*

"He's wonderful, bearded and tan. He's finding himself, I think."

Gwen called it serendipity; I know it's more than that. How can you march into another country and find someone you didn't even know was there unless there's been a little intervention?

"What about finding Nial?" I ask.

"We're making arrangements for a search on the east coast. But it is very difficult. Serena, why don't you come down here and join a brigade? You are so strong and such a marvelous example of self-sufficiency."

God, there she goes again. Sufficiency, proficiency, efficiency—*ciency* words loaded with expectations.

"Of course, you could help these people right from Key West with just a little effort. Ask a school or church to fill boxes with used pencils or paper and have them ship it to the Ben Linder House or to Habitat for Humanity. They will get it to the countryside. But do consider bringing yourself."

She thinks I'm Sister Teresa. There's no escaping the fact that she's going to mention me to Tim. The writing is on the wall. I can only pray he keeps his mouth shut.

"Who else is going to help you look for Nial?" I ask.

"There are young people from all over the world working here. You would find them as interesting as I do. I think you should come here yourself."

A voice in my head says, *nip this, now, in the bud.* "I absolutely can't, Gwen. Much too busy. How are you getting around? How will you get to the coast?"

"I am not sure yet. Not sure who we will be traveling to the coast with either. We may go with Paul in Irene."

"In Irene? What's that, a boat?"

"No, no," she laughs. "It's a pick-up truck with wooden windows."

I don't know this woman at all.

"Right," I say. "What's Tim doing?"

"Oh, he's wonderful. He's working with Paul right now, digging a trench for the new lavamanos they're installing in a little mountain village about an hour from here. They have no plumbing and no electricity. Honestly, it is like stepping back into the beginning of time. These people have nothing but hope and I don't have any idea where that comes from."

"Is it catching?" I ask.

"Hmm. I seem to swing from despair to hope from one hour to the next. But I'll keep you posted," she says, as if I am part of this odyssey, part of this family.

When I hang up the phone, I realize I heard none of the so-called despair she was referring to. No. All I heard was energy.

Talk of Nial seemed to be on the back burner.

I try not to think about the moment when Gwen discovers the truth about me. Tim may not say anything at all. For him it didn't mean what it meant to me. Maybe he has put it in a dusty file and labeled it *history.* But if he does talk, will I know? I don't think so. I think they would be more apt to make it their little secret. That would be the Townsend way.

It doesn't matter. I am giving them to each other and moving on.

Riding my bike down Duvall Street amidst the bizarre and the common, I recognize it's in the extremes of this place that I find comfort. It's the last place to run on the continent, the last sandbar before the great blue plain. Where else would they declare the damn chicken as sacred as a fucking cow? And these chickens aren't wired for dawn. Like everything else in Key West, the chickens are non-conforming. They crow when, where, and as much as they please—so sleep is never as sound as it could be. And then Furbie reacts as if we are under attack when a cock crows close by, barking like it's his job to warn us.

It's the lack of sleep that starts to make me tense and makes me write and rewrite lousy scripts. Scripts that I keep regurgitating in those wide-eyed hours of night. *Tim tells Gwen, then Tim tells Nial. Then Nial and Tim find out they have fucked the same fisher girl. When Gwen knows she was manipulated she takes revenge with Lady MacBeth's passion. She poisons their minds and I die like a fish with a knife in my gut.*

I will have to purge the Townsends from my life, make a life away from them, away from Granite Shores, the Serena Marie and Grandma's condo—all the places that were once home.

But I don't think it will be the little house on Canary Street. It's less mine now that it has taken on Geena's spirit. She has dripped and draped everything in sight with stars and moons, hung mobiles from the ceilings, painted the old furniture we bought with pinks and yellows and greens. Even the kitchen cabinets are now endowed with colors meant for the Caribbean. It is a happy kooky place, very different from my newly claimed Granite Shores home. Much different from the gloom that fights for space inside me.

I was busy taking Gwen's advice when I decorated Grandma's condo, my condo, that is. Gwen said not to throw away the old furniture because it was antique and *lovely*. So instead, I reupholstered the chairs and couch with luscious melon and olive green colors, and put tones of taupe on the walls outlined with creamy white woodwork. Truth is, I feel real comfortable there. It's a little bit of Grandma and a lot of me now.

Gwen contends the classics always outlast fads, and I believe her. The trick, she says, is to use accessories to spruce up a decor. To prove it, she gave me a big pine framed mirror that had once been a window frame from her house, and suggested I hang it on a dark wall where I needed a window. I did. It was exactly what the hall needed. Some old wooden lobster pots topped with plates of glass are now end tables. Cheap, colorful throw pillows light up the couches. Escher patterns of fish and turtles and Homer's prints decorate the walls. I bought a bright white wicker chifferobe for my TV. Voila! Transformation! She loved it, too, said everything was just right. Making a space for myself was like, well, like making a proclamation of independence.

With Geena, I just go along. She is almost always excited about something. Her latest love object is a gorgeous guy who speaks with a Jamaican accent. Elijah. He says he's a Rastafarian but he was raised with voodoo. I asked him about hexes and he says the mind can play dirty tricks on us; I should stay far away from that kind of thinking.

I wonder if he knows what Geena and I have done with the Wicca—powerful stuff. Not only did I cast Nial off, I brought his wife into my circle. Now it looks like I helped return her to her son.

I like to touch Elijah's hair; it's in fuzzy dreadlocks all over his head. "They are a holy man's deference to God," he says, and quotes the Bible—Numbers 6: something or other—to prove it. He uses the Bible like a Southern Baptist would, only he seems to make up his own mind what it means, even justifies the stuff he and Geena smoke. It smells like pot and looks like pot but he calls it holy weed and the direct way to Jah. *Psalm 104:4, He causeth the grass to grow for the cattle and the herb to service man.* He says the world would get along better if everyone would just smoke ganja. His voice sounds like his music, with a rhythm and soul like the songs of reggae and its words of love and warnings against Babylon. I guess he makes love like music, too. When they get going, I take Furbie and walk as far away as I can.

I am never going to love again. It doesn't work for me. Well, not quite true. I love Furbie and he loves me. We don't have to explain ourselves or ask forgiveness. I can wake him out of a deep sleep and he'll come to me, shaky legged and droopy but the shaggy tail always waving yes. How right that woman was when she said dogs choose their masters. I could never have known how right we would be for each other. Furbie chooses me every day. He is teaching me unconditional love. I leave him and he waits. I disturb his sleep and he gives me his wakefulness. I ignore him and he takes care of himself, and ultimately he shows me he trusts that I am able to remember his needs and be a good person. It doesn't matter how predictably I walk through that door at night, he greets me as if it is the best moment of his day. What a dog!

****

When Gwen calls and announces the search for Nial is soon to take place, I decide the best way to help Tim and Gwen is by wrapping them in a protective healing bubble. I begin to design a Wiccan ceremony to keep them safe and make their energies open to receive whatever cosmic messages come their way.

Geena continues to hassle me by reminding me I should let go. I tell her I have, but she insists that we need to consecrate my intentions with a spell of separation powerful enough to reach the Mosquito Coast. So, I create a ritual that will separate me from them in addition to the one to keep them safe. My Wiccan coven also advises me to heal myself first, before the protective energy goes forward.

I choose three candles at the Magician's Candelaria. Black for banishing evil, white for purification, and violet to heal. At midnight, on a stretch of beach, Geena and I draw a pentacle in wet sand. Our Wiccan friends form a circle around it and sway to the music of the clear singular sound of a flute. I have asked everyone to wear white as a symbol of purity. I have covered my white slip with a black cape. I ask my sisters to push evil away as I light the black candle and place it at the head of the star. My black cape is dropped on the ground and left where it falls. Then I light the second candle, the violet candle, for healing powers to take charge. Geena removes the purple scarf from around my neck. She lifts it to the breeze and waves it over my head and it's passed from one person to another, waved around the circle. I light the white candle for purification. Now, as the bride of innocence, I weave in and out of the circle, looping through arched arms. Finally, we all begin to dance in free form. The moon moves beyond a cloud bank and shines on our toes.

For the ritual of protection, the whole group joins in a huddle and we hold onto each other tightly, with me in the center. Geena takes her potion of horehound, alyssum and rosemary, and sprinkles it around us. Then she

111

lights a branch of sage and whirls it above our heads to call on our wisdom and declare our longevity. I feel embraced and safe.

When we re-form our circle, everyone kneels while Geena and I smooth the sand in the middle with our wicker brooms disappearing our footsteps, I ask that everyone look into the smoothed center and imagine a mother and a son.

"I release you, Tim and Gwen, to each other," I pronounce. Words like *be free, go safely, love each other, go in peace, be well,* emerge from the circle.

Geena declares, "You are now free to be your own person," and we sing, *Let the Circle be Unbroken* and wish one another peace.

I feel good. Really good. After our ritual of affirmation, and the reminders of one another's specialness, we go for a midnight swim.

The water is made of seamilk; my splashes break up moonbeams but I don't care. I am baptized into a new morning believing that I've released myself from a web too tangled to have any good purpose on earth.

Life moves on slowly here in Key West. Furbie and I are together a lot. He seems to tell me stories with his eyes. He knows me in a way no one and nothing else does. I wish we could use words, and we try with some success, but look how often words prove to be dangerous. In fact, it may be that the lack of them is the very key to what makes a dog able to be the loyal, deep-felt friend he is. Words are so easily misconstrued. This wooly mammoth of mine doesn't have to ask me what's wrong, he knows. When I look at him and stroke him, let him sleep in my arms or wake to his tongue cooling my feet, I know he knows.

In the coven I learn that animal souls seek out human souls to inhabit. I have no trouble believing this. I've known from the start Furbie adopted me so I can take a look at myself. At the same time he's by my side as I turn in and face the lonelies.

But is *in* where I should go? Often, I feel apart, envying people's ordinariness. I watch a family on their bicycles, tooling around the side streets; fathers and sons fishing on the pier; mothers with diaper bags and strollers. I wonder if I can ever be *normal*. When I ponder the seniors on the glass-bottomed boat outings, encumbered with Nikons and tourist guides, dressed alike in silly hats, polyester pants and glittering sweatshirts that read *Grandmas Do It Better*, I realize, I may not *want* to be like them.

I went to an edgy party down at the pier last night. A guy in a red Hawaiian shirt that could have stopped traffic, took my hand and told me I was beautiful. I liked that. Then he asked me my sign. I told him, Taurus, and he told me he was a Taurus, also, "...a bull and ready to charge." He said, "I always wear a red shirt, when I'm out. That way if someone is looking for me, there I am. Bulls love red."

"Ah," I said. I always wear my red hair for much the same reason.

"Pursuit is the game," he said. "I never give up if I really want something."

As we talked, rather as *he* talked, his eyes kept darting to other faces in the crowd. I needed to get out of this man's line of offense in order to give him the opportunity to pursue someone else. Maybe someone who truly loved red. Ten minutes later, I overheard him saying to another woman, "I'm a Taurus, you know, the bull, always ready to charge..."

Palms swayed overhead, bodies writhed and pumped to Calypso music and between the noise and the sticky heat, (not to mention two margaritas) I became dizzy. I knew I had to remove myself and get to the safety of my bed.

As soon as I got home and stripped down to my bikini panties, I fell asleep without turning over.

I had the most peculiar dream. I was a great turtle with primeval legs, yellow, scaled, and attached in loose folds to a huge thick umber colored shell. Of course, I can't help but contemplate why a person would dream themselves a turtle. Am I someone who is destined to retreat inside herself? I think of the story, *Big Turtle,* a Native American creation story Pop used to read to me. Big Turtle's shell grew into an island for Sky Girl. Am I the island or the sky? The sea? Will I separate the sky and sea or connect them? Or, maybe it means something completely different. Could be this dream is telling me I have a new shell, one thick enough to protect me from reptilian forces.

Wicca meetings add new dimensions to my consciousness. Colors speak to me with their vibrations; the yellow of spiritual power, the indelible green of great moments, the passion and contest of red. I'm noticing auras around creatures, too. Furbie has a golden brown homeliness surrounding him; Geena, a halo of peach. I can smell pink in a Magnolia tree without its flowers, taste the tartness of an apple before I take a bite.

On daily soirees that begin at the Bight and take me into the teeming waters off the Keys, my job is to show off the sea world. But it's more than that for me. It's taken on a new importance. I used to act like a mermaid for the spectators, bumping up against sand sharks and feeding sea turtles. But now, I see myself as a teacher. I want to give people an understanding of how precious the sea is. I want them to realize its design is perfect; teach them to care about the naked brains of coral struggling to survive in the shallows; to regard the graceful skates, those angels of the bottoms, with awe. They should marvel at the tentacles of jellyfish stretching four or five feet, and consider the innocuous oyster's talent at making a house with mother of pearl walls. When large schools of parrot fish move through and around my legs and arms, disappearing me from sight, I want them to thrill at their numbers. If my customers fall in love with the sea and all its living things, then I'll be happy.

Meanwhile, at night I sit under the humbling splay of stars, stars upon stars, and consider the trio who guide me, Pop, Kirsten and Grandma. I say a few words to Pop, hug my dog and know I've had a decent day. Lastly, I trust Gwen Townsend's journey is now in the arms of the Goddess.

Carol Egmont St. John

Thirteen

Gwen

Penny Ruiz and I explore the market place where barrels of beans, strings of fresh fruit, bins of baskets and eager shoppers crowd the aisles. The shelves showcase the myriad products of Central America. I see shoes from Guatemala, hats from Panama, leather bags from Honduras, toy guitars from El Salvador. There's commerce here, and no matter how nascent its existence, it's alive and celebratory.

Sizzling foods fill the air with pungent smells as we wend our way under cascades of colorful clothes. I finger the fluttering Guatemalan dresses and their lovely embroideries of flowers and birds. Such gay colors. Penny urges me to buy some. I would look ghastly in their loose tent-like designs, but I certainly can't wear most of the clothes I've brought with me; they're tight and heavy in this climate. I try on some sandals, zapatos comodos para andar, with automobile tire soles. They will handle the broken streets better than my fine leathers and sweaty sneakers. It is too hot for belts or stockings or fitted waistlines. By midday, I am usually in a meltdown. Perhaps loose bright cotton will work. I purchase a white dress with hot pink and purple flowers on the bodice.

Penny cuts my hair a few inches from my scalp and I can't describe how liberating it feels, despite the new evidence of gray. I only wish I could take off layers of skin or turn mine into the lovely brown versions I see around me. When the sun emerges it is fierce, freckling my face, dampening my clothes defying the powders and deodorants I use. I notice I begin to move slower and talk less. By mid-afternoon, I require a nap so I can wake up to enjoy the relief of evening air—air that is usually preceded by a cooling cloudburst. When the clouds part, colors emerge that turn the sky and the landscape into something new and beautiful. It has a wet sweetness about it. A seductive scent.

Nothing happens quickly in Managua. As I prepare the way for our expedition to the coast, I feel like Columbus must have felt in Spain. First, I must convince someone to enable us, then find advisors, cartographers and connections. Speaking of Spain, we are learning Espanol day by day. Tim is a quick study; I am not.

Penny and I go to Father Joseph's church school each morning at eight. We meet at the Parque de Cortez near the church's gutted sanctuary. Being in the center of town, in clear sight of the community around us, we don't need to advertise our classes. The barefooted ones eagerly join us. Father Joseph declares it a *cultural exchange* because the children are teaching us Spanish as we teach them English. It's charming really. We sit in small circles, introduce ourselves by name and age in each other's language, and then Father Joseph's invaluable slate boards and chalk are passed around.

Our lessons begin by drawing pictures and writing captions beneath them. Then we advance to oral stories. *The burro gets into mischief. He eats bananas, avocados and lemons. He climbs a mountain and swims in a lake with sharks.*

"Sharks?" I ask. "Oh, ellos muy hambre!"

They laugh.

When I tell them sharks don't live in fresh water, that they live in the ocean, the children become excited knowing they know something I don't know. "No, no," they insist, "Lagos tener sharks, tambien. Muy grande."

I am told they are right; their lakes do have sharks—enormous bull sharks from the San Juan River. These moments connect us, both through the words we share and the ones we must mime. We are equally hungry to learn.

I have moved into the posada with Penny and Tim. Our uncomfortable beds are three inch straw-filled, threadbare red plastic mats perched on wooden boxes. The shower is a contraption surrounded with concrete floors and walls to be shared by all the guests, and it only runs intermittently. No water runs on Mondays or Thursdays. I don't understand this shortage of water since it rains daily, despite the so-called dry season I hear is almost upon us.

Maria Morales, the woman who runs the guest house, is industrious and amiable. I see she has no husband and Penny says this is typical. Many of the husbands are dead or gone. She is an immigrant from El Salvador and perhaps this is the reason she keeps her family behind the walls. I surmise the children who play in the rear courtyard are her grandchildren, and the young woman at the kitchen sink is her daughter.

Maria is proud to house Americans and, although she looks older than I, she gets up before the cock crows, cooking tortillas and collecting eggs, swabbing the front porch's concrete floor, then the back. Always humming. Her hair hangs in a thick dark braid down her back. She's about four-foot ten and as strong as a mule. One of her front teeth is missing and the thin plastic thongs she wears on her square feet can do them no good. I would be happy to pay her more and even buy new sheets and blankets for all the beds, but Penny told me it would be exactly the wrong thing to do. She said it would imply that the house is inferior to my standards, and I will appear not to appreciate her things. Right now, Maria has a position of importance. She has the beds and the house, and we honor her by living there in the Sandinista neighborhood.

My first night in the posada, I couldn't sleep. I was sure I heard gunfire in the streets. I got up, looked out the barred windows, and saw nothing but shiny blackness. They kept firing and I tossed and turned, wishing for the modest luxury of the hotel I had naively vacated. Penny told me to stop worrying, that the neighborhood was closely guarded. By morning my nerves had snapped. I knocked on Tim's door and announced we must go to the hotel. I tried to bribe him, promising to pay for his room. It was clear we had to get out of this place. When I told him why, he said that the sounds were most likely from firecrackers; bullets were too valuable a commodity to waste.

"Fireworks are commonplace here. It's one of the ways people celebrate. Kids light them all the time. Relax, Mom," he said, as he hugged me. "I won't let them getcha!"

Father Joseph listens carefully as I tell him about my plan to look for Nial. Then he surprises me by reiterating the words of the men at the embassy. He says it is one of the few times he has to agree with the likes of Trainor Steele.

"The coast is unpredictable," he warns. "Remember, it was the home of the notorious Edward Teach and hasn't changed much since. They're a lawless bunch out there."

"Who was Teach? I don't know him." I ask.

"Oh yes, you do!" he laughs. "His nickname was Blackbeard, and he was only one of the pirates who plundered the Spanish ships along the coast."

"But that was during the seventeenth and eighteenth centuries," I point out.

"It's still a perfect place for hiding bounty and people. You'll find the rules are different there—there aren't any."

"Are there any pirates left?"

"I think so, yes, if you believe the stories—and that's often all we have here. The coast is a maze of lagoons meant for wild things—a dropout place if there ever was one. The only people who choose to travel in those waters are adventurers or characters with questionable motives. It's a dangerous region for outsiders."

"Someone must go there occasionally," I point out.

"A number of missionaries have ventured into the Bluefields area and brought back valuable information," he acknowledges.

"At the embassy, I was told they were murdered."

"The story of the nuns played big in the press. They used it for scare tactics to keep Europeans, missionaries and U.S. reporters out. I think it's because of all the covert forces at work in the place. It's hard to know who's responsible for the atrocities that have happened there. They're *all* extremists."

He leans back to relax, but his body is tied in knots—arms folded, legs crossed. Then, as if he notices, he stretches out and makes wings of his elbows, puts his hands behind his head and extends his legs. His feet are large; his soles worn. I don't suppose he cares.

"The one true thing is that they want their own government. You know, the suffering started five hundred years ago when the Spanish first arrived. Two thirds of the natives died within the first hundred years. It's been home to despots ever since."

"But the revolution..."

"The Indians mistrust the Sandinista. And the United States is bribing them to join the counter-revolutionaries, the contras."

"But why? I'll never be a quick student of politics."

"The Indians don't want to conform to the new Nicaraguan laws. They believe they'll be forced to change unless the counter-revolutionary movement wins."

Father Joe is clearly sympathetic, but he isn't the iconoclast that Penny has become. She sees anyone who opposes the revolution as uninformed.

"Is the new Nicaraguan government repressive?"

They've outlawed the death penalty and pardoned the contras who are willing to go along with the government. They're holding free democratic elections. I don't think either of us would call that repressive, do you? For Nicaraguans, it is more freedom than they've ever known."

"Is this true for the coastal people? Why don't they feel liberated?"

"They weren't involved with the revolution. Shrimpers and fishermen depend on foreign trade and at the same time cherish their tribal affiliations. They're used to their autonomy and still celebrate their own folklore and myths. They believe in witchcraft, hexes and alternative realities."

"Are they violent?"

He looks away. "A priest who was murdered was found with his testicles in his mouth."

I shudder at such barbarism. "Is an end to the horror in sight?"

He lifts his shoulders and talks with his hands. "If a warrior has his gun and his hate, and no containment, how does war end? At this point, Bluefields is an angry hotbed with scoundrels who have vested interests in keeping it that way. You have to remember the Mosquito Coast represents forty-eight percent of Nicaragua. In other words, there are two Nicaraguas and in that part of the country the revolution is not resolved."

"Why do you stay here?" I ask.

He looks around at the dry dirt of the floor, the broken pottery out of which bougainvillea pushes its pink up the crumbling wall. I follow his eyes toward the broken clouds above our heads. "I'm not in Bluefields," he says smiling. "I stay here because I am needed. I know who I am here and what needs to be done."

"What is that?"

"Everything." His smile penetrates my eyes and I am absolutely sure that, if there is a God, he lives in this man.

"I must go to the coast," I say.

"Yes," he answers. "I'll see what I can do to help you, but you must, at least, wait for the dry season."

"It's here!"

"Should be, but the rains seem to keep coming, don't they?"

Days have gone by with no opportunity to start our trip to the coast. Heavy rains have caused mudslides, closing the roads we plan to take, so we are forced to wait another week. But we're not idle. Tim is completing the plumbing project with Paul in the countryside and alternately works at the *colectivo* the rest of the time. Paul, in turn, has given Tim a hand with organizing the harvesting of the abaca during these critical weeks. They are quite a team. Gone more than not. Penny and I, meanwhile, remain engrossed in the school.

We take little trips around the city now on the fuming busses, which are driven by hombres with a clear sense of machismo. Like cabellaros, they kick up the dust of streets with their vehicles and rarely come to a full stop for passengers. People leap from their doors as they exit, and race alongside to hop on. I must say when they see Penny and me standing primly at the bustop we are honored by their discriminating courtesy. I like looking at the drivers' seats best. They're surrounded with personal objects ranging from embroidered versions of the Virgin Mary to Sandinista propaganda. Some seats are decorated with velvet cloth and paper flowers. Rosary beads jingle from the backview mirrors. They need whatever they can find to bolster them as they wind through the hodgepodge in the streets.

Casa Ben Linder is our home away from home. This center for volunteers was created after the assassination of Ben Linder, a young idealistic mechanical engineer from the northwest, who worked to bring hydro-electricity to the northern regions of Nicaragua. He was brutally assassinated—martyred by the contras. Penny and I heard many stories about his wonderful nature. He was fervent, smart, and a clown for the children, adding laughter to their hard lives. The entire nation grieved his death.

We are presently behaving like mamacitas for the new crop of volunteers at the house. We concoct homey things like cornbread and pies in the kitchen and, when we can get the ingredients, other special meals, too. The young people come and report their adventures to us like they might to their own mothers. We understand, encourage it even. But when one of the kids called Penny *spry,* I thought she might hit him over the head with a rolling pin. We don't need reminders that we're among the elders of the group.

In an attempt to treat the volunteers to a meal of coq au vin, I decide to order some chickens from the little hacienda down the street. Walking there, I strain to remember the key words I will use. But as soon as I see the woman who I assume owns the place, I feel flustered. I manage to ask her name. "Como se llama?"

"Rosalita!" she answers.

"Hola, Rosalita," I say, without entering her yard, which is really more of a pen. Using gestures as well as words, I ask if I may buy three chickens for eating.

"Si," she says again. As she points to the yard of birds, I assume she wants me to choose which ones I want.

"Oh, just tres pollos," I say holding up my fingers. "Tiene lavar? Will you clean them for me?" I add.

She flashes a beautiful smile and nods. "Oh, Si! Uno momento. I watch stupidly as she picks up a bar of soap, grabs a chicken and shoves it in a pail of water. It isn't until she begins to give it a shampoo that I realize my

Spanish and mime have failed me. "Oh, no. No, Senora," I say. She hands me the live dripping squawking creature. "Es no good?"

"No, no, it's not that!" I say, and try to use use my brilliant linguistic talent again. This time I try, "Muerto. Dead! Por favor?"

"Oh! Si, si," she says, and with a deft twist of her wrist, wrings its neck.

I am weak-kneed at the sight of the bird's feet still kicking in protest.

But it's not over yet. I proceed to mimic the act of plucking. Gingerly, I pull a feather from the carcass and say, "Por favor? Todo?" Finally, she understands, and I go home with three broken-necked bald chickens. It has taken me hours, it's mid-day and I all I want to do is take a nap.

Nothing comes easy for me. I am on a balancing beam from the moment I wake up each morning. Penny has become a Godsend. Our friendship deepens as we share our stories.

We are in the kitchen making dinner when she tells me about her lost husband, Manuelo Ruiz.

She says, "I was an overworked, underpaid social worker in Lawrence, Massachusetts, when I met Manny. Many of my cases came from the islands, so I wasn't ignorant about the lives of people in these cultures, and I surely never intended to marry into one of them."

I can see her as a social worker, unaffected, deliberately plain, prepared to be a spinster. I watch her square hands chop celery in perfectly spaced pieces as she talks.

"I was single, forty, and thinking marriage wasn't going to be in the picture. I took a vacation I'd dreamed about for years: the Virgin Islands, St. John, St. Bart, you know—the Love Boat scenario. I felt like I was someone else out there under skies meant for charter ships. But the appeal wasn't just the aqua sea and the dreamy music under the stars. When I first saw Manny with his twinkling black eyes, his Clark Gable mustache and white uniform, well, he just about took my breath away."

I thought of the stewards on the cruises that Nial and I had taken. We would amuse ourselves watching them operate, knowing they were expected to give the single women a good time; ask them to dance, introduce them to others, escort them to the Captain's table.

"It was heady for me. He led me onto the dance floor and before I knew it, I was Ginger Rogers. I was wearing a black satin dress that night, a true departure from any dress I've had before or since. I should have had it framed for posterity."

This unadorned Penny, with her espadrille-clad feet square on the floor, once pretended to be Ginger Rogers. It's a hard picture for me to imagine.

Her short fingers place an onion on the cutting board and I watch, fascinated, as she turns her knife into a chopping machine.

"Manny was the most tender lover, the sweetest man...brought me chocolates and flowers, even jumped ship to be with me when we got back to Boston. I had to marry him. Not because there was a baby on the way, there wasn't, but because he was my last chance."

Tears run down her cheeks. I doubt they're caused by the onions.

"We lived in Boston at first, and when he wanted to return to Nicaragua to see his family, we did, and then made the monumental decision to stay."

"You must have loved him very much." An understatement if there ever was one.

"We came at the tail end of the revolution and stayed through the reconstruction, if you can call it that. We knew change had to come hard and believed the Sandinista were the only viable answer."

Still trying to understand, I say, "It seems it isn't over yet. What do you think of the situation now?"

"Manny's family has nothing. They're no better off than they were before, but they think they are, and I suppose that makes all the difference. In the States we take the psychological gifts of freedom so lightly. It's hard for us to understand what the absence of repression is like."

I feel myself drawn to Penny in a way that would not have happened back home. Here, we speak a common language and share our losses. And I find her Massachusetts accent comforting in the midst of so many things foreign.

"Daniel Ortega is a man of the people. The aristocratic families, the former ruling families have too many attachments to the past. It's a hard transition. Without the farms operating and without the precious bullion of the West, I don't know if they can do it. This embargo thing is just about defeating the country. Manny figured he would be important to the reconstruction, maybe even a link to the States. But things weren't that simple after the war."

I ask why.

"Why? We worked with the Sandinista, started organizing the people and building roads, putting in power lines and digging trenches for water. I think the establishment was afraid—thought the whole thing might actually work and that Ortega would become an icon for revolution in other Central American countries. So you see, the war hasn't ended; it's just become covert. The United States decided to replace Daniel Ortega and went to work to make it happen. Instead of helping rebuild Nicaragua, Reagan's men trained and paid *freedom fighters* to rock the ship of state. It makes it hard for me to go back to Massachusetts. I'm so angry—so outraged that the government behaved this way. It's painful to blame your own country for your husband's disappearance."

Her body has grown tense from talking about it. She attacks the lemons. As she slashes away, I wipe the juice from my arms.

"Rural schoolrooms that we helped establish are being shut down, one after another. The contras blew up bridges and even medical centers and set us back. There's more unemployment, now, than work. Another stab at an already vulnerable back."

"The place *does* feel desperate to me," I admit.

She lays her knife down, thank God, and looks at me.

"I don't think you can know how exciting life was in the first years. We were turning an illiterate country into a literate one. In one year, literacy improved by ninety-five percent. I was part of that; so was Manny and people like Father Joseph and Father Tom and many of the native people who could read and write. Everyone was playing a part. We all went into the countryside and made things happen."

"What about Violeta?" I ask.

"Violeta Chamorro is old Nicaragua. Her husband was shot by the Somoza military and that makes her closer to the people's cause. But I don't believe her speeches; I only look at what she does. I don't think she can break her ties with the patrones and let the country move on. It will depend on the States, and we know better than to wait for good news from there. Meanwhile, one by one, the schools are closing."

"Why are the schools closing?"

"The contras killed three hundred teachers and there's no money to pay those who survived. Chamorro's government has made rules that demand children wear shoes. Imagine! They also have to provide their own school supplies. Rules like that will stop most of the rural children from showing up. The teachers are giving up. They haven't been getting paid their thirty-four dollars a month, so who can blame them for walking? Without pay or the zeal of the reform movement, you can understand why they're disillusioned and demoralized.

"My husband wanted to help. I think he was going to make a difference. That's probably why he was disappeared."

How terrible for her. To not know, to never know. I mustn't allow myself to hang on too long.

"There must be something we can do. Tim and I will ask everyone we meet about Manny, I promise you that. But you and I, meanwhile, we can do something to get the children in school. Maybe we should invent shoes that children can afford, or import school supplies from the States."

"Ha. You see what happens? You're catching the Nica bug. Of course there's something we can do! There's too much for us to do! You see the children waiting each morning.

When are you going to the Atlantic coast?" she asks.

"Soon. It's a matter of weather. We could fly to Bluefields in a little plane or we could take the overland route. Both are complicated. If and when we get to Bluefields, we have to navigate through some uncharted waters. I am just not sure what is wise— looking for transportation when we get there, or bringing our own—and where would we get our own?"

"If money is no object, I would fly," Penny says.

"It's not."

"Then fly and pay for help when you get there. I can't imagine people have many opportunities to make real money in such a remote area. You should find someone willing to help you fairly easily."

"Do the planes have to meet any safety regulations? When we land, will the natives just steal what we have and kill us?"

"Possibly," Penny says as casually as if we talk about making a wrong turn.

****

It is Tuesday, January 17th, and I've been here over a month. It hardly seems possible. I'm becoming more acclimated to the place. Other than the celebrations that surrounded Constitution Day, I am able to sleep through the fireworks now. Sandinista Police no longer intimidate me, either, with their fatigues and their rifles. Instead, they give me a sense of safety. I actually take walks with Penny in the evenings and they slowly roll along next to us in their Army Jeep—our protectors. I have learned to trust the foods, too. I actually like the taste of beans and plantains, can live with raw sugar and tolerate the smell of cooking oil at six in the morning. My cot is now a bed, although I do suffer from night sweats. I have secretly added a quilted coverlet to the plastic and found a small feather-filled pillow. Penny laughs at me as I hide them in my suitcase each morning.

Tim arrives with detailed maps and a plan. He seems decisive as he tells me we will take the land route north to Honduras, then east to Rio Escondido. We are renting Father Joseph's truck and will provide it with a tune-up and four new tires in return for a week's rental. Tim has already made arrangements for the tires to be shipped to Honduras where we will pick them up and put them on the truck. I learn that shipping tires to Nicaragua would be difficult and time consuming, and might not even be possible in the end, so I agree to these plans.

The Rio Escondido flows into the Caribbean Sea in Bluefields. I am anxious about our trip into the highlands and the truck's ability to handle hills of any magnitude, but Tim insists the motor is good and we can make it. I decide to trust him; what else can I do?

We have made contact with someone who knows of a reliable person to help us explore the river region on our way to the coast. Our vehicle will be a barge named Paulina. Its captain, Roger Sheffield, works the river regularly and is considered knowledgeable. We will leave Father Joseph's truck in the highlands with some volunteers. They'll return it on a trip into Managua for supplies.

Most of our money is hidden in a peanut butter jar in the cooler. Some, we put into thin leather purses that strap around our waists, the rest into our wallets for ready use. Our passports will be necessary at the borders and so we tape them in the tops of our hats. I feel like we're anticipating the worst and say so.

"Well, just remember not to tip your hats to strangers!" Penny teases.

It's not exactly what I want to hear.

We head for the town of Leon for our first night. I'm surprised at what we discover. Leon doesn't wear the same "scars" that I have seen elsewhere. I might even venture to say it is lovely despite the bullet holes I see in the walls.

The houses are colonial with red tile roofs; their surround walls are splayed with trumpet vines and bougainvillea in exotic pinks, oranges, and yellows. Purple wisteria grows around and through cracked stucco. The peeling painted doors leading to secluded courtyards remind me of the Costa del Sol as I first saw it, before it was reclaimed.

Bands of children walking home from school are dressed in crisp white shirts and wearing shoes. Obviously this town has something the others I have seen do not. Murals of the Sandinista victory adorn village walls but common graffiti is absent. We are amazed at the size of the cathedral that dominates the town. Twin domes tell us someone in Rome must have wanted to affirm God's presence in Leon. It must have once been prime property.

It's easy to find a charming posada. We check in, then go outside to sit in its cool garden among pheasants and banana fronds. The innkeepers join us. When we tell them where we're going, they reply excitedly, "No, no, no. Murderers live there!"

Unfortunately, I do not understand them so they graphically add meaning to their words by slitting their throats with their finger tips. They tell us we need protection along the way and, if anyone tries to rob us, we should claim to have Nimo Suarez as a friend.

Tim explains that we have made contacts and we will be traveling very lightly. They seem skeptical.

We have clean sheets and decent beds. I sleep like a bear in winter and visit Nial in my dreams. He's wearing a long green skirt and has flowers in his hair. He holds a branch filled with olives and eats it- the whole thing— fruit, branch, and leaves. He looks wonderful—young, strong and happy. I make love to him.

"I could go by myself, Mother," Tim says, as we start to roll over the rough terrain the next morning. "You could stay in Leon until I see how difficult this is really going to be."

"I will not," I answer. End of discussion.

The mountains are lush, their volcanic peaks like arrows of hope. Toucans and luminescent parrots splash color into the dark greens. Unintentional harvests, como llovido del cielo, (gifts from heaven) hang from forgotten vines. Mangos and wild grape, avocado and papaya. Calla lilies appear like roadside angels, clusters of white tucked inside wide waxy wings.

"These people are surrounded with beauty. At least they aren't deprived of nature's finest gifts," I say. My voice trembles because of the road's washboard surface.

"Maybe that's what makes them so accepting," Tim says.

"Maybe people have to have next to nothing in order to appreciate such treasures. Do you think these people understand the extraordinary abundance of their natural world?" I ask.

"I don't think they think about *their* world. They can't do that kind of thinking because they don't know how the rest of the world exists. The excesses of our lives are unimaginable to them. And, so is the idea of a common person possessing the land, its food or other resources. They're untraveled. Uneducated. Their concerns are simple. They rest in the food they'll eat today and the clothes they'll wear tomorrow. We could learn something from them."

"Tim, you're becoming more and more like your father. Your looks are even morphing into his. It's very comforting to me to have you here at my side. What made you come?"

"Mother, how could I not have come?"

"You surprised me so. I truly thought you were in Arizona on a motor bike."

"I was, for awhile. But nothing worked for me. I waited on tables in downtown Tucson, on the strip where kids play dress up and don't know the seventies are long gone. I felt like a goddamned fish out of water."

"Yes, I should think so."

"Drugs, dogs and backpacks. Punksters. Teenie boppers. Unreal and empty. It started to embar...whoops!"

We plow into a sinkhole and my head hits the cab's ceiling.

"You all right?" he asks.

"I think so," I laugh. I'm just grateful Irene is still upright.

He rocks the truck between drive and reverse and we seem to dig our way deeper into the earth. He climbs out of the cab to examine our situation. I think about our food supply as I realize there are no tow trucks to call. Tim sticks his head in the window.

"Got your boots on? We're going to have to build a ramp. Let's get some sticks and stones under our tires. Take these gloves, Mom."

I leave the confines of the truck and face the tangle at the jungle's edge. To the east and west of the dry river bed there's plenty. I begin to haul the larger pieces.

"Better pray it doesn't rain," Tim warns.

The thought charges my energies. I have seen what happens to these seemingly harmless gullies when it rains. Torrents of water appear with the power to sweep cars and trucks away.

In minutes we build a rough surface in front and behind the tires. I stand back as Tim climbs into Irene and starts her up again. He shifts the gears and the wheels start spinning. She starts rolling slowly, forward and then back. Stones fly and a few hit me, but there's no pain. "Okay now, old girl, you can do it," he says. The "old girl" growls at the effort; she rocks, spits, splays dirt, and then burns some rubber as she begins to pull herself out of the depression. Tim's smile tells me he's relieved. I hop back in and believe I'm smiling, too.

It doesn't take long before we realize the road we traveled yesterday was a *good* road. Water and rock have had their way on the roads we now traverse. It is no wonder Father Joe kept warning us to wait for the dry season. The only thing that convinces us we're headed in the right direction is the absence of choice. There is only one road, and we're on it.

I see men and small boys walking along the road's grassy edges carrying machetes.

124

"Where do you think they're going?" I ask Tim.

"Looking for work," he says.

"But the farms are shut down," I say. "Look at all the abandoned equipment we've seen. Rusted beyond repair. Don't they know it's hopeless?"

"Guess not," he says.

I suppose there is nothing else *to* say, no reason to ask how these people will survive. Who's in charge? With the patrones gone, who's left to pay them to cut coffee beans? I just can't fathom how young boys, as small as the ones we see, can manage the huge knives they carry.

We go over a crest and are brought to a stop when we see a tree lying across the road. A group of men wave at us. "Oh no. What now?" I ask.

"Could be an ambush. You stay in the truck no matter what. My Swiss knife is under your seat."

My fingers, which I smoothed this morning with exotic oils, now fumble for his weapon. It is where he said it was. I place it in my lap, extrude the blade and grip the handle while he is calling cheerfully out of the window, "Hola! Desea aiguna cosa?" He is acting naively polite, offering to help them. I know who really needs help here.

The men are armed with machetes. They stand four abreast on the far side of the tree as if it is *they* who cannot cross. No light penetrates the dark jungle of fauna on either side of the road. I imagine an armed battalion of bandits watching us from its interior.

"You must pay for us to lift this tree," the men demand. "Fifty dollars."

"Oh amigos," Tim says. "Gracias." Then, in Spanish I can almost understand, he acts utterly grateful. "I am so glad to get your help. I don't think I could have lifted it myself, but unfortunately I have not got fifty dollars." He puts his hands up in despair. "Would five American dollars be enough?"

They lift their machetes. Their leader speaks. "Fifty dollars or we will take everything you have. How much do you have?"

Tim pulls out his wallet and opens it, still smiling. "I only have twelve dollars," he says.

"If you want the tree to be taken from the road, it will be fifty dollars."

"But," Tim protests, "I am on my way to see my good friend, Nimo Suarez! I must stay somewhere tonight. How about five dollars and some Coca Cola? Is that a deal?" he asks, as if they are doing business.

"?Nimo Suarez? For friends of Nimo Suarez, eight dollars and we have a deal," they say.

"...and Coca Cola!" Tim adds.

The ambushers are mollified but my heart sinks. I think when they see the cooler, they'll take the whole thing and our money will go with it. While Tim metes out eight dollars, I quickly remove the cans of soda from the cooler and pop their lids. Once the tree is moved, we make a great ceremony of the Cokes, shake hands all around and thank one another until the men move to the side of the road, obviously satisfied with their enterprise.

"Hasta la vista!" Tim calls to them as we drive away.

They wave and hold up their cans, toasting like businessmen.

"How did you stay so calm?" I ask.

"I figured it took them about an hour to cut down that tree, and two dollars an hour around here is a hell of a lot of money. Then I thought of Father's favorite expression: *Make it a win-win situation.*"

I slip the knife back under the seat. Tim starts to sing *De la Sierra Morena Cielito Viene bajando.* I join in. *Un par de ojitos negros, Cielito Lindo de contrabando...*I am positively high on the fact that we're alive.

After we drive a while I verbalize my thoughts. "I think these people are not as innocent as you give them credit for being."

"They're acting out, Mother. You can't blame them. They see our truck, see our skin, our clothes and they want what we have. It doesn't make them bad."

"Well, they're not innocent. And...possibly dangerous."

"Mother, it's not too late to go back to Leon. You were comfortable there."

"And leave you in this wild country without your mother? Most certtainly not!"

He laughs. So do I.

Father Joe had given us the names of people to contact in Bluefields and told us to use them if we should need to impress questionable characters with our connections. But we were unprepared for this trouble so close to *home.* I am grateful for the innkeepers' advice about Nimo Suarez, whether it impressed the banditos or not.

We reach the Honduran border without another incident, but at the border, guards go to great lengths to inspect our vehicle. They demand our papers, look under the cab, in the engine. They open our duffel bags. I am rather amused they think that a middle-aged woman such as myself may be a drug runner, but not so amused when they demand papers for our car registration. We have nothing other than our passports and they don't seem to be enough. Tim speaks his best Spanish. He appears to be prepared for the occasion as he hands them papers with a seal on them and officious print ending with signatures, his own and others, at the bottom. It's actually the warrantee for his Kodak camera but it does the trick. They look at it carefully, rub the raised insignia, pass it around and say, "Twenty-five dollars for fees, fifteen dollars, insurance." Tim doesn't ask what the fees are about; he just hands them fifty dollars and they wave us through.

I am now thoroughly aware of our vulnerability. If a rogue army should choose to butcher us for the truck or our cooler, or for anything whatsoever, we could be disappeared and who would find us? I think of Manny Ruiz and Penny's long and futile search. Now I wish we had flown. Slipping in and out of countries through surreptitious means is not something I had expected to be doing with my life, and a small plane seems safer than a pair of Americans using trickery to survive.

In Choluteca, Honduras, we meet with the man who was supposed to have our tires. He has shown up but only has two tires. *The others are on the way,* he tells us. We should come back next week. Little does he realize it has taken five weeks from the day I landed in Managua for us to get this far. I, for one, would rather lose the tires than return to this place.

"Let's find a different way to take care of Father Joseph," I say.

Hondurans seem distinctly different from Nicaraguans. The people in Honduras appear solemn—as if they have lost their music. I feel negative ions in the air, a darkness in the brutal sunlight. Little children have swollen bellies. There's no sign of the spirit I've seen in Nicaragua. And here, the military police are omnipresent and unpleasant. People's eyes don't find mine.

We head south, southeast, back into the rugged mountains of Nicaragua. The terrain is difficult. I begin to identify with the shocks on the truck as each disk in my back rattles. Tim stops at a roadside stand where we buy papaya and avocados. I would prefer to eat fresh fruit than chance e-coli or typhoid at some unclean Mestizo stand, which doesn't exist anyway.

We reach Matagalpa by late afternoon. It's a high, quiet place. The streets are narrow and mostly unpaved, but, compared to what we have seen for the past six hours, it looks like Greenwich, Connecticut. We look for the hospice being run by some workers from the Casa Ben Linder, and are excited to find it is a lovely old plantation house overlooking thickly forested mountains—mountains upon mountains that fade away to pale blue. Its foundation is tucked into tropical spiky plants with large bold flowers. Orange roof tiles match the blooms and catch the late rays of sun to warm our welcome, as does the large porch and open door. I am thrilled as I anticipate a safe night with a little graciousness thrown in.

"*Bienvenidos!*" calls a pale blond young man in the doorway waving a bottle of Tequila. "Step in. We've been expecting you!"

The insides of the hacienda are stripped of all luxuries. There's an old sink that can hardly remember its porcelain days and walls where only a few tiles are left to indicate what once was. The floors are holding up pretty well but no one has washed them in years. There is not a comfortable, cared for spot anywhere. I wish it was mine to love and do well by.

"Who owns this place?" I inquire of Lars who has come to Nicaragua via Sweden.

"Somoza's family owned it. I guess the bastard himself lived here from time to time. He owned about a fifth of the country, after all. A hundred and sixty other farms, each similar to this one."

"How did it come to be a hospice?" I ask, trying to imagine the life that once made the rooms sparkle.

"When the going got rough, the family who ran it moved to Miami and the Sandinista took over. After the war, the government let us use the main house as a place to live while we taught the people who remained how to build their own houses. They're getting parcels of land and some support until they're settled and their crops are planted."

"But what if the owners come back? What will they do?"

"Somoza's people? I don't think so. That's why we're here.

"The land rightfully belongs to the workers now and we're showing them how to reclaim it."

His conscience is clear.

"But where will the people work? How will they earn money?" I ask.

"Come with me," he says. "I want to show you something."

Well below the main house, a huge wooden barn sits in a field of dirt. To one side is a concrete slab as big as a baseball field. I soon learn this was the drying table for the coffee beans.

"See how it is slanted so the water will drain off? That holding pond, over there, is the runoff. It was also the only water supply for the people who live here. This was once a huge operation."

We look down at the water and see it is full of insects and God only knows what else. A goat wanders over and takes a drink. A dog relieves herself in the same water. Rusted farm equipment sits nearby, beyond repair, no more usable than old cars in a junkyard.

On the other side of the barn, chickens and pigs cohabit. Lars opens the barn door, and because it is dusk, the darkness inside is almost total. I hear children giggling above me and I blink to elicit my nocturnal vision. At the far end of the barn in a hole in the earth, a slow-burning fire yields noxious fumes. The smoke burns my eyes as I look upward.

"You should tell them to get down from there; they could fall!" I say softly to Lars. Tim nudges me.

Lars explains, "This is their home. They will be careful. The families who live in these stalls go back thirty-five years. Most of them were conceived here. They have never slept in a bed, climbed a stair, or used faucets. Notice there are no windows, only the narrow spaces between the barn boards to let in light."

"It's a good way to convince people they are less valuable than animals," Tim says.

Lars nods in agreement. "You see those planks sticking out of the wall? They scramble up them to get to their sleeping quarters. If they can't make it for some reason, they have to sleep with the animals in the lower stalls or under the stars. Climb up and say hello to Luis."

Tim makes the climb easily and shakes Luis' tiny, out-stretched hand. I don't trust my agility and wait for another time. Tim tells the little boy that I am his mama.

Luis leans out of his stall to get a better look, like a pigeon might peer from its perch. He regards me with eyes that deserve sun and smiles a docile smile that lights his face. He and his family of three sisters, a mother and a father all live on the top row of the first stall in an area no more than eight by ten feet. There are sixteen stalls like theirs. Each has been a home for a growing family.

"They eat at the end of this building, I'll show you. Gloria, their mother, Ramon's woman, washes their clothes on the stones by the new well. That pail over there is used by everyone who lives here. It is always busy."

The stench of old oil cooking someone's beans proves a little too much for me.

"The well is already contaminated. They don't believe in what they can't see. It is a constant battle to fight the ravages of parasites. We are starting from scratch here, telling them not to pour dirty water back into clean."

He points to the tiny woman at the fire.

"Gloria has lost at least two children. I don't know if she even bothers to count the miscarriages."

"Hola, Gloria! Meet my friends from the States!" Lars says in his Swedish accented Spanish.

Gloria looks up and says something I can't comprehend, but I attempt my version of her language. "Hola, Gloria, como esta usted?"

She smiles and nods. I am not sure if we have communicated.

Tim and I dutifully follow Lars through the rest of the property, past some adobe casitas where I hear and see more people moving about.

"Those are the houses we're building for the people who live in the barns."

They are simple block buildings with crude doors and a few unpaned windows sitting squarely on small sections of raw earth. I suppose they must be castles compared to stalls.

When we are back to the house I enjoy a stiff glass of tequila and then another. It must be youth that thinks they can turn this injustice around.

A leggy brown spider the size of my palm sits comfortably in the middle of her finely crafted web suspended in a window that once knew lace. I consider killing her but decide there's no point. If she goes, there always be another and another. And she's worked so hard at her art. Who am I to say my life means more than hers? If I give her her space perhaps she'll leave me to mine.

I feel old and sad and selfish. I want to go home now. I want to climb into my big sleigh bed with its carved roses on the headboard and firm Posturepedic mattress, pull my down comforter over my head and sleep. I want to wake up to hear the bells in my church's steeple, see the harbor sparkling its diamonds, and make footprints on the beach blanketed with snow.

I want to walk down familiar streets and see faces I've too long taken for granted. It's time for me to get to know those people, my people. Find out their names, how many children they have, if they're doing well. Ask what they dreamed last night.

As soon as I get back, I will call Lizzie and Sally.

Can you forgive me, Nial? Can you forgive me this longing for home?

Carol Egmont St. John

Fourteen
Serena

Worship is an imaginative act and imaginative acts should be worship.
It's the Wiccan way. I want everything I do to reflect my new consciousness.
It should, because Wiccan philosophy has filled my head and pushed away
old ideas. I've even decided to reread books I once loved, just to hear them
with my new ears.

It only makes sense to revisit Hemingway. A person can't live in Cayo
Hueso (Key West's original name) without knowing something about Papa
Hemingway. He wrote *For Whom the Bell Tolls* in the '30s, right here in the
neighborhood, and *To Have or Have Not* around that time, too. I like the fact
that I breathe the same lusty air he breathed, but what interests me most, is
how direct his writing is. I don't think he cared if anyone thought him literary.
He told his stories his way and be damned with the critics. Key West is like
that. People can do things their own way, or no way at all. It's all about the
rising and setting of the sun, the barometer's reading, the oleander, the sea
urchin. Addictive personalities gravitate to this freedom and the attitude.
Here, at the edge of the earth, they can be exactly what they choose. And
that is where I don't quite get it, because something in me is made up of
Cape Ann and it doesn't fit here. It's something as basic as salt.

I try not to think of what I'll do in the spring but I know it'll be unnatural
for me to stay in the world of Tiki bars and lemon trees—especially when the
wharf is buzzing and the Serena Marie is dry. My friend, Geena, says I
should stay—that a person can't be depressed down here. I don't try to
disillusion her, but even Poppa Hemingway said, happiness in intelligent
people is a rare thing.

I try. I dance and sing and play dress-up with Geena, which is actually
dress *down* because, when we're not working, we wear little more than a
sarong and a bathing suit. Yet, despite all the fun and games, my sense of
direction feels fuzzy.

Lately we're in love with the movies. We even watch silent films. I'm
hooked on the quirkiness of Charlie Chaplin and she can't get enough of
Bob Hope and Hedy Lamar. Elijah, Geena's fluff, laughs his big bellyroll
laugh as Bob Hope clowns around and Hedy waxes exotic in Hollywood's
version of the tropics. Elijah's laughter is contagious. His aura is orange.

I like him. He's a mellow fellow. A dude. That's what Geena calls him,
her *Dude*. In Granite Shores, a match like theirs would cause a stir. Down
here, they don't cause a ripple. It's even true among the Granite Shore guys
who have winter whale watching businesses nearby. Back home a black
and white couple would would get them pumped. Here, they don't notice.

I saw Frankie Haskell the other day. He was strung out on something at
the Tiki Bar on Pine Key. Makes me sick to see him wasting himself that

way. Pop used to call it the lonelies. He said that seamen tend to be *lonelies* by nature and booze and drugs are the connectors. If I tell the truth, I'm a lonely now—well, more like, alone in the middle of a party. Hey, I know; I conjured it up for myself, so I can't complain.

Ah, the world of herbal remedies. I don't really believe it can be that easy, but there's a Wiccan consensus that believes St. John's Waart improves a person's attitude. I take it. Nothing changes. I still struggle to stay out of an ebbing tide.

One night, Elijah insists I try the *holy weed*. I'm afraid of it because Pop's warnings play in my head, and I remember his friends who moved from grass to heroin and coke. Then again, Elijah and Geena seem well enough. They aren't looking for anything more powerful or dissolving in the sand, imploding into nothingness the way I am. So, I decide to eat the brownies.

Whoa, I can hardly bear the laughter. I laugh so hard at some dumb expression on Furbie's face that I can't stop. I am doubled up, holding my sides with tears streaming down my cheeks. Gina and Elijah laugh right along with me; it is as freeing as an orgasm and far less dangerous.

I suspect Pop was wrong. I feel like pure spirit—colors intensify; objects embrace one another; sounds blend and my thoughts are as soft as velvet.

And now, Elijah and Geena and I become one as we eat our sweets and drink a limeade that is nothing less than nectar from the gods. It's delicious. We strip and dance to reggae as if we invented it. My arms move in magical rhythms, my hair and legs and breasts and hips. I am music.

Elijah puts himself behind me and gyrates into my back. Geena comes up close to me and turns us into a sandwich, myself the meat. Her breasts are soft against mine, then her lips on one side of my neck and his on the other. It feels so good. I can't believe how easily it all happens. We make love to each other and the night ends with us sleeping like peas in a pod on the queen-sized bed I call mine.

In the morning, the queerness of it all comes down heavy on my head. I think Geena anticipates my return to separateness because she remains quiet as she prepares breakfast. She puts on the radio and cuts up a honeydew melon. I watch how deftly she scoops out the slimy seeds and lets them slide down the sink's drain. With the pulpy interior gone, she cuts into the firmest green of the fruit. It's ripened to perfection. No need for salt or yogurt. It's just right as is.

We don't speak.

I imagine we're having a contest. Who goes first.

You go.

No, you go.

Then she starts singing to herself as she cuts up a lime. "*Lemon tree, very pretty, and its lemon flowers are sweet...*"

"*But the fruit of the poor lemon is impossible to eat,*" I sing back.

She slices the fruit into six parts as neatly as I can shuck an oyster, then puts sprigs of spearmint on each side. It's so pretty.

131

I fill the blue coffee mugs and we move in our familiar morning dance around the kitchen. Sunlight settles on the bunch of hibiscus I picked from our garden. They're a touch of the Orient in our truly funky, folksy kitchen where my very own genie has cast her spell.

We sit down and face off. "Don't even think, *a penny for your thoughts*," she says.

I smile, and swizzle my spoon around and around in my blue cup.

"My mother's favorite line," she groans, putting her forehead in both hands.

I nod and don't tell her she doesn't have to remind me. I remember approximately every word she has ever said.

"Hell, I love you. We both do. So who is to say we shouldn't act on it?" she says, looking through the palm fronds tickling the sliding glass door to the errant pelican standing on our patio table.

I rest my hand on hers. "I know. I know you love me."

Why should I remind her that I realize, better than anyone, that three *is* a crowd? That it wouldn't be long before two of the three of us would hate the third. I don't want to be in any more triangles. What a hopeless mess I could find myself in all over again. Lucky for me, this time I have history to teach me and a better option to take. I'm pulled somewhere else.

The coffee's aroma fills my head. Soon its roasted magic flows like a waterfall from the cup to my lips to my veins. I enjoy the rush of energy, and note how things take a clear shape as the caffeine careens through my system. "Listen, Geena, I love you, too. I do. There's nothing I wouldn't do for you if you needed me...but I can't stay. I have to take myself back to New England. It's been great here with you—great enough for me to feel it doesn't have to be over. I just think, I think...."

"Oh no, you don't. Shit, woman, you aren't going to walk out of here and leave me alone!"

"You will never be alone. Elijah loves you. You have the coven and the job and it's *your* world. Something in me needs to go back to mine."

"Last night was just natural, no big deal."

"It isn't about last night, it's about all the nights to come. It's time for me to go home now. My wings are twitching. It's just like that for me. I'm the peregrine who has her radar set on go. Even the stars are telling me it's time to fly."

Actually, it's early for me to return, but I'll drive home this time, slowly; take the opportunity to let surprises happen, let the Goddess have her way.

My new car is weighed down with all the things I decide to take back to Granite Shores. This year, Furbie makes no bones about the fact that he's coming, too. It will be his first summer at sea and his ESP tells him something special is in store for him. He's a moving obstacle course as I pack. It doesn't matter where I am, I find him in a wad in my path. He actually sits on my luggage, head between his paws, eyes doing that pitiful thing. He worries my pillows and hides his bones in my laundry. I start putting his toys in the car so he gets the idea that I understand he's coming along this time. He buries them even farther inside as insurance.

Geena is furious. She threatens to buy a cockateel, something I will never take from her. She says she will clip its wings, lock it in a cage, and call it Serena.

I don't see her shopping for it, however. She's just excellent at feigning gloom.

Leaving Key West is not conclusive in that I can't say I won't return. I refuse to put a terminal face on it. There's been enough finality in my life.

Geena wraps her long arms around me and wets my cheeks with tearful smooches. She hands me two snack bags, one for Furbie, one for me, and warns me I better think hard before I swallow. Her revenge will be sweet. I know she's okay, though. Geena is not one to choose misery for long.

Calm settles in as my overstuffed Blazer picks up speed on the highway. Loud vibrating music gets me on down the road just like the clickity clack of wheel on rail. I am free of an agenda; can drive in the draft of the geese or take detours. Maybe I'll check out Savannah, walk along the river, or stay in Charleston; take in Monticello, maybe hang out in Jamestown a few days, look at the caravels moored in the harbor. Pop would approve.

But I don't seem to stop anywhere for long, despite Furbie's bad breath (which smells like yesterday's pizza) panting into my neck from his perch in the backseat. I resist the inviting signs along the way. Something keeps pushing me due north, through swamp and then pine, through *hollers* and hills into the heart of Tennessee. Listening to Nashville radio converts my hands and feet to musical instruments. I belt my own tone-deaf version of *Amazing Grace* across the highway. Even Bill the Blazer seems to sing along. *I was blind but now I see.* He's doing just fine on this long haul for a big ole boy on his first road trip, and Furbie, too. Bill is just the rightest name for these wheels. Bill: no-nonsense, reliable, large and comfortable. Just plain Bill.

I hit the haze of the Blue Ridge Mountains listening to tirades about Jesus and the inevitability of Judgment Day. Bill, Furbie, and I are not afraid. We groove and move like three old friends until we hit D.C., and then something makes us want to stay awhile.

Little had I known about cherry blossoms until I saw the capital. It was then I learned the same spring breezes that wake the worm and sweep winter away on Cape Ann arrive in Washington, D.C. a month earlier. They start as pink tips on treetops, then open and fly like perfumed moths. Street after street is swept and sweetened by their softness. Beauty fills me so full, I give everyone I see the right to be happy. I even forgive the newlyweds who ask me to take their picture near the obelisk for unknown soldiers. I make sure they turn their faces so they are looking at each other, placing the erect white phallic symbol right between them. The adoration I see in each face makes me wonder what they have done to deserve such love. How must that feel?

I take a walk to the Ellipse, the same green park where Pop and I saw the AIDS Quilt unfolded lifetimes ago. Today, there's a large group distributing placards and passing out water and buttons to anyone who walks by. Someone has set up tables for selling books and videos. Furbie and I begin to wend our way through the crowd. Ollie North's picture with a stop-slash symbol across his face catches my eye.

With a certain excitement, people are queuing up for a walk down Pennsylvania Avenue. No marching bands for the parade appear, just a silent band of Latino women waiting to walk. They have bouquets of paper flowers and pictures of sons or husbands or daughters pinned on their bosoms. No one wears costumes either, except for a unicyclist dressed as a wicked Uncle Sam, spinning around, carrying a burlap bag marked with dollar signs. When I look up the avenue, I wonder who will stop to watch.

Now I hear jeers and cheers and songs breaking out. I see people holding hands. Babies are caught and strapped into their strollers. Announcements over megaphones direct people to certain stations. I am thinking how diverse the crowd is. It's the amalgamation of the spirits Pop always said make up America— everyone different and yet all of us seeking a common ground to make things work. He would have liked the faces of this crowd. "Look, Sam—Latinos, whites, blacks, businessmen, farmers, homosexuals, Christians, communists all working together!" I could just hear him.

"Where you from?" asks a tall, balding, man whose nametag reads SIMON. His eyes shine like fireballs; he has designer teeth. A powerful magnetic field surrounds him. His aura is red.

"Oh, I'm just looking!" I say, instead of asking if Simon is his name or his company.

"Are you a sympathizer or someone the Feds threw in to stir up the pot?" he asks back. He's joking. With my purple threads and hand-painted boots spangled with stars, my hair permanently blown to a frazzle, a Fed I am not.

The loudspeaker tells people to prepare to start the march. "Find your organization and remember to have fun, bring a water bottle and put all your refuse in the blue garbage cans before you leave," the voice says. "We will stop at key points along the way. Remember, it is in solidarity that we make a difference!" she shouts.

"You with a group?" the man asks.

"I don't really get what all this is about. I'm into cherry blossoms, basically."

"They're early this year," he says. "The march is to express support for the people of Central America."

"I have a friend in Nicaragua, actually two. Actually, maybe three..." I must be sounding like an asshole. "My friend, well, she's working in Managua, well, sort of."

He doesn't walk away from my babble. Instead, he leads me to a group of people I soon discover are from Massachusetts. They're a mixture of advocacy groups. Ministers for Peace, Doctors Without Borders, Habitat for Humanity, and others I don't quite get the names of. A man named Daniel Kiernan is with them and speaking with authority.

"Pete Hamill said it best," he says, 'We're exposing a body bag of lies. The decision to train the Contras was a decision to kill. Those who kill people in the name of lies will eventually face retribution."

I understand that well enough, but *who* is lying and *why* they are lying is not yet mine to know. I'm not even sure what these people are protesting, what these people want.

"The government is not going to participate in any more covert wars. The struggle in Latin America belongs to everyone. We are marching for the best reasons on earth. We are marching for justice! Let Brotherhood begin right here, right now, with us," Mr. Kiernan shouts.

Applause and cheers fill the air.

"We are marching for decency!"

More hoots and hollers.

"We are marching for those who cannot march for themselves."

Someone shoves a placard in my hand. I look at what it says. *Nicaragua for Nicas.*

This sounds perfectly plausible to me. The crowd from Massachusetts pulls me into line and the man with the smile stands at my side.

"Good girl!" he says. We need every warm body we can get. Let's put a Sandinista scarf on Fido here, so he feels a part of it.

"He's a Furbie," I explain. I think Furbie gets the idea. He's wagging his tail like it's a flag.

As we march down Pennsylvania Avenue, I feel the warmth of the crowds that have appeared from nowhere; return their waves and smiles, their thumbs ups, their V for victory signs.

Simon tells me the President is at Camp David, but he explains, and I realize, it doesn't matter whether the President is at Camp David or if the Congress is on spring break. We are the people. The real people. The marchers and the spectators from Everywhere, USA.

I believe, because of the numbers and the signs, they have come from cities in the east and west and from little villages in between.

Simon goes on, "We have to take responsibility not just for our own freedom but for the freedom of others, as well."

We march past four huge trucks that look like railroad containers. I ask Simon what they're for.

"They're a small compensation for the U.S. aid we promised and didn't give. They're stuffed with flashlights, soaps, pads of paper, blankets, and simple tools—instead of ammunition and TNT."

I can see people wearing t-shirts saying *Witness for Peace* and *Quest for Peace* on their chests. Many balance on top of their cars cheering for the paraders as we cheer back.

Three men in dark suits with crisp white shirts yell epithets. I think they tell us if we don't like it here we should try Nicaragua. Meanwhile, the banner that reads: *America First* keeps blowing in their faces. It's comical.

The woman on my left points to the trucks. "There are the tractor-trailers that were driven across the country from Oregon and California. They went clear to Maine and then south to Georgia and every little town inbetweewn that wanted to contribute. One of the drivers is marching with us. She's seventy-four years old!"

Bridget Tesorerio wasn't much more than that when she gave up. Grandma might have been with the America First gang, though. She didn't believe in questioning authority.

"How will they get all the stuff to Nicaragua?" I ask.

"They'll all leave together in a Caravan for Peace at the end of the rally," she says. "The trucks will hold more than soap. They'll carry people to witness for them."

A chilly wet wind sweeps in while we march, but warm feelings prevail. I'm actually attaching meaning to the words I hear sung as we stand in front of the White House facing the flag...*crown thy good with brotherhood, from sea to shining sea.*

The world feels a little smaller...a little more like family.

Furbie turns and checks to see I'm still with him. He cocks his head as if to say, "Are we there yet?" I squat and he runs to me so I can ruffle his fur coat while he slobbers all over my face. The rain begins to fall, but gently, very gently, and we march on.

*America, America, Goddess shine your light for thee...*I sing.

Fifteen

Gwen

The Rio Escondido's steam smothers the air of this alien place. Humidity presses on my skin. Pungent green smells assault my nasal passages. Our boat, a crude barge, moves slowly downstream. It is a craft with no grace other than durability.

Roger, our guide, assures us we're safe, but he obviously prefers to navigate midstream, away from the low jungles on either side and I try not to imagine why.

It helps to know his boat is a familiar vehicle on these sultry waters; waters that ooze through lands too flat to push a river. Wildlife oozes, too. We see the slow swimming manatee, a huge slug Roger insists must be saved from extinction, and then further downstream, a rare caiman floating just beneath the surface; its lazy periscopical eyes winking and rolling around in search of a new victim. His long camouflaged nose covers teeth that could tear a person's limbs apart.

It's all about hunger here...for every creature. Insects sit silently on the water's surface; unsuspecting targets for the piranha below. Imperial white birds with crowns on their heads stalk the shadowy edges, expecting food to arrive. I feel like an exotic bird myself—too white, too tall, and too naked. I want to cover myself and at the same time wish I could remove everything touching my skin. My skin itself.

Tim and Roger are immersed in men talk about history and war. References to places are bantered about and I try to remember the names. Puerto Cabezza, Rosita, Betania, Kukalaya—names that never appeared in any texts or travel guides that I've studied.

Roger talks about about the indigenous Indians who inhabit the waterways—Miskito, Rama, Sumo, and Garifuna—and explains why they regard themselves as the true, legitimate Nicaraguans. He informs us that mestizos and Creole occupy the controlling end of the spectrum in these parts. Many are descendants of the slave ships that preceded Spanish colonization. He says western Nicaragua measures prestige by the closeness of one's connections to Spain, but in the east it is by the length of tribal history.

I quote Father Joe. "A priest I know described Bluefields as populated by castoffs, fragments of defunct cultures."

Roger says, "Aye, that pretty much describes meself!"

We pass a marker with a gravestone beyond it. Roger brings us closer to shore, saying that the headstone marks the graveyard of Spanish pirates and their children, children born from native women. I wonder where the women went. Were they buried anonymously, without markers?

En route, there are no people to observe—no movement or villages in sight. Occasionally, trees appear, so tall they hide the sun, with trunks like tentacles that crawl across the ground and bury themselves in the muddy banks. Their gray legs fold into smooth pleats beneath umbrellas of leaves seemingly too small for such extremities. Outstretched limbs drip with mosses, vines, or snakes, I'm not sure which, but I'm grateful for the moments of relief when we glide beneath their lacy shade.

Calls of creatures I can't see conjure up stories of the wild. I must say, our guide has no fear despite being a white man in a dark world. He is not as white as I, however. His arms and bare chest shine with a bronze earned from weathering sun daily. He belongs here, this river man. His beard is bleached gold; the hair on his chest glitters in the sun. I wonder how he can live this way, in isolation from the world. But I cannot speak. It is too hot, my own voice would annoy me; put more weight on the oppressive air.

Roger tells Tim that the pride of the Misurasata Indians is their reputation as warriors. "They're bent on protecting their way of life." he says. "They refuse to be a part of any nation other than their own. They have already seen what a central government can do. They saw it burn their villages and kill more than a thousand of their people. Despite the killing, the Sandinista never won a battle because they couldn't penetrate the mindset of the tribe any more than they could take control of the jungle."

I imagine eyes watching us through the huge fronds. A mosquito the size of a hummingbird lands on my wrist and takes a blood sample before I swat it, and mix its remains with my own.

Tim asks Roger what people do for work. I think how American that question is. Here, work must be about maintaining a subsistence level of life. Work can't possibly apply to a place with thickets too dense to see light, a world meant for ocelots and anaconda. Can it?

"Some are caiman hunters and others are shrimpers. But the wars have cut into their business," he says.

Too hot to move, I let out an involuntary sigh.

The man appreciates my suffering. "You better get out of the sun. We don't want to burn you to a crisp. We have enough burnouts around here," he laughs.

My lethargy lifts when I hear voices, actually see what looks like a family of four people on the bank. A wooden canoe rests near their feet. They are waving and speaking in a tongue I can't decipher; it's definitely not Spanish.

Roger waves and puts his thumb up. They shout excitedly at him and he says to us, "Looks like we have a problem here. Hang on."

The barge makes a laborious turn toward the patch of black volcanic sand that might be called a clearing. It is, perhaps, ten foot by ten foot. We hit it with a thump and lizards race for cover. Roger throws a small anchor over the side. I am sitting under a canvas tarp hoping to be indistinguishable from its bulk.

A small dark woman with knots of velcro hair and slow yellow eyes in a face as wide as it is high does the talking.

"Meestah Rogeh, sah," the woman says. "You help boy? Take heem down to medicine mahn?"

Roger leaps from the side and I see the boy's leg wrapped with grass and leaves, tied with strands of hemp.

"Is bahd. Machete deed it."

Tim has been watching from the bow. He grabs his backpack and jumps over the side to join Roger. The two of them unwrap the primitive grass bandages. The boy is obviously weak. I'm preparing to faint when Tim calls, "Mom, get that sewing kit out, the one in the side pocket of your duffel bag!"

Roger feels the child's head, then holds him down and tells Tim to lift the leg. Tim, meanwhile, has taken off his tee-shirt and sponged water from the river to wash the wound. Roger yells my way, "Get the rum. It's in the red box—in the stern. I don't think we have to worry about gangrene. It's looking clean enough."

I simply react. Before I know it I am overboard, too, walking in water I wouldn't dream of entering if I could think. I have taken off my scarf and am pouring rum into it when Roger grabs the bottle and literally pours it on the wound. Tim pulls the bodies of headless ants out of the boy's leg, blood spurts out as a result. Fascinated, I no longer think about fainting.

"Those ants stitched away while they lost their heads. If you ever need to sew a wound, place an ant over the cut and squeeze its head. Its legs will do the stitching. Everything you need to survive is in the jungle," Roger says. "But ants are only a temporary solution. We need to sew this mess together and make sure it doesn't get infected."

"Thread a needle, Mamacita," Tim orders.

I try to calm myself. The nylon thread we've brought for repairing gear will have to do. I shakily thread it through the finest needle with the largest eye I can find. Roger takes it and lights a match to sterilize it. He hands it back to me.

"Think sheets, Mother," Tim coaxes. "Think of mending the sails on the Endeavor in the storm of '87."

"How in the world can I think of sailboats and New England while my feet are covered with volcanic waste in the middle of a place I can't begin to understand?"

"Just do it, Mother," he says.

I do as I am told, muttering, "God help me." The child's face grimaces with pain. I see his pink tongue wagging as he opens his mouth to scream, but no sound emerges. Instead he freezes himself in the scream. I feel the same scream inside me as I pull the taut skin of the sticky wound toward its counterpart. When the needle punctures his skin, he jerks away.

"Here, take this," Roger directs the child. The boy drinks.

"Now, you too!" Roger says, placing the bottle on my lips.

I drink.

Tim is pinching the boy's big toe. "Think about that toe, my good mahn," he suggests. "You're doing fine, Mother," I hear, as I penetrate the skin for stitch number three.

They continue to hold the boy's leg up in the air. After the first three stitches, it becomes easier for me. I make thirty-one in all. We take my scarf and wrap the boy's leg in it. Then Tim pulls some grass, takes large leaves from a bush and cuts a green vine while Roger rewraps the boy's leg until it cannot bend.

"You are good lahdee," the woman cries. She reaches her gnarled black hand to touch my hair. Bee-u-tee-full lahdee." She is smiling. Her left front tooth is missing.

"Do not get the leg wet," Roger says to the boy, "and do not uncover it for this many days." He shows him ten wriggling fingers. Now, what is your name, my man?

"Jorge."

"You are a macho mahn, Jorge," Roger says, and shakes both of his hands by crisscrossing his arms. Their palms meet in a fraternal slap, like they are a part of a secret club.

The other two family members squat passively at the edge of the jungle. They have not spoken. One is a very old man with bowed legs, bent so badly it is impossible to imagine how he can squat. The other, I presume a brother of Jorge's, wears a Mickey Mouse shirt. He is a few years older, perhaps. The old man rises only when we have left, then gets into his dugout canoe. In a mere instant, the mother or grandmother of the children fades into the vegetation with them.

I climb back on board, sit on the deck, and indulge in another shot of rum.

"Imagine these children carrying machetes," I say.

"Imagine them carrying AK 47s," Roger says. "Every boy's a warrior."

"But that child was no more than six!"

"Jorge? He's more like ten. They are little people."

Tim adds, "Little and tough. The kid didn't even cry."

Despite the elixir of rum, I am wide awake and noticing the adrenaline my body has pumped. I imagine this is what a man must experience when he faces the battlefield. Now I have seen the human face of this place, met a boy who must become a man early, seen his blood as red as my own son's. It's obvious his mother cares for his safety no less than I worry about Tim's. She must find it hard to watch him suffer, and to be a mother who has to encourage those things that cause his suffering. He must find it hard to be a boy who faces pain silently.

Roger has announced we will be staying at what he calls a town. It is really just a clearing where bohios have been built on stilts with grass roofs and bamboo ladders. He says it's a place for us to sleep comfortably and take time to enjoy the fresh fish cooked on the beach in front of the huts. "You will like the authenticity of this place, Mother," he says.

"I am not your mother," I respond curtly. My indignation gets across without any more words said.

"And a good thing, too," he smiles, his large tanned hand lifts me gently to the shaky boards he calls a dock.

I am not sure if it's me or the rum but the motion of boards and boat turns my legs to rubber. Roger escorts me with his arm around my waist and his hand resting much too close to my breast. Tim lugs our bags from behind.

Children run up to us. "Meester Rogah, Meester Rogah," they call. "What did you breeng us?"

"Ha!" he cries. "You will see soon enough. Make room for a very grand lahdee."

I feel like a dish rag. Is he mocking me? I can't bother to argue. I have to hold on. All the sailing I've done and I've never experienced vertigo like I did on this river.

We cross the black sand to a shaded spot under a grass roof. It has no chairs, no towels, not even a bench. I collapse onto it anyway. A child brings me a wild flower that looks every bit like an orchid. I manage a smile and put it in my hair.

Tim asks which of the huts will be ours.

"I think, my mahn, you shall have your pick!" Roger says easily. "Doesn't seem to be a lot of traffic today."

We are looking silly and I am feeling even moreso because I cannot move. Not yet. More children arrive and touch my hair, which must be sticky from the wet heat. They say things that are almost English but I can't understand them. I know blonde hair fascinates them. Little fingers float around my ears.

Roger leans over and tells me I am the Queen of Santa Marta. They have crowned me with flowers. I don't know what he means until I reach up and feel the flowers they've stuck in the top of my head. I must look bizarre.

I need to urinate, so I manage to rise.

"You are a walking-talking bouquet, Mother."

"Maybe talking, but walking—I don't know."

Roger says to las ninas, "Take the queen to the latrine. She has to make water." He may appreciate his poetry. I can't.

The children, dressed in everything from their birthday suits to hand-me-down playclothes from Benetton, lead me down a tight path into a tunnel of thick green leaves. They fall back, giving me what I believe is some privacy. I see a wooden box in the middle with a golden seat cover. When I lean to lift the cover, I realize it is moving. My scream brings the children from behind the bushes.

"No problem, Lahdee," a little girl with a big smile says. She picks up a large stick and hits the lid as hard as she can. Hundreds of cockroaches, at least two inches in length and perhaps three quarters of an inch wide, scramble down the hole. Now I am expected to squat above it.

"Go on, go on," I say to the children. I wave them away with my hands. "Shoo, now! Salir!"

Desperately, awkwardly, I relieve myself and pray that the time will never come again for me to use this "modern" facility.

141

When I return to the beach, I have two little girls in tow, and I don't know how many children behind. I feel like the Pied Piper. Rather, the Peed Piper.

"Are you all right, Mother" Tim asks.

I don't elaborate on my experience.

"I'll get Katya to prepare your room. You stay here," Roger says, as if I have a choice.

A young woman with shiny brown hair and skin the color of tea approaches us. Roger moves quickly to embrace her and she him.

"This is Katya," he says. "She will take care of you." They seem to have a history, these two. Perhaps love is free here. I imagine he has his pick no matter which village he visits. I certainly don't care. Why should I care in the least? He is simply a vehicle to get us closer to the Atlantic.

The two of them turn away from us and enter a building with a tin roof and wood siding. It is not on stilts, so it looks more familiar but less poetic at first glance. I wonder what is happening inside.

"You were wonderful, Mother," Tim says.

"You were equally so," I answer. "Who will understand what we are seeing and doing here? It's as if we've entered a time capsule and gone back ten thousand years."

"It is like being on another planet, isn't it?"

"Kind of."

"Not quite safe."

"Not quite."

"Fabulous, though. I haven't felt this adventurous since I was sixteen," he says.

"Not that many years ago," I note. "You talk like an old man. Imagine how I must feel! Having such adventure at my age."

"Hey, you're just getting started. You're second only to Wonderwoman."

"Hardly," I say, but his words have made their mark. I feel flattered.

"You know, when I was a kid my favorite fantasy was Robinson Crusoe? I was the king of Penny Loaf Island, before the water taxis and tour boats fucked it up."

"Tim, really, such language."

"Fucked it up? Christ, Mother, let it go. We might be somebody's dinner tonight. What's a stupid word got to do with anything?"

"I'm sorry. Of course you're right."

Obviously, my Wonderwoman status is over. Didn't even last a minute.

"Mother. The language thing...you're afraid I don't respect you. Is that it? I respect you and I love you, but I am not your Little Lord Fauntleroy and never could be. It's time for you to respect me."

"Tim, I..."

"I know, I know, you're a mother first. Always the mother. Even in the wilderness."

"No. No, I really don't want to be. I am tired of all that. I want my own Penny Loaf Island," I say, surprised at my words. "Maybe my own jungle. You know, as in, Me Jane!"

We both need some food. I am suddenly starving.

Someone lets out a howl from the trees behind me.

Along comes Mr. Rogers with an entourage of small people, the villagers I presume. They set about building a fire and, while I remain supine, they create a table out of sticks and a mat of fronds at my feet. It is remarkable. Before long, a fire glows in front of the evaporating sun. Roger teaches the children how to make a cat's cradle with long blades of grass, and then casually asks them if they have heard of a plane crash or met an American stranger in the past few months. They shake their heads, no. "This lady has a husband who had a plane go down. She is looking for him."

Katya and the villagers stop their work and look at me, sadly. They tell Roger they have heard nothing and then they continue to cook our meal. Their silence is sweeter than words.

Roger and Tim start to sing songs and before long, the air is cleared and wrapped in melody. I tell myself I must remember. I must remember this. Roger's hands look gentle as he strums the guitar, his voice awash with diamonds. The stars come close, closer; they fall and drift, and I feel the vastness of the sky against the smallness of our little cluster of humanity.

When Tim walks to the water's edge, I am reminded again how like his father he's become—his stride, his courage, his ability to see a bigger picture.

Roger lifts a bottle of Victoria Gold and guzzles it down without so much as suggesting I might like one. He burps with satisfaction.

I cannot deny I think about the firmness of his frame. His face is aged by time and weather, but his shoulders and arms are toned and strong. He's no boy.

"Nothing like the Queen's beer to make a beast into a man again. Been drinkin' this ale for more than a quarter of a century."

"Did you go from mother's milk directly to the brewery?" I ask, thinking he was too young to have been drinking beer for so many years.

"I think you have just paid me a bloody left-handed compliment. As a matter of fact I had to break with my family before I indulged in the Devil's brew. Mum was the original teetotaler."

It is hard for me to imagine this man was ever someone's little boy.

Another howl erupts in the background. "That child has been screaming since we arrived!" I point out.

"Howler monkeys. They're just like kids—start acting up at dinner time."

Once again, I have proven my ignorance, but there's no need for pretense or excuses; Roger expects no more or less.

"Have you had children, Roger?"

"Hundreds," he smiles. His eyes have deep laugh lines at their corners.

I suspect he's impregnated more women than he knows. I blush. Why does this foolish thing happen to me? At least the sun is gone. No one here can tell.

The howlers continue to scream. I turn to see if I can spot them.

"They could be a half mile away. They're a noisy bunch."

"How big are they?"

"Oh you'll see—anywhere from a few pounds up to fifteen or more. Baboons with an attitude. They travel in troops, eating flowers and fruit, but they can be bloody nasty. They'll shit on your head or aim piss at your face to keep you away.

"Lovely. Will they attack?"

"No. But they're curious. They'll take a look at the three of us whiteys before too long. Maybe you'll be lucky enough to catch a glimpse if you keep your eyes up. They like the canopies."

"I find their calls chilling."

"Well, enjoy it; there's not much opportunity for chills out here."

Chilling does seem like the wrong word. Although it's cooling down now; I actually feel the air move.

"How did you get here?" I ask.

"I was born here."

"You?"

"My parents came as missionaries, well, almost. They were really running from Hitler. Religious zealousness got them out in time."

"But you're not German?"

"No, my folks were Brits. I'm Nica."

"And you and Katya... ?" (Have I actually posed this question?)

He shakes his head from side to side and says. "No, no, no, no! She's more a daughter. A Mayangna daughter. The Mayangas think they are rightful heirs of Nicaragua. They claim they arrived long before Columbus. Some say Managua is a bastardized version of the name Mayangna. It was once their capital city. Katya is not only a Mayangna but the mother of four children. I'm their compadrazzo. A compadrazzo is like a godfather in these parts."

"She looks so young. Her name, Katya--it sounds European."

"She was named after a missionary that was loved and lost. Kat was only fourteen when she had her first kid. That's how it goes here."

"Your parents...they never went back to England?"

"No. They couldn't. Their way of life had moved too far away from the reality of post-war England. They believed they were meant to stay."

"How did you deal with their deaths?"

"It was a long time ago. I was twenty-two when they died. It happened during a bout of dengue fever. Most of the other villagers died, too. I was away at school in Leon."

The howlers are chattering somewhere near by. I look up and see a black primate the size of a small child hanging over the edge of our grass roof, rubbing his chin and smiling at us. I grab Roger's arm.

"Hola, ol' boy," he calls. "Hold onto your piss, won't you?"

The ape's lips form a pink oval and he answers back with a piercing sound. I don't breathe.

Then he makes a new sound, similar to the roar of a lion, deep and ferocious, and is gone.

"Me, Jane," I say.

"Hmm. I don't suppose that makes me Tarzan?" he asks.

After a restless night of listening to the mysterious cackles and caws, scratches and screeches of the night's chorus, we ready ourselves for our exploration of the estuaries at the mouth of the river.

I am hoping it will be possible to find information about Nial nearer the coast where people may have been witness to whatever happened. Roger believes it's not unreasonable to think there's a chance we may meet someone who knows about the crash, someone who has evidence of a victim or a survivor. There are only thirty thousand people in Bluefields. News travels mostly by mouth, but it *does* get around because talk is the favorite pastime...that, and booze and drugging.

Roger's transport business is as much a water taxi. He takes on cargo and drops it off at designated places. Knowing one's whereabouts in this maze of tributaries is an art unto itself. He knows where to hang dead center of the water and where to find the invisible little villages that depend on him. To me, one bend looks like another. We have seen remarkable birds, red-footed boobies, blue-footed gannets, and huge pelicans with wing spans larger than coffins. We even saw a tapir drinking at the water's edge. He looked like a miniature elephant with a sawed-off nose. A homely animal maybe four hundred pounds or more. A remnant of prehistoric creatures. Then aren't we all?

If I could, I would wrap myself in mosquito netting, but I have none. I am mentally recording the number of bites I've suffered so I will remember netting should I ever return to this place. Tim and Roger manage to repel insects naturally. Is it their maleness? Another of nature's inequities? I am a mess. I'm glad I have no mirror. Roger says abstention from scratching is the only way to prevent itchiness. So far, it isn't working.

Our meanderings create hours of silence. This is a place where human voices seem intrusive to nature's hum. Strangely, it is comforting not to need to talk. At noon, while munching on the last of our peanut butter and jelly crackers, we talk about life on the water, any water, and how it pares a person's needs down to basics. Our conversation reminded me of Serena and her lifestyle. I told Tim about her, "I have met an amazing young woman. We spent quite a lot of time together before I left. I am impressed by her singularity. Her fortitude and honesty. Actually, I invited her to come down here with me, but she refused the invitation."

"Where did you meet?"

"She has a little lobster business and moors in our cove. You must know her."

"Not Serena?" His eyebrows shoot up with surprise.

It interests me that he seems so flummoxed.

"She's half your age."

It's her youth. "Well, that's true, but you know I am not dead yet. What has age got to do with anything. I needed a departure from my other friends. Surely you can imagine that!"

145

"I can imagine a lot of things but you and Serena hanging out. That's cool. She's cool."

So he tells me he's known her since they caught guppies together as children, but his interest tells me there's more to the story. I doubt any red-blooded young man could avoid admiring such a woman.

Tim takes turns with Roger at the tiller. They work comfortably together. Natural friends. We wend our way from one village to another. Each place has something for us to carry to the port and Roger asks the same questions again and again about a plane crash or news of a tall blond stranger.

Today is our day for returning to civilization. Leaving these endless snaking waters and infrequent sightings of human existence. I must say, I am excited and afraid. Afraid of disappointment and excited to make some kind of connection. Roger doubts we will have as much luck in Bluefields. He believes the out islands are our best bet.

"Ee-aa-hoo" we hear calling across the water. A group of boys appears on the shore to our left. They are standing on a tiny spit of sand making birdcalls and gestures to come toward them. Their thin arms wave bunches of fruit, perhaps to sell or transport.

"Don't believe I know these lads," Roger mutters to Tim. Despite the fact that he doesn't recognize them, I am afraid he will make a snap decision and heed their calls.

"I don't think stopping is wise," I caution.

I can see Tim feels skeptical, too, by the way he looks to Roger while ignoring the boys.

Our captain decides to find out what they want. "Come now, mates? Let's give it a go!" Roger says in his best British yo-ho voice, and he takes the wheel from Tim.

It is not that I am afraid of the ninos; it's just the stories I've heard make me hesitant. I know we're not liked here, no more than anyone else who is foreign. The Contra's guns are still in the hands of children. High-powered guns could turn up anywhere. And there's desperation and hunger. Roger himself pointed that out.

"If I were a child in these jungles, I would think, *here come more gringos to do more harm than good*. I might even use them as target practice."

"Mother. It will be all right, Roger knows what he's doing."

"Heave ho! We're comin' about," our Captain calls. Roger doesn't consider himself anything more or less than Nica. I swallow my fear; he's the captain and this is his river.

"Stand back," he calls as we turn toward the shore. No sooner do we hear the thud of hull to sand than about a dozen scrawny boys of assorted ages scramble out of the bushes and clamber all around the boat. First, they rock it free from the bank, then they check it for guns and ammunition. Roger tells them the boat is the property of the Mission de Paulina and he is just a river man. He tells them they must not do anything to harm the boat because, like himself, it is a servant to the people of the river. He speaks in two tongues and, truthfully, I can read his hands more than his lips. He tells them the Paulina has the blessing of the madres and carries a curse for anyone or anything that brings harm her way. He says all this as if he's explaining the rules of the road.

"Where are you going?" the leanest meanest looking one of the group asks.

"Bluefields. We have an important mission, a very great and good gringo fell from the sky and we are trying to find him. We are picking up food to take up the river on our way back."

"We will come with you to protect you," the boys say. "We sell bananas."

Skeptically, I think a few bunches of bananas are just what the people of Bluefields need. I look at Tim and he smiles at the boys as if they are kindergarten children. He must not notice how their knives hang on their sides. Does it occur to him they may be a rogue army lost in the jungle?

Roger bows and asks the boys, "When do you plan to return to your village?"

They explain that they have no village. All of Bluefields is their home.

"Must be Boy Scouts," Tim says to me with a mischievous expression on his face, "on an overnight."

Roger tells them to sit on the floor and he will have them in port in less than an hour.

The boys sit down obediently and remain huddled in silence as Roger heads downstream.

Tim chooses to interrupt the quiet. "Hey, Roger, how about a song? Why don't you add music to this ferry ride?"

Surely, he's kidding. I can't believe my ears.

"Ah a ditty for the kiddies!" Roger says.

Tim takes over the tiller and Roger grabs his guitar. He props one foot up on his storage box, holds his guitar like a cowboy and begins to play. These hooligans are being treated like guests and to my amazement they start to respond as such. Can they possibly have forgotten to plunder and rob us blind? Roger's seaworthy voice sings,

You can trust the moon to move the mighty oceans,
You can trust the sun to shine upon the land,
You can take the little that you know
And do the best you can,
And you see the rest with the quiet faith of man.

He sings it again and again, one line at a time until he gets them to repeat it, then goes on to the next verse.

There's a storm tossed ship tonight out on the water
There's a soul that sails alone out on the blue
There's a dreamer with her eyes upon the heavens
They're all looking for a way to make it through

The boys start to sing gingerly.

"Hey, we have ourselves a choir here!" Roger says. "Now how about this one? Maybe you already know it?"

The boys giggle and their bodies relax against one another. Terra cotta toes start keeping the rhythm.

Roger plays the song I first heard him play last night in Santa Marta under the stars, with me feeling so foolish. I liked the song then, but it makes more sense to me now.

Somos el barco, somos el mar, yo navego en ti, tu navegas en mi
We are the boat, we are the sea, I sail in you, you sail in me.

We are moving closer and closer to the port city. The back rivers seem contained compared to the wide canals of Rio Escondido's delta. Her green waters turn brackish and soon our destination comes into sight.

When we were back in Managua and working at the Casa Ben Linder with the volunteers, Penny and some other Americans made flyers for us to bring to Bluefields. The flyers have a picture of Nial, dates and descriptions of the plane and a list of contact people to contact if anyone can provide information about the crash or the pilot.

As the boys disembark from the boat, Roger passes them and gives each boy a cordoba to place the flyers around the city. He tells them if they see Nial or hear of him, there will be a very big reward. I notice the name, Roger Sheffield, has been added to the list of contacts and the barge, Paulina, as a place of contact. I am learning goodness has many faces.

A few women wait for the baskets we have brought from inland villages, and in the background, men with donkeys watch the activity. Roger jokes and barters with each of the women, he evidently gives them some information about me because they point and giggle, then discuss with each other what he has said. Roger delivers the heaviest baskets to the men who place them on their donkeys' backs. I have no idea what's in the baskets, if they're filled with fruit or carved ebony, cocaine, beads, or seeds. I don't ask and would never assume.

Our own debarking is less swift as we reorganize our supplies to haul them through the streets of Bluefields. Miraculously, our money is still safely rolled inside the peanut butter jar in the cooler, and we pull out a significant part of it to pay Roger. He takes it without checking the amount. Tim and I had decided to give him considerably more than he had asked. He is quiet as he walks with us to the tourist bureau.

I find myself not wanting to step away from him into the haze that is Bluefields. The air is steamy; the streets rough. I can smell clay baking and fish drying. Tin roofs burn brightly but the small dark skinned people don't appear affected by the heat. For me, it hurts, along with the bright white empty question of Nial's circumstances. I now must face this reality with my dear son, and am struck by an overarching sense of helplessness. I turn to

Roger to ask him something, "But where?..." and he's gone. He's pre-occupied with some people on a side street selling water. His face is the only one here that I trust other than Tim's. I want him to stay with us, wish I had been more pleasant, but it is too late.

I wave to him and he crosses back to us to say goodbye. I actually consider embracing him but we're sweaty and I feel awkward besides. I reach out my hand instead and he surprises me by enfolding it in both of his. "You're a courageous and fine woman, Mrs. Townsend. A rose among the thorns. It is a privilege to know you." He bows, like a knight to a lady.

His words restore my energy and straighten my spine.

"I have something for you," he says. "Well, actually, it's not from me. It is from one of the old crones in that group across the street. They heard about your healing abilities. Do you see her over there?

I look across the street to see a brown weathered face smiling at me. She is wearing a black skirt with pink embroidery and a big straw hat tied under her chin.

"She asked me to give it to you, to protect you. She says you are compadrazzo, family."

I unwrap the gift tied with pampas grass and folded into a leaf. It is a purple crystal.

"I doubt crystals are common here," he says. "It is probably very valuable to her but she wanted to please you. You understand, on the Atlantic Coast women are considered powerful. They're regarded as witches by the men who they seduce, and the people they heal. Looks like you have been recognized by los mujeres as one of them. Probably the story of your stitchery got to Bluefields faster than we did."

I am moved. I look toward the old woman to see if she is watching. She is. I grasp the crystal in my fist, place my hand close to my heart, and tap it three times. She nods in acknowledgment and turns away.

"Some say crystals have magic," he says.

"Well, I believe in magic," I tell him, wondering if he does too.

Once the Tourist Office has found us a place to stay, Tim and I begin to navigate Bluefields. I am struck by the utilitarian nature of this city, about the size of Granite Shores, with the shipping industry dominating it, just as it does at home. Of course, it's a bastion of maleness, except for the female vendors in their bright brocaded skirts and straw hats waiting for produce to be delivered in the pangas from points south.

We go to the Police Department, which appears to be a local paramilitary group distinguished by their fatigues. They ask us how long the plane was missing, and tell us they have no records of a plane wreck or of any tall Americano trying to reach someone during the past year.

They direct us to the boatyards where we meet with Father Joseph's point man, Victor Hernandez. He says there are more islands than are recorded in the shoals off this coast. Some are inhabited but most are not. If a person had made it to one of the islands, he could have survived. But if he was clever enough to survive and wanted to be found, he could also send out signals to the passing boats. He says there are hundreds of trawlers and cargo ships that navigate these waters regularly.

I have to agree with Victor Hernandez, that a man could signal one of the passing ships if he wanted to, but I am still intrigued by the out islands.

"Is there any way we could rent a boat and island hop?" I ask.

Tim interrupts, "Wait a minute, Mother. I don't think so."

"Hop islands with a boat?" Victor asks. Again, my words don't translate into sensible Spanish.

"I don't think it's wise to try to search these waters, on our own, Mother," Tim says. "Not without knowing the islands or the customs of the people who inhabit them. I think we should find a local navigator."

Tim's right; we can't set out on such unknown waters. What am I thinking of? But I am sure Victor can help us. He agrees to look for such a person.

In each of our connected rooms in the miserable little hotel, we have one small shuttered window. The walls are built out of cement block; the door has a dubious lock and the ceiling, a noisy fan. The toilet doesn't flush. Our mattresses are thin and covered with more red vinyl, which smells like spoiled milk mixed with ammonia. Bugs and spiders sit confidently on the wall. I am tired. I am so tired I am afraid to let go of what consciousness I have left. Afraid I won't be able to wake.

I knock on Tim's door. "Tim, I'm thinking we should go on one of those charter tours before we target our trip. Let's work from a broad base and then narrow the field. If we learn someone is out there who has a recall of the plane we will know where to begin. I mean if we hear anything at all. What do you think?

I hear him snoring. He's out cold; gone for the night.

This trip has introduced me to the most amazing companion and wisest friend I could have hoped for, my own son. I move toward his bed and remove his shoes. His lips are slightly parted, sweet and soft, reminiscent of that little boy I was afraid to put down. His hair falls over his brow and his hands curl in little cups, still gentle and refined. He is a man now. I am proud to see that he never cowers or gives up. He trusts his mind and it's serving us well. Nial would be proud. I am proud. I lean over and kiss his cheek. "Night, Mom," he mumbles from the otherworld.

Morning is barely moving when we hear a loud knock on our door. I grab some clothes and open the door slightly to find out who's there. Two armed men in uniform tell me they are officials and we must show them our luggage. I don't know what to do. I beg for a moment to dress properly. Tim puts his Swiss Army knife up his sleeve and then we open the door. They go through everything and ask why we are in town. My hands tremble as I show them the pictures of my husband and then I relax when they appear to believe me. It's then I realize that Tim and I being together on this journey is precipitous. We look like legitimate family members seeking another family member. Tim alone would have been distrusted by the police; I, alone, would not have made it here at all.

We remove ourselves from our horrid rented cells and walk down the early morning streets. We pass metal shelters that heat up like aluminum pots under the sun. It is no wonder these people are brown; they're braised. Children, chubby and dear, sit on the ground near their mammas. They do not whine or beg. They're at ease in the dirt, some with flies stuck in their coarse black hair or on their runny noses. We are greeted with smiles from faces so soft, a bad thought behind them seems impossible. I have already learned to ignore the mothers' outstretched hands, but I have yet to master guilt.

On the edge of the land near a quagmire of houseboats, I see a sweet clapboard church with stained glass windows and a steeple. The Moravian Church, it is called. I am astonished by its crisp whiteness, its clean lines, painted walls and simple elegance. A Quaker might call it home. We can't pass up this opportunity to talk to someone who might be able to help us. The large doors in the front of the church are open and so we enter to be greeted by a tall thin rather Dutch looking man. He wears a white robe and a black collar. We comment about the beauty of his church and ask if we could speak to him for a minute. Soberly, he leads us to his study and his words disturb us.

He has the nerve to suggest that Nial's work may have been more sinister than we thought. That he could have been working for the CIA or perhaps running drugs. He even had the unmitigated gall to suggest that Nial was carelessly cutting the mahogany forests to grow abaca, acting as another destroyer of one of the endangered and most precious resources of the region.

Tim and I assure this so-called *man of the cloth* that all of these things couldn't be further from the truth. Nial had only a respect for the earth, the people, and the future of Nicaragua in his heart. I added that the colectivo is merely utilizing farmland that was left fallow after the revolution.

The reverend goes on to say that, unfortunately in worldly struggles, everyone thinks he or she is on the right side, God's side. He says he believes this perception has made the indigenous people outcasts in their own land.

"He may have been shot down because he was from the United States," he says. "It would be reason enough; at least to these people, who claim this is their land and the rest of us are invaders."

We try to explain Nial's long-term interest in the progress of the democratic movement, but we don't seem to make an impression on him. Given that, we're surprised when he sticks out his tired veined hand and agrees to do what he can to help us.

"I will take some of your posters and place them in the church and in the Garifuna's hands. Perhaps, you'll learn what you need to know. Perhaps, you will not. God bless."

With this questionably pleasant conclusion he dismisses us. Neither Tim nor I feel our words can change the reality of the perception here. So, we meander to the docks, furtively, like two stray cats and look for a place to eat.

It's a busy harbor with great container ships from Japan and Brazil in port. A fish processor from Singapore waits just beyond shore.

We find a metal-clad diner and order hueuvos rancheros y cafe au lait, tortillas on the side. We tell the restaurant's manager about our missing person, then ask if we may post a sign on the wall of her place. She kindly agrees. This gesture seems grand in contrast to the negativity of the minister, and I feel a glimmer of hope, of confidence returning.

After gorging ourselves, we search for water taxis and pleasure boats, and considering it isn't exactly a tourist's town, we're surprised to find them both. We've passed many more shacks made of found materials along the way. It is as if everything in this town is temporary.

By nine in the morning the heat is intensifying. I strip down to as few clothes as possible and buy us two round-trip tickets for a boat ride to Rama Cayo.

While we wait for the boat to leave, we distribute our flyers in offices nearby and hand them out to the other excursion boat people. We circulate them in the streets, give them to the harbor police and the street vendors. We ask people to ask their friends. It is not a friendly place. We know we aren't connecting. Even the roads lead away, to the water, not the land. It is all about water, business, and fish—not retrieving lost souls.

I imagine we appear more foreign than we know. I will be happier on the water and am grateful for my protective crystal. Tim remains focused, his head into the task, not wasting time on irrelevant observations.

Our tour boat takes us to an island where about six hundred Ramas live. They are isolationists and island life makes this possible. It surprises me we are allowed to pull into their port.

While we are on Rama Cayo, I am hit with a severe headache. I lose my breakfast and then my intestines decide to erupt. By the time we get back to Bluefields, Tim is as sick as I. We are a pathetic pair in our hot hotel rooms with no flushing toilet. We try to laugh at how disgustingly intimate our suffering is. We can hear each other retching through the masonry walls and knock on our shared door to commiserate. We pray we will live through the night. In the morning, despite the fact that we are feverish and still sick, we stagger to the tourist bureau and make reservations on the first plane we can get back to Managua, to medical care and safety.

Once we arrive back in the capital, we check in at the Intercontinental Hotel and use it like a hospital. For three days we are disabled, this time more privately, too sick to care. When we come out of it, I decide it is time for me to return to the States and Tim decides to stay at the farm, oversee the replanting of the fields and figure out how he can best expedite another shipment of the harvest. Paul has joined forces with Tim now to help with the work. He's a positive influence regarding Tim's decision to stay because his enthusiasm is catching. It looks like Tim's more inspired than ever to make his father's venture work. I promise him I will do whatever I can on the home front to ensure smooth sailing. At the same time, I feel obligated to remind him how tenuous the situation is at the plant. He reminds me nothing could be as tenuous as life in Nicaragua.

I do want to see Penny before I leave, but I am still not myself. We have a brief meeting at the hotel. Visit long enough for her to note that I've lost weight and insist I look wonderful. She tells me I must not lose faith, that hope is enough to keep a person going. I praise her strength and we promise to write as we separate.

Sixteen

Serena

Cape Ann in April is disappointing. I left the blooming of the capital in denial of how long winter actually hangs on in Massachusetts. I understand now why pansies and petunias shriveled up in Grandma's window boxes every spring. Like me, she probably forgot the cold rains and chilly nights that produce frost instead of petals. I resist making the same mistakes she did, and lock her trowel in the toolshed for a while.

The town clean-up crews are grinding through the streets sucking up winter's casualties, but the potholes aren't mended yet and blue tarps still hide boats stored in the yards.

My condo feels cozy and welcoming. At first, I love the privacy that Key West didn't offer and I'm at peace with the sloth that sets in because there's not much I *have* to do. Unfortunately, too many days alone and too much television, and before you know it, the lonelies creep in again. Where am I going? How can I really erase the people I've loved, get over the pain and start over? Maybe my penance is to suffer alone. But how long?

After five days of rain the sky opens up and I know I have to get out of the house or I'll begin to look like the mole I'm becoming. The sunsets at Halibut Point have a way of reminding me of the bigger picture, the one that extends way beyond this rocky coast. So I take Bill as far as I can, park and walk to the point's farthest edge. On a smooth bed of flat golden rock facing east, I watch the tide come in and consider how the waters rise no matter how low they fall, each tide rhythmically coming and going, delivering and taking at will. I slowly inhale and just as slowly exhale trying to make a rhythm of my own. As usual, the conscious act of breathing relaxes me, and by the time the sun drops into the sea, I let go of my stuff and just am.

Ipswich Bay still smacks of winter, its Prussian blues and hard edges are unrelenting. Last year's dead leaves clog the wedges between stones, although, I see a crocus or a tiny new shoot testing the air here and there. On my way back to the car, I make my way along the water's edge placing each foot carefully on boulders where only the most catastrophic events have made an impression. I walk past a tidepool without succumbing to my habit of looking for things to rescue. Something in me used to feel fulfilled when I reentered creatures to the sea; watched them sink into deep water and get another chance. Now, I suspect they are exactly where they should be; caught for gulls and terns and horseshoe flies.

The guy I met in Washington, Simon Delacroix, has called me twice since I got back to Granite Shores. He says there's a need for networking on Cape Ann. Wouldn't I like to gather some people who are like-minded and join forces with their Cambridge group? Truth is, I have nothing better to occupy my time but I can't imagine who I'd call. I liked those people, the ones I met in D.C., but I don't know much about Nicaragua, and I don't know anyone who is "like-minded" here on Granite Shores.

Simon invites me to a meeting on Sunday in Boston where they will show a film and discuss plans for organizing work brigades to go to Guatemala and Nicaragua in January. These trips must be what Gwen was talking about.

I haven't seen her. I know she's back in town. She called Geena who told her I was taking the long way home. It's obvious they didn't find Nial; I'm sure she would have said something. I heard the big news through breakfast talk at Sailor Sam's, that the Townsend Rope Company bought itself, and the Townsend's stone house is on the market for almost two million dollars.

At Beacon Marine the other day, Ted Peterson said it was all true. Nial's company is a cooperative now. Tim has been named operations manager, Mac Huff, manager; Ted's president of the new board with Gwen taking on the Vice President's role.

Ted spoke like a proud father where Gwen was concerned. I have to say his tone ticked me off. It's more of the patriarchal crap that history passes down. I wanted to ask why *she* wasn't president of the company but kept my mouth shut. I figure if I ever have the occasion, I will ask her that question myself.

At the risk of growing old alone and blaming myself for it, I force myself to go to Simon's networking meeting, which takes place in a church basement near Harvard Square. About twenty-four people are present, all of them at least ten years my senior and three of them ministers. This puts me off some, being an avowed Pagan. We are shown a trio of films that cover three organizations working in Nicaragua. Their missions are similar to each other—to raise the living standards of the poor and help the people help themselves. I feel certain that Christ is on the agenda somewhere, but he's never mentioned.

I have to admit it's impressive to learn how volunteers help families build their own houses. The film of children learning in dark classrooms taught by skinny young male teachers in white shirts with only a few workbooks and no pencils or paper was what everyone else was impressed with. I suppose the schools are a major achievement, considering these children had no schooling before, and neither did their parents.

I'll bet I'm the only person in the room who hates schools. Even though educating the peasants is at the head of these people's priority lists, it wouldn't be on mine. I think the Nicaraguans may have been happier before the revolution and before all sorts of programs were forced on them. They are simple people, used to guaranteed work and grateful for a place to live. It's my guess that private houses and education are outsiders' ideas of well-being—wanting to make the peasants more like us, make them compete, make them want.

The second film features a scene from one of the horrors of the Hidden Wars. It actually shows the massacre of children in a peasant village by military soldiers on horseback waving machetes. They lob the children's heads off, children standing on the road—two and three year olds—and they let the screaming mothers live so they can mourn. It's hard to believe someone could film such an atrocity, but I saw it myself and I'm sure it was authentic. It makes me feel ill and stupid. Changes my mind. We sit quietly when the film ends, in a blackened room where words are not enough. Perhaps we *could* do something. Maybe there's something I can do.

Unlike me, the people in this room are formally educated and I know some are professionals, pretty prestigious, too. Dr. Daniel Davidson, the anthropologist, is here; Barry Dukakis, the social reformer; Cecil Peabody who funds grass roots movements for social justice. And Ken Myerson from Doctors Without Borders. I don't know the others but all of them knew about this situation before they came tonight. I have no intention of opening my mouth and revealing my ignorace.

Simon works me into the group by making a joke about how he corralled me at the march in Washington and isn't about to let me out of the pen. I am surrounded by smiling faces, each wanting to tell their version of what they saw or heard on their recent visits to Central America. I can see they are connected in a way similar to fishermen. They love the tales of hardship just as much as the ones of victory.

Simon suggests we get together soon in my *neck of the woods*. He says I should invite some of my friends and think of a good meeting place. There's a woman I should meet, he tells me; her name is Gwen Townsend.

It's like a buzz saw starts screeching in my head. I know my flirtation with this thing is over and can't tell him why. I'm afraid Simon may disappear if I don't get on his bandwagon, and he's nice, might even be good for me. But...I can't go any further. He would like to make everyone think they have something to contribute. But, if I get involved, there I'll be again, putting Gwen Townsend in the middle of my life.

I tell Simon I have already met Gwen and we come from two different worlds. I try to explain that our relationship has dark holes in it and it's better for me to leave them alone. I also try to explain that pulling a group together on Cape Ann is not for me. He says he wants to talk to me about that.

"No. I just can't participate. I really am not that type. Shit, I'd like to help, but you have me all wrong. I don't do groups." I tell him.

"Well, how about a cup of coffee then?" he asks. "Do you do coffee?"

It seems harmless enough, so I agree. Thing is, he says, he wants to meet me on my turf. I try to think of a place other than my apartment. I won't invite him there because it could be misinterpreted. I definitely won't bring him to Sailor Sam's because it would be like bringing him home to family. I decide on Barnacle Bill's where only the tourists show up. Great environment down by the big trawlers, stench of dead fish and live bait, and all the colorful array of fishing boats you could hope for. He'll love it.

"Well, if you're willing to drink a cup of coffee with me, how about dessert?"

"All right, although Barnacle Bill's is better known for chowder."

"Well, if you're willing to have coffee, dessert and chowder, how about a main dish to tie it all together?"

I agree to that as well.

We make a date for dinner on Saturday. A date. Here I am, in my mid-twenties. and I have never had a bonafide date. I have no idea what to expect. I suppose I should just plan on hearing a pitch to participate in the Central American Advocacy Group. But he's the nicest man I've met in a long time, and he can form complete sentences. He's sober, has a job, is over six foot tall and likes me. What can I say but yes?

The extent to which I go in preparation for this evening is embarrassing. I actually search for the perfect outfit and wind up with a new skirt and blouse in a wonderful soft jersey that moves as I do and hugs where it should. I sprinkle Grandma's old necklaces on the bed and play with the amethysts, the citrines and tourmalines, her favorites. Like lilacs against a blue sky, the amethysts work their magic on my blue jersey. I put them aside, laughing at the thought of wearing jewelry in Barnacle Bill's, but determined to wear it anyway.

I hardly know who this man is or what his intentions may be, but I wish the week away, regardless.

Saturday finally arrives. When I hear the phone ring, I'm sure it's him canceling our date and resist answering. But the caller turns out to be Gwen Townsend. I listen to her careful way of enunciating, like there's a thought in front of each syllable. I think how friendly her voice sounds, but I am not going to open that door again. I need to stay out of her life. She only *thinks* we are friends. She would hate me if she knew the truth.

It is time for me to go forward, fill up all the cracks in my heart. I need to start thinking about who I want to be next. I've learned a lot outside of the classroom. One of the things I know is that the ride feels best when I'm at the wheel. That's why I didn't care about going to college despite Whitey's prodding or Grandma's urging. It seemed more like their idea than mine. As far as I could see, colleges were no more than young people's homes, holding tanks for kids until they'd figured out what they wanted to do with their lives.

I'm a fisherman. It's been a fine way of life for a girl who grew up by the sea. What I didn't anticipate, and what no one could have convinced me to believe, was that a day would come when I wouldn't be sure pulling pots was enough.

Seventeen

Gwen

I've been back two months now, Nial gone for eleven, and I can't find terra firma. The supermarkets I longed for during my months in Nicaragua still look glutted and excessive. The house feels ridiculous, so much wasted space meant to harbor things, not life. These crazy roads filled with rage, glutted with large gas eating cars occupied by one person going somewhere their feet could take them; people misbehaving, too distracted or self important or angry, throwing fingers at each other instead of bouquets. Even Mother is reduced to angry words. On the one hand she's losing her speech; on the other she's saying words I never heard from her mouth before. I asked the doctor if it was some form of Tourette's Syndrome, "No," he says, "it's just that her masks are down."

I guess Mother has been storing up curse words all her life!

When I look at the stone walls to the rear of the house, I have to ask what kind of people would build a wall fourteen feet high for some fruit trees? Even the Townsend pride grates on my conscience.

I am not sure what to do with myself. In Nicaragua, I had no doubt. That's why I'm going back. I think the debilitating intestinal thing is over, although I still suffer bouts of discomfort. Tim says he's acquiring all the right parasites so he can eat the wrong ones, and he's feeling well. The new crop of abaca is planted and thriving and Ted and I have seen to it that the Townsend Cordage Company goes on, for a while at least.

Tim has agreed I should sell the house. It will pay off the loans Nial took out, and leave us with more than enough for a modest place. I will look for a house that provides Tim with private quarters. He seems amenable to that idea although fairly neutral about all the rest. I think he's so immersed in his project, he has little psychic attachment to this old house right now.

Speaking of psychic, I have a gnawing concern about Serena. I haven't seen hide nor hair of her and I know she left Key West a month ago. I thought she was distant the few times we spoke this winter, but it is hard to tell what's going on if you can't see a person face to face. It's in the eyes, the innuendo, the shadows of language we discern the intention of words. In Serena, despite her staunch independent spirit, I recognize a wanting— something like my own—whenever we meet. From the beginning, I felt her energy pushing itself on me and withdrawing simultaneously. It is that very duality I'm drawn to.

I suppose it's foolish to be anxious about her whereabouts. I'm not her mother, and yet I am not sure a woman on the road, alone, is safe these days. Who looks out for her? I must ask who she contacts to say where she is or if things are well.

I've been invited to share my impressions of Nicaragua here on Cape Ann. I want to make sure Serena comes to the meeting. A surrogate minister at the Granite Shores Unitarian Church has made a room available for the presentation. It will be sponsored by a Cambridge group that works to benefit Central America. This will be a major challenge for me. I am not sure what I want to say, but I know I must find the right words, words that will educate and inspire others. It should be a call for help.

Old friends have called, planning to attend, but I hope above all that Serena will come. If it hadn't been for her prodding I wouldn't have climbed aboard that plane going south in the first place. I think she will be responsive if she understands the needs of the people. There are all sorts of ways she could get involved. Her quick mind is as remarkable as her strong body and she's looking for something, I know it. She must be.

No word about Nial from anyone in Bluefields. Penny says she got a telephone call from a man named Sheffield. She asked him if it concerned Nial and he said not really.

I should contact Roger myself. It's just I don't know what to say to a man who is so different from my world. He must realize this. Perhaps he will call me when he has a practical reason. But, I do think about him. When I remember his hands around mine, it stops my breath. I should be ashamed of myself. Nial is the issue here, my darling Nial. Lord, what was it he said to me that last day?

As I work on my words for the meeting, I realize the degree to which Nicaragua has taken hold of me. It's as if, in that Godforsaken place, in its primitive, steaming broth of struggle, I participated in the discovery of fire. There, with Gloria, cooking meals on the coals brought down through the millennia. In playing with the children, games that preceded the written word, singing their music, looking into those big brown unspoiled eyes, I found the meaning of being human. This is what I want to tell anyone who will listen—that when I stood back from my world and regarded these faces, I found myself. We, all of us, are no different than the chips of glass in a kaleidoscope, any which way we turn, the design is beautiful. My own gift of crystal is a fortuitous reminder.

But this is so melodramatic.

Probably more telling is the significance of the red plastic pail on a knotted rope. I saw it in El Crucero where the slash in the pail's bottom was not enough to make it disposable. It was, and I am sure still is, the sole utensil for scooping water from a thirteen-foot well, a flawed but valuable access to the village's water supply. Or perhaps it was the blue ribbon tied on the end of a stick belonging to a six year old named Roberto. It ornamented his hobby horse and was a great source of pride. So many soft, innocent images flood my mind as I try to write. I realize I have been harsh on the land from which I ran.

Realtors are salivating for the sale of our house. It is easier than it should be to keep everything in perfect showing condition; what else have I to do? I could push things along and boil apples or fill the rooms with fresh cut flowers to give it a sense of liveliness and homeyness. I could open *House Beautiful* to the page featuring our gardens, but the truth is, I believe the someones who buy this place will have to see past its present to earlier, better days. I hope a family with messy children and two dogs, a cat and a passion for sunsets will find it. Someone who will fill it with new spirits and lots of attention and make sure it stands forever.

I talk to Ted at a board meeting and he tells me he's seen Serena, reporting that she was full of questions about me and the company. I, meanwhile, haven't seen the Serena Marie yet, neither the boat nor the woman she's named after. Such a puzzle, that one! Not so much as a phone call from her.

My talk takes place in two days and I am going to impose myself on her. I really must see her. She's been an inspiration to me, now it's my turn to inspire her, include her some way in this journey of mine. How adorable she was when she came for dinner that night and looked at every detail in the house as if it was a museum or something. Of course, it *is* a museum; that's exactly why I must leave. Perhaps there's something she would want of these old things. I wonder.

Phones used to be my main line of communication with people, beyond letters or drop-ins or e-mails. Now I dislike them; the long numbers, answering services, tele marketers, prompters and call waitings—all of it. But I will call Serena, anyway. She would probably like to have some of the things I plan to give to Goodwill.

When I dial her number, I hear, "I'm sorry I can't come to the phone right now, but please leave a ..."

I don't. Instead, I hang up hard, then wrap Grandmother's tea set and the silver Chinese cricket box I've never used and put them in the car. Serena's apartment has the pizzazz of the new and the charm of the old. The sweet Irish tea set will look charming behind the glass doors of her kitchen cabinet or on the glass tea table near the sliding door to her deck. I suppose she will put a pair of those dangling earrings of hers in the cricket box.

I ring the doorbell and she opens the door simultaneously.

"Hi! I saw you parking the car," she says. "I am just about to meet a friend. But, come in, come in for a minute."

I don't think a minute will be enough. "Ted told me he saw you and I tried to call but...well, I am moving you know, and I just thought you might like these little things from the house." It is as if she doesn't want to let me past the foyer. I am flustered because *she* seems to be.

I explain further. "The Irish tea set was my grandmother's. It dates from another century. I thought you might like it because it is reminiscent of your grandmother's past, as well."

"I don't know what to say. It's so kind of you to think of me...you even remember that Grandma was Irish, Gwen, but, shit, I can't accept this. It...it doesn't seem right."

"What could possibly be wrong? I want you to have it. There's no one who I would rather give it to. Of course, if you think it is too old or you don't like it, that's all right, too."

Serena is obviously not used to receiving gifts. I suppose I am going on too much, babbling, but I must tell her about the box.

"This little box is Chinese. It's a sarcophagus of sorts, they used them as coffins for their prized crickets—especially those that brought them good luck. It's a little treasure, don't you think? Of course, you can use it to store matches or earrings, or stuff it with nothing more than memories."

She stands there staring at the gifts as if they were stolen from the Gardiner Museum, as if they're too hot to handle. She is startled by a knock on the door and becomes agitated. This is not what I expected. I certainly didn't mean to be the cause of upset.

"I'm, it's..." she starts.

"I'll be going, dear. You must consider the gifts as thank you notes for helping me get on that plane to Nicaragua. I will be speaking about my trip tomorrow at the Unitarian Church in town. *Please* come. Three o'clock. Jay Street. You might find it more interesting than you know." I slip her one of the church bulletins.

She takes it and, before she answers the knock, she passes the old mirror I gave her, musses with her hair, and frowns into the glass. It is the first time I have seen her appear vain. Then, as I step aside for her to open the door, I see a tall attractive male on the other side and realize I've stepped into something. She's too nervous for it to be an established relationship, but then maybe it's because I'm on the threshold.

Her smile brightens the doorway. "Why, hello, Simon. Come in."

Her power is back.

"I want you to meet the person you wanted me to meet in the first place, Simon. This is Gwen Townsend. Gwen, Simon Delacroix."

I am impressed how she has shifted gears in seconds moving to what appears to be utter composure. But who is this? The man who has been calling me?

"Simon, aren't you?..."

"Mrs. Townsend, aren't you?..." we say at the same time.

Simon takes the lead.

"You are just the person I've been looking forward to meeting. Ready for the lecture tomorrow?"

"But how could you have..." I start to ask. I am just too confused.

"I'm in the process of trying to talk Serena, here, into getting involved in our group!"

Our group. I have no idea what he's referring to.

"Serena? What...what in the world?" I don't mean to stammer. I am really lost. What in the world could Serena have in common with Simon Delacroix?

"Yes. She was willing to march in Washington, so I'm hoping she will become an organizer here on Granite Shores. She's told me about you."

This does not sound like Serena. I have to put some pieces together to believe what I'm hearing.

"Serena? Marching in Washington? I just find this..."

Serena interrupts, "Amazing, Gwen. I was passing through the Capital, and...."

"And she saw our demonstration and told me about your work in Managua. Of course, she was proud to know someone who was working with the children. Thing was, we never actually mentioned your name until the other night at the Cambridge meeting. This is how these things keep evolving, through our connections. It's pretty common," Simon Delacroix says.

I can hardly explain to him how *uncommon* this connection is, for either Serena or myself. It is as if we had gone to India, myself from Boston and she from Sydney, and we bumped into each other in Bombay.

"We're headed out for dinner. Would you like to join us?" he asks.

"Oh no, I couldn't possibly," I explain, "I'm still working on my little talk."

"We're both looking forward to it, aren't we Serena?" he says, giving her a big wink.

She looks totally perplexed and doesn't do much more than give me an enigmatic smile. I must admit I'm stunned and deeply touched by her unanticipated interest.

"You two go on now and have a lovely evening," I manage.

On the way home, I smile at the thought of Serena's surprises. She seems to be becoming more and more a part of my landscape. Her involvement could connect us in a profound way.

Eighteen
Serena

Romance is in the air tonight, right alongside the low tide's foul fumes. We're sitting on the winter porch at Barnacle Bill's Restaurant next to a noisy heater. The conversation grows easier as we down a bottle of good Merlot.

I ask Simon what he does in his real life.

He tells me he's in the mortgage business, that his work is about money and figures. Sometimes it's so dry, he thinks he can't do another day. He says he needed a higher purpose, something to throw himself into, something he could care about. That's how he got involved in Central American issues.

It's as if I am hearing Nial all over again. I wonder what it is about me that attracts lost boys? But as I listen, I realize Simon's not lost. He's not tormented either. This man has obviously found his purpose. And who am I to judge anyway?

He sips his wine and studies the menu. The flapping of plastic sheets where windows should be, doesn't phase him. I like this, and I like the looks of him in his tweed jacket and loafers. He dresses more like a professor than a banker. Pop might have liked him, too.

I order the beer battered shrimp and get a kick out of his excitement over a two pounder. Lobster is the most popular dish in this place. We're in *lobstah* heaven, afterall.

Simon pulls the salt stained sheet back to get a full dose of the night's landscape. I can see boats turning into Townsend Cove. Beyond them, the crooked rooftops of the old chair factory flatten against the evening sky. It's a clear cool night with good weather expected tomorrow.

A full moon rises. A piece of its edge begins to darken.

"The eclipse," he informs me.

We watch as a great black thumb starts to smudge the moon's mottled face. Little by little, light is stolen from the sky.

By the time we leave the restaurant only the moon's penumbra remains.

"Chicken Little, the moon has gone out. Just another reminder of forces so mysterious they'll have their way with us," I say.

"Imagine how mystifying eclipses must have been to the Arawaks. They probably terrified people before they knew what caused them," Simon says. "Naming things is the true gift of science."

I shake my head. "I'm not so sure. It must have been awesome to be in the world when everything was magical. Now, we have to hold onto whatever magic we can find; reinvent ways of celebrating nature, ways we lost with modern times. When everything finally has a scientific name we'll have lost the mystery."

"Oh, you think words are reductionist by nature then?"

I don't think he's being condescending. "Reductionist? Yes, I guess so. I think there are too many words, too many explanations. A shell is a treasure to a kid until it becomes just another mollusk. A pebble is a precious stone until it's reduced to *gravel.*"

We walk along the pier toward the boats, their rusty hulls and stench create the sea zone that identifies Granite Shores. Prowling wharf cats scramble to new hiding places. How can cats get that ugly when they start off like blue-eyed puffs of cotton?

He puts his arm around me. "I like to think of myself as a man of science. It's science that keeps people from helplessness; from dying unnecessary miserable deaths or being conquered by destructive forces that could take the pleasure of a night like this away." He hugs me a little.

"Yes, and science is also responsible for creating the weapons that could end moments like this for all time."

"Ah, but you are seeing only the dark side of it," he says, easily. His fingers play notes on my arm.

It's only because I'm enjoying the discussion that I taunt him with what I consider to be true. "Science has a superiority complex. It insists it's right until it proves itself wrong."

"Ah. That's the beauty of it, my dear!" His index finger makes circles in the air. "We are always on the lookout for improvement."

"But, don't you see? Science suffers from righteousness? Believe this, oh no, now believe that. Scientists expect the whole world to shift the truth, time after time."

"And what would you prefer? A world of magic? Is that what you find satisfying? Look how magical thinking gets twisted in places like Haiti where hexes are used to terrify people into submission, or in the punishments meted out to men like Galileo who contradicted church canons. Look what superstition did to the so-called witches of Europe, killing, hundreds of thousands of them."

"But you're talking religion and politics. The occult is outside of either politics or religion. It's more continuous, like the universe itself, with rhythms and moods. It's sourced in nature and so it shatters less easily than theories do. Its roots forever attached to the flower."

He lets my words go. His arm has now comfortably looped itself through my arm, while both his hands dig in his jacket pockets. I hope he realizes I am liking him and my arguing with him is really about that. About how safe he feels. How much I respect his mind. I would never talk to Tiny or Frankie this way. It couldn't happen.

"You a witch?" he asks, right out of the ether!

"Yes," I admit, holding my breath for his response.

"I thought so," he laughs. "You're doing some bedazzling right now."

I look into his eyes and cross mine. "Razzle, dazzle, frazzle, bedazzle!" I tease.

He squeezes my arm and points to the sky. "Hey, you've returned the moon to us. You must be a good witch. I think I'd like to see you again. Give you the opportunity to put your powers to work."

"Maybe. Maybe, I'll see you again. Depends on who you are."

"I'm a warlock," does that help?

"You're joking. I want to know something about you, that's all."

"I'd like to be a person whose life starts here."

"Does that mean you're someone with a past you're ashamed of?"

"It's a past I'd rather not share right now."

"Sounds dark."

"I think the better way to describe it is, it's the past. I'd like to leave it there. Lay it to rest. I'm moving forward, onward and outward from what was."

"Are you married?"

"Used to be."

"Children?"

"One."

So, here's the rub, I guess. There's much more to know.

"Boy or girl?"

"A son, five. He lives in Tuscany with his mother. You know, I don't want to spoil a good evening. Could we hold this interview somewhere down the road after many other evenings? Slowly, with a reference point in the present."

"I have a past, too."

"I would hope so," he smiles.

"Believe me, mine isn't perfect either. I just need to know more about you before I see you again. I don't want to waste my time in situations designed to hurt someone, particularly, me."

There. I put it on the line. We're not going to pretend our relationship is about good works in Central America.

"Okay, then," he says. "Let's turn the tables. Married?"

"No and never."

"In love or committed?"

"No."

"Never?"

"Twice."

"Kids?"

"Both of them."

His beautiful teeth shine as he laughs. I'm aware that he wants to be a good guy. We turn from the docks and meander home, up past St. Peter's Hall and the Burnham Tavern. There's music pouring out of the American Legion Hall across the street. Those people sure do party.

"I love the architecture and the little towers on the houses," he says, looking up at the widow walks where women waited and wept for husbands whose ships didn't return.

"It's almost mythic, the houses the stories and the pain. We've lost over ten thousand fishermen in this town and every year new names are added to the list. My own father is one of them."

"You from a fishing family?" he asks.

"I am a fishing family!"

"You mean, you fish?"

"I *think*, too. I have my own lobster boat."

"I'm impressed. It's a pretty hard life, a solitary life for a woman."

"Not when you've been raised on the sea, when the sea is your home. I was nursed and educated by her. It's hard to think of another way to be. That's not to say I'm not paying close attention to what's being put in my path."

"Does that include a guy with a kid and a past?"

"It doesn't exclude him."

"Have we earned a kiss for making magic tonight?" he says, and I see his lips coming toward mine.

I'm ready and not disappointed.

It's a gray Sunday morning and I stretch into the memories of that very appropriate, very warm kiss from Simon Delacroix. His name pleases me. I wonder if he's made it up. Serena Delacroix. Maybe there's a future here. He seems to want one, but I'll tred lightly. I won't rush into anything this time. It's a fatal flaw I intend to fix. My imagination trapped me in nets of my own making.

But what about the coincidence of Gwen and Simon meeting? Why did that have to happen? She must think I'm interested in her work now...Simon saw to that. He couldn't know how much he was trespassing on my ground despite my trying to tell him. I'm sure his enthusiasm sent out the wrong message. I'm not going to get involved with Central America. I'm only interested in the people who are interested in the place: The Nials. The Tims. The Gwens. And now the Simons.

She, obviously, wants me to go to her talk later this afternoon. Our relationship continues to be beyond my understanding. I'm never going to tell her about my affair with Nial. Never. What good could it possibly do?

It's less than a year since I forced myself on her, and here she is, acting like it's so important, almost an obligation for me to hear her speak. I'm kind of flattered and caught in the trap of two wrongs or two rights, depending on which way I turn. But, now, she wishes I would show up at the talk and it's what Simon wants me to do, too. If I don't go, both of them will be hurt.

I consider faking a headache, a twisted ankle, a sore throat, or worse, but decide to row with the tide, swim with the river, sail with the wind and ride the horse in the direction it's going.

Bill and I sit in front of the little white clapboard church. I keep his motor running as I look for one more sign that this is really what I should do. Tacked to the side door are the words, INSIDE NICARAGUA - TONIGHT. I imagine Gwen's name is the smaller print beneath.

Light rushes into the street as the door swings open. Simon looks out and I see his face brighten when he sees me idling there. "Park in front of the library," he calls.

I do as I'm told and then make my way back up the short hill to the church. Simon leans out the door and I see his arm stretched toward me like a great hook. I am not even inside before he thrusts a bunch of flyers into my hands and tells me to *man the door.*

The early birds noisily arrange folding chairs in a circle and decorate a long table at the end of the room. I see Gwen's touch in the white cloth, the flowers and sparkling jugs of juice and water. Dainty flowered napkins are folded and placed in circles around platters of store bought cookies.

You wouldn't know it was a church. Statues and crosses are missing. There's no altar or pulpit in sight. Instead of Jesus and the saints, corkboard covers the walls. On the boards are lists and notices, pictures of the church members and their new babies. Under block letters that spell KUDOS are newspaper photos of Green Belt People protesting, a peace and justice parade on Martin Luther King Day, and the messy faces of children at an Agape Feast. On the big corkboard next to the door, is an advertisement for a Wiccan drumming session at Halibut Point.

At least twenty-five people have shown up by the time Simon launches into the meeting.

Joe Greensleeves marches in last and takes a seat right across from Simon. It's my first clue the meeting may have some controversy. Joe is the ultra-conservative voice of the Gazette. Simon begins to talk and Joe interrupts him right off. Pop used to hate this guy. I think I could, too.

"Do you realize," he asks Simon, "that Russia poured at least five hundred million dollars into Nicaragua, last year alone? Have you forgotten or are you uninformed about what happened in Cuba?"

People shift in their chairs. They turn to look at Joe like he's a nut case. But, it makes little difference to him.

Now he's pointing at Simon, his nails are bitten, and his finger shakes in a kind of rage. "Have you forgotten that as soon as the commies had an ally in the west, they built missiles to blow us to smithereens?"

Simon leans back in his chair, relaxed, hands behind his head, one leg over another, and I see how his eyes move warmly around the circle. "Well. It looks like we have a dubious guest here tonight. And your name, Sir?"

"Greensleeves."

"We're not talking about Cuba or Russia or missiles, here this afternoon, Mr. Greensleeves; we're here to talk about a brave young nation."

"We'd better talk about missiles," Joe sneers.

Simon lets the antagonism roll right over him. He says, "We're the ones with the missiles. We have missiles capable of reaching around the world. One of our warships could eliminate fifty-five million people. American spy planes fly over every country in the world. We've got an arsenal capable of destroying the world ten times over. We have nothing to be afraid of except some crazy religious despot who's bent on terror. We certainly don't have to fear a bunch of peasants emerging from the stone age, trying to learn the meaning of freedom."

"Freedom?" Joe shouts. "You damn pinkos better wake up! You're kidding yourselves. The commies are lining up on our borders and you're bent on helping them. You don't get it."

"I'm afraid sir, you're right about one thing. I don't get it. Are you talking about our borders with Mexico and Canada? I haven't noticed tanks on either side. Why don't we quit the rhetoric and move this evening on."

Joe's been dismissed but I don't think it will last long.

Simon turns his attention to the group. "We're here to talk about Nicaragua. It is a country with few resources and many problems. But, the Nicaraguans aren't beaten. They're full of hope. If there are any more fears about these people's intentions, let's talk about them. Get them out of your system, justifiable or not. That way we can open our defended hearts, and go beyond our paranoia about creeping communism. The cold war is over folks."

The people laugh and nod.

Simon must be deliberately igniting Joe's temper. The man is almost erupting. His face is flushed, he's snorting, and he looks helplessly foolish. If anyone is here to choose sides I can't imagine they would align themselves with Joe Greensleeves.

Joe stands up and shouts, "You're going to learn the hard way, you and all the rest of your lefty friends," and leaves.

"Amen. Thanks for sharing!" Simon calls to his heckler's back. Everyone applauds and I see Gwen come out of the kitchen, her hands clapping, softly, as she moves into the circle taking a seat across from mine.

Simon begins his introduction. As he does so, Gwen lowers her eyes and looks at her hands. When she lifts her head, she smiles at me and then around the room. I see a new kind of confidence. I wonder if the others notice how aristocratic she is, with her high thin eyebrows and small straight nose. Her nostrils flare a little as she talks as if to compensate for breaths she forgets to take. Her chin is so high she has to look down. It's not an act, it's who she is. I like her new hair, short and casual. Her formality and elegance are such a contradiction to the poverty she's trying to describe, I'm almost embarrassed for her. But, she engages the whole room with her obvious enthusiasm for her message.

Something important has happened to Gwen Townsend. She's clear and forceful telling us about it. She wants us to learn what she's learned. She talks about the scarcity of goods and the richness of spirit in Nicaragua and no one can doubt her sincerity. She says the people's needs are urgent.

"They need aspirins, towels, soap and things as simple as forks and spoons and pencils."

A person can't help but want to do something.

I am interested in her description of the school where she and a friend named Penny taught. She says shoeless children line up early in the morning waiting for a chance to learn how to read and do numbers. She says they stood in reverence when she showed them what their names looked like in script and brought their madres to see. Finally she gets to Nial and describes what he would have wanted to see take place there.

It is my first chance to hear her talk about Nial. To learn answers to questions I dared not ask. I breathe slowly, deliberately and try not to move.

"My husband had a dream that started when he was a very young man." There's love and light enough in her eyes to fill the whole room. "This dream propelled him to work with the Peace Corps during his college years, and most recently to work with the revitalization of the farms of Nicaragua. He was so hoping to help the people help themselves by providing them with a ready market for their cash crops. On his last trip he was on his way to celebrate the harvest of that crop. He was terribly excited to be part of the new Nicaragua; to participate in its free enterprise."

I realize for the first time, that Nial didn't fly away because of that awful fight we had. It didn't have anything to do with me. It was a business trip, with flight plans that were made days before he took off. She explains how the flight plans led the Coast Guard to a spot where small pieces of the Cessna were found. She says he was taking the trip to celebrate the harvest.

Her voice trembles as she goes on. "I don't want my husband's death to be the final word. I want to see him triumph over death in the well-being of those people he loved so much.

"Nial Townsend died so others could live. He was trying to fulfill a mission, a vision he'd had for his entire adult life. His affinity for the people of Central America, particularly Nicaragua, was constant. Nial's project was the manifestation of his unflappable belief that we are all our brother's keepers." In her closing remarks, she says, that she and her son Tim are committed to continuing the work he began.

I, meanwhile, try to push back Nial's last words to me. Try to forget that he said he didn't think he could pay for the crop. I never saw the great confidence Gwen would lead a person to think was Nial Townsend. My knees and hands feel cold. I feel tears slip from my eyelids. She thinks he's dead. This is her way of commemorating his life. I am overwhelmed by her acceptance of his death and realize there will be no ceremonies, no grave, no coffin, no reckoning. No way to affirm the awful truth of his passing. It's over. Nial and Gwen, Nial and me, Nial and all the secrets. It comes down to this—a four letter word—over. Gwen sees me crying and thinks I am a sister of compassion. She begins to cry, too, but we cry for different reasons.

"I am going back," she announces. "I am going back to see what I can do. I need your support, your prayers, and your contributions. A little, will do a lot, to help the children and their courageous mothers. I plan to find a way to begin, one child at a time, to make their world safer and healthier. Will you help?"

Murmurs around the room are followed by a round of applause and Simon announces that if anyone wants to be involved at any level, the sign-up list will be in my hands. I look down at the clipboard on my lap and see it as an anchor holding me in place. I can't run from the room and disappear into the night.

Gwen, Simon and I stay until the very last person leaves. I've collected eleven signatures from people willing to get involved. Gwen is glowing like an altar candle. I've never seen her like this, but if I could, I would do whatever it takes to keep the flame from going out.

Simon asks if he can take me home. I remind him that he brought Gwen and he says, yes, but wouldn't I like a ride, too?

"I need to be alone, Simon. Bill's in front of the library and he'll be hurt if I leave him there all night. Some other time. Okay? Thanks for the offer, though," I say and turn to leave, letting them rehash the success of the evening together.

"Hey, wait a minute, there," Simon says. "I'm putting this list in your hands so you can form that little group you said you couldn't pull together. Your witchcraft could create miracles.

Call me, my number is on the bottom of the sheet."

What can I do to convince this man I do not organize groups? How little he knows. I never joined a church, a club or a union. I know less about groups than anyone I've ever met. He just can't be more wrong about me. I'm a lonely.

It's the purple hour and my footsteps are hollow as I walk down the quiet Sunday street. I walk right by Bill. Main Street is very different in the absence of the refrigerated trucks hauling fish from the fisheries and the noisy traffic of daily life. One glowing window showcases the predictable line of sobering fisherman waiting for coffee in the Donut Shop. In the glare of the street lamp two teenage girls smoke their cigarettes looking furtively up and down the street for boyfriends or parents.

I take a detour, slip down a few stairs past the bank's parking lot, through the Building Center to the Harbor Link. The boats rest on their great sawhorses waiting for summer.

What am I feeling? Grief, for losing a person I never quite found? Sad? Yes. Sad. Sadder than sad.

The ocean, Nial's grave, laps up against the wharves. A shiny green dory taps its side against an abandoned dinghy. Otherwise, it's so quiet here even the gulls are on hold. Across the harbor the chair factory leans in on itself. It will implode one of these days. Someone has to save it soon. There's no more time for nostalgia. That's the problem here. Granite Shores loves itself just the way it is. It doesn't want change. Outsiders come in and demand sewers and parking facilities, better schools and the closing of the gurry plant, and the city resists. But, it will be forced to change just like we're forced to breathe. Suck in all the air in the world, hold it for a record time, and before you know it, you'll give in. The world pushes itself in on you and breathes you whether you like it or not.

Nial is gone. His whole beautiful self is gone, and I am here. So many people gone and I am still here. Why is that? What am I meant to do? Is it time for me to become something else? Maybe, someone who used to fish.

Someone who has learned the world on her own terms and knows when its time to widen her horizons.

I'm free. But I don't feel liberated. Could it be that my chrysalis has dropped and I need to shake myself out in the sun to discover my wings?

Out of nowhere a feather floats to my feet. I pick it up and touch its perfection. Is it a sign, a pen, a plume, a brush or a heavenly gift? It's whatever I want it to be; I just have to name it. That's what Pop said again and again, "When you can name what you want, you can have it." He also said I would know when the time was right to make a choice. "Sam, you have all the gray matter it takes to be whatever you want to be. It's up to you to decide what that's going to be, no one else."

Simon said on that first date, "Let's begin here; no past, just future."

Why would I do that? I want all my life, the continuum. The present is today's gift, but why would I throw out the gifts of the past? What kind of gratitude is that?

A merganser moves silkily through the water. Her family follows in aviarchal order. I count on seeing them come and go on their migratory expeditions; watch them return to full color in the spring and don their white feathers in the fall.

I will not see Nial again, not in this life. He will never return to this place and look to the North Star or nuzzle my neck or turn my skin to mush. There are no more migrations for him. No more corners to turn. No more maybes, or ifs, or wishes. There's only never and forever. Only this great gulf between what was and what is. He is beyond the caring and the pain, beyond needing Gwen or Tim or me.

Penny Loaf Island's light goes on. It's blinking eyes send out mixed messages. Watch me. Keep away. Watch me. Keep away.

I am struck that I am sending out my own energy, receiving light and sending it back. The whole world is of two voices and I am no different. The dark and the light. The in and the out. The up and the down. The lost and the found. As I stare across the harbor, a curtain opens and I see with perfect clarity. The purples deepen. Stars shoot across the sky and the night holds me in its arms. A beam from the lighthouse shines my way, illuminating everything around me. My heart pounds in my chest, my legs weaken and I don't need to think to understand. I experience symmetry, grace and purpose. The whole universe is a dear and perfect home, incredibly close. I'm one with it all, I know everything and am everything; past, present and future.

Nineteen

Gwen

Thick heat curtails the simplest movement but I am here and in motion. I was forewarned; Bluefields in late spring is close to unbearable. I had no choice but to come back because there was rumor of a stranger inhabiting one of the out islands. Although the source of the rumor is three times removed from Roger Sheffield, he carried it to me on the slim chance that it could be true. I couldn't ignore such a lead. Especially since Roger had promised to facilitate the search and went so far as to find someone to help us, someone who knows the islands. Roger says the man is a native with firsthand knowledge of the reefs and a familiarity with the indigenous people.

Strangely, I feel more confident this time around, not so much in regard to actually finding Nial, but of being able to negotiate Bluefields. I flew into the tiny airfield rather than take the long excursion down river. It was easy to find my way to the same horrid hotel where Tim and I were so sick, and, surprisingly, it didn't seem quite as dreadful without the cholera. Knowing the landscape makes it easier, too. I have no intent of getting sick again. I won't eat anything that isn't packaged or thoroughly cooked. I definitely won't drink the water.

Tim has promised to come immediately if I find significant evidence. I can't expect him to follow up on every lead. So often the leads have been vague, based on scraps of information. I have only received two reports that sounded anything like our descriptions of Nial. One turned out to be a French kayaker and the other a strange blend of buccaneer and booze hound. Roger pointed out that although the two were definitely not my husband, they were proof positive that people here are responding to our ads. I'm grateful to Tim and Roger for following through with the preliminary investigations while I was in Massachusetts. Now, without the desperation and fear I felt on my first trip, I think it's fair to say my expectations are more realistic.

It has been a convoluted journey to return to this place. I'm seeing how each step of the way led to the next, including the talk I gave at the church which heightened my intentions.

Roger lifts my spirits the minute he comes into view. He carries a bunch of bananas in his arms that might as well be roses. His smile is easy. It says he likes me. I like him, too. There's a dressy quality in the flowered silk shirt he's wearing; he might as well be going to a wedding. But, I think it's sweet. I'd like to think he dressed up for me.

We go to the docks to meet our guide. Hand-tooled pangas filled with fruit for the south, smash into each other as they deliver their cargo. Vendors add to the hustle and bustle at the docks. We intend to take a motorboat to an out island. Kukuloe Cayo lies about ninety kilometers northeast of Monkey Point. (Such peculiar names!) The island is protected from intruders by sharp coral reefs and an aggressive display of defense when strangers approach. Only a handful of native families live on Kukuloe and off-islanders respect their isolation. Our visit is based on the unlikely story that a white man now lives among the people. No one knows any more than this, and Roger admits it's hard to believe the tribe would permit an outsider on its sacred ground.

I am immeasurably grateful for Roger's company as our boatman and guide seems either too unimpressed or too afraid of me to speak. He is a short, square man whose genes obviously make him more native than Spanish. I learn he is a Mayangna, referred to as Sumo, by locals. Roger says he can speak English but I doubt it. I can't see his eyes because they're narrowed into slits from squinting at the sun. He wears a headband that holds down his straight black hair which ends up in jagged points just above his shoulders. His shorts are the color of the sea and his hands on the wheel are reddish brown. Like a stout barrel, his neck connects his large head with a hard square chest.; his unsmiling mouth forms a straight hard line on his face, perpendicular to an imperious hooked nose. Wooden and stolid, like a rough hewn block of oak, he chooses to stand in his boat rather than sit.

An old man carrying baskets approaches.

"We need somebahdy give we a hand, go to Monkey Point," he says.

"No got boat big nuff to take de tings dere," our boatman answers." "No go to Monkey Point."

The man turns and as I watch the baskets bob along in the opposite direction, I realize our boatman talks. But not much. We don't need conversation, however; we simply need this man to take us where we need to go. I listen while Roger explains our mission. Using words that are simple and clear I can only assume they are understood; Nimo doesn't choose to respond with a grunt or a nod or any recognition at all.

Our boat is made of hand-tooled light wood. It's watertight and comfortable in the water, although I am not. The seats are hard. We have no cushions to protect our backsides or shields to stop the spray. But we know this motor of his is the dream of many men in Bluefields and reason enough to make a simple craft a coveted item.

After skimming across the water for more than two hours, we reach Kuku, the nickname of Kukuloe Cayo. As we quiet the boat's motors, I look at the stretch of beach which must be a mile long and realize how unruffled it is. We are locked out of its shoals because of the coral, but we parallel the edge, watching all the time for a break in the reef. The aqua waters are topaz clear, clear enough to see its treasures—fish meant for coloring books, sands bearing pink pearls and shells too rare to be named. I look down into a kingdom where grasses flow like ribbons and the sun plays on the bottoms. The shapes and pathways below are no less mysterious than clouds.

We putta-put along about one hundred and fifty yards from the shore. A covey of children run out from behind a leafy glade. They shout excitedly at us. I can make out their little hands waving.

"The children seem friendly enough," I say to Roger.

"Ah, what you don't know is they're screaming, 'Off with their heads. Off with their heads!'"

I half doubt him, but don't need to say what the other half believes.

From the bushes some men emerge followed by a young woman with a small baby. The men yell something and our boatman grunts.

"What are they saying?" Roger asks the boatman.

"Dey say, dey no like. Go way."

I am listening so intently, I don't notice that one of the men, the tallest man, has shot an arrow at the boat. It splashes in the water about ten yards from me.

"Take us to the other side of the island," Roger orders.

"How about home?" I suggest.

"No can go to otha side."

Now the boatman gives the orders. "Sit." he directs Roger. "You bote sit," he commands.

I turn my head away as he commences to remove his pants and sandals and dives into the water. When he emerges, it is with the arrow in his teeth. We follow his strokes as he swims, stark naked, toward the group of islanders. "Watch out!" I scream, when the tall man takes aim again.

Fortunately, one of the islanders places a hand on the bowman's elbow and I see his arm relax. All stand still while the boatman emerges and plants his feet on Kuku sand.

When the older natives see the boatman's face, they move toward him. I can interpret motions, recognize shapes and sizes, but can't hear conversation from this distance. I realize they have communicated in some common tongue because there's an eruption of voices and gestures when a disagreement of some kind ensues, causing fingers to point in many directions. Then, just as quickly as it began, the argument ends. The island men close rank and stand as one, a buttress to their island, their children disappear behind them.

The tall man removes himself from the group and accompanies his woman and infant toward a stand of trees. He is the only one who bears a resemblance to a white man in this crowd. The other men are squarish and short legged. But that is all that would make the taller man suspect. He is much older than Nial, with wild white hair and very dark skin. He has a peculiar labored gait and, what's more, it's obvious he is connected to the young woman and the baby. I watch as she passes him the child and he lifts it like a trophy to the sky. The differences between cultures is not that great. Parents love their children, want to protect them no matter where they are on earth. It is all the same, only the context changes. I see the girl's arms reach for her baby and pull it toward her, adoringly, as she reclaims her role. The man and woman face one another and he leans closer to speak. It cannot be my husband she sees. I would know him if I saw him. Even from a distance.

Our boatman reenters the calm sea, dives deep and surfaces near the shoal. His lungs must hold twice the air as mine. Roger leans over to help him into the vessel. "Hell, man! You've got nerves of bloody steel. What happened out there?"

"Mans tink you dangerous. Dey no want you neah dah islandt."

"Makes perfect sense to me! What do you think Mrs. Townsend?"

"Did you ask about my husband? Ask if they have seen him or heard about him?" I ask.

The boatman does not look at me, only at Roger. "Dey all point in ehbrey which way; dah sky, dah sea, dah nort, dah sout."

"Did you mention the plane?" I want to know.

"Dey say planes dey go up, dey go down, ebrey way."

"And?" Roger asks.

"Dey know no white mahn!"

All the way back, I try to recall that tall man in my mind's eye. I start to believe he could have been Nial. Could have been, if he were white and larger, younger, blonder and moved differently. I admit my thoughts to Roger. "I could hardly see him, it is probably wishful thinking," I say.

"Could be. Could be it *is* your old man. Could be he's gone native, chosen the primitive life. It wouldn't be the first or last time such a thing happened around here," he says.

"That would be preposterous. I can't believe a man would come on a mission to save a company, help rebuild a country and wind up a...a...native...a fugitive. My husband is a rather remarkable person, you know. He's always been responsible; proud of his work."

"I'm sure he was. That's not to say a man can't change. Can't wish for something else. There's this guy thing, a guy thing that wants to be basic. That's why we go hunting and climb dangerous mountains. Why we head for the wilderness, take risks we shouldn't. I'm almost there myself. I see people playing at it all the time around here. I've had to save their asses more times than I'd like to remember. Not too long ago, a bunch of chaps dressed like pirates came along the coast in their rich daddy's sloop— probably on college break. Bloody fools! I imagine they were having a hell of a good time until they hit a reef and, down they went, like bricks, to the bottom. Only three of the seven were saved. The other four gave the sharks a feast."

Roger need not tell me stories of what happens to men lost at sea. I ask him to spare me the details in the future.

Our trip back to Bluefields seems shorter that the one that took us away. When I reach my hotel, I collapse on the bed and sleep soundly until I'm awakened by a dream I can remember only vaguely. A baby screams in its mother's arms. It has a man's face—not a face I know. It's a ghoulish, skeletal, unidentifiable face of pain. I wrestle with conscious and semi-conscious thoughts throughout the night. People similar to those on the island appear and reappear. I try to speak to them, but they can't hear me screaming.

By the time morning comes I am convinced I have to go back to Kuku. I cannot let my questions go unanswered.

It is with a clear head that I meet Roger down at the docks. The Stalwart Paulina is tied up. Her bulky self knocks like a clumsy wooden shoe against the bumper tires strung along the concrete pier. She's strange here, obviously meant for riverways where she's protected from the ocean's whims.

Roger leans over the bow. "Howdy, Mate. What brings you out so early on such a miserable morning?"

"I couldn't sleep last night for wondering who that tall man might be. Why he looks so different from the others. I have to go back and find out."

"I think that's doable if we can get our lad to join us."

"You are referring to the merry boatman, I presume?"

"None other."

"But Roger, I must call my son. He should be a part of this expedition. At least, I have a feeling he would want to be. And you have already done so much. More than I could have dared to hope for. I would hate to put you at risk again."

"Mrs. Townsend, that's my middle name. If risk were an issue, I'd be in England."

I think, *except that England is not your home and you would probably feel a greater risk there.* He is being gallant though, I must say.

"I appreciate your unselfishness. I really do. I want to pay you, give you something extra—you've been so helpful. Is there anything you need from the States?"

"Indeed," he says. "If you mean it and are willing, I'd like you to persuade your rich American friends to support the Mission de Paulina. Have you heard of it?"

Surprises never cease. Would I have dreamed of such a response?

"I haven't, but I don't know why I haven't. Father Joe should have mentioned it; knowing I was headed this way. Knowing, Tim and I could have contributed something."

"He may not have heard about it. We're in a country where the right hand knows little about the left. The mission is a home for homeless boys. We need just about anything you can think of— money wouldn't hurt either. But, it's *things* we need. And people. Have a friend who's a nurse, perhaps? Someone who'd be willing to pay us a visit and stay a lifetime? We are looking for the West's answer to Sister Teresa. We could use an optometrist, too and some specs."

This passionate appeal for a boys home throws me. Here I am, facing my husband's possible survival, wondering if Nial is indeed the man I saw; living a mere two and a half hours from where we stand, and he is talking about a home for lost boys. I'm so taken aback, I'm not sure what to say next. Not wanting to dismiss his request, I promise that we will talk more about the mission when I get back from Kuku.

"Thanks, Mother You don't meet too many ladies from the States here, you know. Not too many gentlemen, either." He looks around as if he should go somewhere but he's stuck on his own boat.

I forgive him for calling me mother and try to say the right thing. "I am really curious about the mission. I didn't mean to be short. Perhaps I can visit the place someday? Perhaps with a friend? My friend Penny is intrigued by this part of the country, this forbidden territory. And...we both have contacts in the States for eyeglasses."

He throws back his head and laughs out loud. "You're good for this bloke, Mother. I should have predicted you'd respond just as you did. But, let's get to the business at hand. What you need to do right now is to get out to that island and put on your own specs to see what's there."

"Good point. I must tell Tim to bring his field glasses," I say, my hand fingering the crystal again.

"I see you remembered your crystal."

"I wear it all the time."

"Let's go find our Sumo swimmer. You can't expect Tim to handle these waters alone. The lad's a fine specimen of manhood, but he doesn't know the hazards. By the way, you might find it amusing to hear our boatman's name is Geronimo."

"As in Geronimo of the Alamo?"

"As in Suarez."

"Geronimo Suarez?"

"That's the one."

We walk together along the edge of the wharves, past the loaded pangas and the shrimpers, the lobster boats and a few excursion crafts. The air has the texture of foam caught on sand. We walk in slow motion. The bright bold shapes of trawlers and barges are the only relief in the haze. It is wetter than rain.

I worry our boatman won't be at the dock when, there he stands, right in front of us like an apparition.

"Geronimo!" Roger shouts.

"Name, Nimo. You wahn de boat?" he asks.

I realize I have heard that name before. Nimo, Nimo Suarez.

"We need your boat for a return to Kuku. Tomorrow morning. Good?"

"No. No good. The Rama dey no like you. Rama people, dey no like nobahdy. Dey been heah one hundred, hundred yeahs. Dis is dare landt."

I see the men hauling crates from the Isabel, a Portugese lobster boat. It could be the harbor in Granite Shores but for the heat and a few other minor details.

I must make this man listen to me.

"Geronimo, Nimo, I think one of those people on Kuku is not Rama. I think he may be my husband."

177

"No go to islandt," he announces, his lower lip fixed on his jaw, his arms crossed against his chest like a Sioux instead of a Sumo.

Roger pulls out his money clip. "We'll pay," he says.

I see Nimo's eyes travel to the money and almost hear the wheels in his head going into reverse. Seconds pass and we have our captain.

Then I call Tim.

"Of course," he says. "I'll come. But could you wait a few more days?"

I withhold my initial thought. Instead I ask him, "What does Nimo Suarez mean to you?"

"Sounds familiar. Wasn't that the name we were supposed to remember if we had trouble?"

I touch my crystal.

"I think I should go right now, right away."

Tim insists that a day or two won't matter and says he can't just hop a plane. I will have to wait a few days, that's all. He's in the middle of exporting the harvest and has too much to oversee. Two days and he'd be free. "Two days, Mom? You can wait two days!"

I tell him that I will call him again and not to worry. Roger Sheffield has offered to go with me. I don't point out that he, Nial's own son, is the one person in the world who might be able to see what I saw, only better.

Roger, Nimo and I decide that we need not wait the two days. We pack some water and staples and leave within an hour of the call to Tim. It is a relief to leave the stench of fish and oil hovering over Bluefields Harbor. But it is not pleasant air we find out on the brackish blue-green sea. It seems to become heavier, more oppressive.

During the two hours it takes us to cross the waters to the chain of islands in the southeast, Roger and I have lots of time to talk. He tells me about the children who live at the mission. These are the children lost in the revolution, orphaned, hidden, wounded and abandoned. Some severed from their communities, others from their limbs. Roger's second wife, a missionary from Germany, made this home her life's work. She died of breast cancer four years ago. Six converted Christian women carry on. Trained by Paulina, they remain dedicated to her dream.

"And you carry it on, also?" I ask.

"I do what I can."

"Did you live there with her?

"I did, at first. After the building was complete and the rooms full to overflowing, I became superfluous. Her greatest love was the cause. I was lost somewhere in the effort. If I showed up at all it was on the bottom rung of her priorities.

"And you left?"

"Not entirely. But, yes, I left. My religion is the river and the life around it. Paulina and I didn't agree on our priorities but we did support each other's work. She knew that man-made religion had crowded me from the day I was born. Too many words, too many answers. I believe in forces beyond mortal imaginings—and that's about it.

"I don't know what I'll do if Nial is out there on that island."

"This is a good time to think about it. You may be in for a disappointment one way or another."

"I was thinking that."

Kukuloe Cay emerges on the horizon like a gray humpback. The boatman heads east of her this time, but as we look to the shore, we find access to land as difficult as it was yesterday. Rugged rocks plunge into the sea from this end and constant waves smash against them. I wonder what it's like to the far south. Evidently Geronimo wonders, too.

Our first challenge, however, lies in getting out of the churning current and into negotiable waters. We head due East and are still challenged a mile beyond the island. The waters seem to be rising and angry. Whitecaps begin to hit us with unusual force. My arms and back are reacting to the impact of one wave and then another. I must not have been thinking straight to have ventured out here, placing these two men in danger and myself in a quandary.

A strange green glow tints the clouds and the sky has turned too dark for this time of day. Part of me is grateful for the cloud cover, the other concerned. We turn back toward the island again. This time the force of nature carries us in. Our Captain Nimo deftly controls the wheel and I silently thank God for that.

Out of nowhere a gust of wind rips the sun visor from my head and climbs under my blouse pulling it up to my shoulders. Roger stumbles and grabs a hold of the rail. "Christ! That wind had to be eighty miles an hour."

Then, like glass on granite, lightning fractures the sky and seems to open a million spigots. One bolt follows another, each followed by the menacing roar of thunder. Silver pellets pulverize the water around us.

"Now what?" I scream over the motor and the angry sky.

"Prayer is good!" Roger calls.

I think of, but am unable to clutch my crystal as a rogue wave lifts the boat up and onto a reef. We hit hard and stay only a fraction of a minute, the bow of our boat pointing to the sky until another wave comes and takes us from behind, hurling us toward the coast.

We can't see. We can't manipulate the craft. We just hang on as best we can until we hit something.

"It's a sandbar! Get out and hold on to the boat!" Roger yells.

"Storms no come dis time o' yeah," Nimo announces.

Neither Roger nor I point out this fact appears to be moot.

As we prepare to climb out of the boat, another wave comes. Despite our proximity to the craft we are catapulted into the lagoon, pushed between the sandbar and the land. This water is calm compared to the tide we came in on. I float, realizing without the force of the entire Atlantic at our backs, we may survive after all. We begin the long reach to shore.

By the time we crawl upon the white sands of the beach, I'm exhausted. Roger and Nimo. who have pulled the boat behind them, put down anchor within wading distance and climb slowly out of the water. Our boatman does not collapse, but he does allow himself to sit and Roger makes no pretense as he lies, spread eagle, sweating through his water clogged clothes. I know I must retreat and cover myself. The sun is starting to climb out of the leaden sky. In fact, it is now in full blast, and my wet salty skin will fry. I move to shade, sitting beneath the wide green fronds that trim the beach.

A bird with a green crewcut and golden green and scarlet plumage ending in an extraordinary sweep of tail, maybe three times its body, sits on a branch of the tree beside me. It is a spectacular creature, unlike anything I've seen before, save a peacock, perhaps. His yellow eyes study me. I return the gaze, making sure I don't move so much as my big toe.

Nimo sees the bird, too. He whistles and the bird takes flight. When it lands on his shoulder, he talks softly to its cocked head.

Slowly, I feel my strength returning. I can hear the sky shuddering in the distance—only an echo now. The storm, a tease compared to the notorious storms of summer, has left as quickly as it came.

Roger gets up and goes back in the water. At first, I think he's planning to start up the boat but then I realize he's trying to retrieve the oil can. It is bobbing like a red shark fin on the surface. Sharks! I didn't have time to be afraid during our calamity, now my breath catches. I don't want him to go any farther. "Come back!" I call. "Please, come back. We'll get it later."

He is beyond hearing.

From someplace above my head, I hear the excited voices of children speaking in a clicked tongue that bears no resemblance to English. They scramble down the cliff, deft as mountain goats. Some throw coconut grenades that land beyond my little shelter.

"Quetzal!" they cry when they see the bird, and stop dead in their tracks.

I stay in the shade. Nimo signals silence to them. He speaks to them in his wooden, unsmiling way and then, to my surprise, each child bows a little and backs away. Nimo's headband was lost to the sea so his hair is sticking out all over his head like a black crown of feathers. I think of Quetzalcoatl, that ancient bird god, and wonder if the children think he has returned one more time. This time as Geronimo Suarez.

Roger emerges from the water again, sporting the oil can.

I am startled to hear movement behind me and turn to see the tall man standing there, a man I almost know. He is as brown as any native, angular to a fault. His collarbones almost protrude through his skin, his scarred legs, hairless, and the hair on his face thick, only a shade darker than the hair on his head. When I find his eyes and he looks at me, I know he's mine.

His knuckles grow white around the bow in his right hand. I look for the wedding band on the left.

The trees above us make a music too foreign for me to enjoy. The tumultuous wind sucks the air around us into itself and leaves my chest empty, unable to so much as gasp.

"I don't know you," he says in English, his eyebrows doing what they have always done when they're angry.

I must decide how to approach this new Nial. I look at the others who seem light years away. Is he mad? Is he afraid?

"Nial?"

"You must go away. You're trespassing."

Perhaps he thinks we're in danger.

"Don't worry, everything will be all right. We're safe," I promise.

"*I* am safe. *You* are not. You are not welcome here. You must leave."

I see how his skin must have blistered and healed. How his eyes do not want to look into mine. I lower my gaze, afraid of what's missing. His feet are bare, leathery and bruised. White scar tissue stands out against the brown freckles of his skin. He's been burned, my poor darling. Burned and saved somehow.

"Nial. When you were missing, we never gave up. That's why I'm here. You can come home now. You have nothing to fear."

"Fear? I am not afraid. I'm not who you think I am. I belong here. This is my home."

His accent is peculiar. Has he not spoken English for the entire year? Could it be that he believes he is someone else inside his head? Does he actually expect me to believe he intends to stay on this little island with fish and coconuts and a few natives to keep him company? Perhaps the shock of my presence is too much for him to process. I should sit down and remember to breathe. *Hope is the anchor of the soul.*

"Please, darling, let's sit and talk awhile."

"No. You must go."

"Nial?"

"Go. I am not Nial."

"Nial. You are Nial Townsend, my husband."

"No. Your husband is dead."

"You have a son, Tim, and me, your wife." I start using my hands as though my words aren't enough. "Tim is here, in Nicaragua. He's working with the people, continuing your work and harvesting the crops. You would be so proud, darling."

I see no expression whatsoever on his face.

"Nial, you would be so proud of him. We love you. We are all just fine, but we need you. You must come home."

"I am home. This is my home."

As his arm rises to direct my eyes to the hillside behind him, I see his wedding band is still on his finger. I hold mine up and point to it.

"Look. This ring is like yours. Our wedding bands."

I can't touch him. He's enclosed in an electric fence of his own making. I look up to the sky for an angel, perhaps, but all I see is blazing cobalt. No sky should be this blue in the face of such a storm.

"Please, darling, look at me."

"I don't know you," he insists.

I can't imagine how to penetrate the mask.

Hope is the anchor of the soul.

181

"Nial, I've been waiting so long. Come home. I love you. Tim loves you. Things will be better. Better than they ever were."

"Go away. I don't love *you*. This is my home. I *am* home."

This cruelty can't be real. I try another tack.

"You have a responsibility to come home and clean things up, Nial. Even if you don't love me, or your son, you must do what's right. Then if you wish to come back here, you certainly may."

He turns, looking at the sea. "Do what's right? I am doing what's right. I am living my own truth, not someone else's."

I wonder, now, if he's gone mad. This man with whom I've shared most of my life is foreign and hard. I look at his long boney body, smell his sweat. Did we ever sleep like spoons? Did his knee hairs ever tickle mine? I once tuned my breathing to his, my hours, my wants and dreams, I trusted his instincts as easily as my summer garden. I thought we were forever; indelibly pressed on each other's soul. Inextricably bound. What can I do to remind him, to convince him to come with us?

If I could just reach out and touch him, help him to respond, but I'm afraid of what's alien, fierce. I wonder if he is capable of understanding where he is.

Hope is the anchor of the soul.

"We're in Nicaragua, Nial. Tim is working at the farm with the farmers and the abaca is being harvested. I'm staying in Bluefields, and I've been looking for you and believing all the while that I would find you. Truly, I have."

"Go home. Your husband is dead. Leave it at that."

His jaw is set. I hear the finality of his voice. Could it be that my husband *is* lost?

I start to beg. "Nial, there was a terrible accident. You're not dead. You've been traumatized. Please, let me take you with us. If not today, it can be another day.

"Your husband is dead. There was no accident. His plane was shot down. When he woke up he was free."

So he remembers this. "You were shot down?"

"Yes."

"But why? Who shot you down?"

"I am meant to be here. It was my destiny. I was brought here by fate. These are my people, my island, my paradise. I have found what I have always been looking for, Paradise. My woman and Rama child are with me. I'm Rama now. Your husband was gone long before the crash. You must have known, Gwen."

My name. He remembers my name. "But, I didn't know."

"It doesn't matter now, Nial Townsend is dead."

I used to let him lead, thinking myself wrong to question, to think my own thoughts. What price have I paid waiting for him to work things out?

Beside us, deep in the brush, I see a woman with a baby in her arms waiting in the shadows. This must be the woman I saw from the boat. She is probably waiting for him to send me away. Maybe not. She is young and brown. Innocent. He is distant and bizarre. So strange. The poor girl. It strikes me suddenly, that what he is telling me is true. He's not himself anymore. I don't belong here. I should walk away. But what if he has amnesia or post traumatic stress or some other mental illness that can be treated? Then again, what if I persist and force him from this island? What then? Who will I ultimately find on my hands?

"I can't leave you like this, Nial. Come with me. I will get you help and we'll find a way to make things work."

He shakes his head no. Then he turns away from me and nods to the woman to come forward. She floats into the intense light that is now all around us. Her caramel skin glistens, her brown eyes look up at him as if he were a god. Their healthy round baby is tied to her belly; its little feet tucked in like a bunny's and chubby arms reaching for a plait of her long black hair—thick, straight, young hair.

The quetzal opens its wings. It rises from Nimo's shoulders and then dips in a sudden swoop over Nial's head. The ground starts to move and I reach for something to hold onto. I feel myself going down when Nial catches me. Still holding my arms he says sternly, but quietly, "Gwen try to understand. This is real. It's my choice. This woman saved my life and I'm bound to her. I want her. I am not as mad as you are thinking. Let the past be the past. It's only a dream now. My child, Kuloee is real. She's two and a half months old. Her mother is real. A good woman and my woman. You must go away and let us be. No one need ever know. You were never here. Leave things as they are. Let me go. It is for the best."

He is asking me to relinquish our life because he has buried it and made up a new one. He wants to share what's left of his time to be with this exotic girl who doesn't even speak English, who can't know anything about the world he came from.

What can I say?

I look at the young mother and try to explain. "I had a little girl once, too. We named her Sabrina. We loved her very much."

She smiles at me and looks doe-eyed to Nial for an interpretation. He gives her none.

Roger approaches. "I think, old boy, that we need to sit around a fire, pop a Pacifico and talk some of this through, What do you say?"

"I say you are trespassing on my land."

The tribesmen must have been gathering at the foot of the hill. They begin to approach. I have no idea how long they have been watching this white man and woman bringing their lives together to an end. Nial begins to back away. His last words are cold and clear. "Leave, please, leave. You cannot find what you are looking for ...there are only Rama here."

The men in the tribe absorb and cover him. I watch, helplessly, as he and his little family retreat into the same fauna from which they had emerged. What was it—minutes, hours, or twenty-six years ago?

Nimo declares, "We go now."

183

But I am immobilized. "We can't just go away and leave him like this. Can we?" I ask Roger.

"Do you really believe that we should force the miserable bloke to come with us? I don't see how, and, personally, I think we should let the ole boy be. He's had a sea change and you're not part of it. You could get the Coast Guard or the officianados in on this, but then what? You're dragging him back to whatever made him miserable in the first place."

"I take offense at that Roger."

"We go NOW," Nimo insists.

"We were never miserable. I admit it seems impossible but if I could just talk to him one more time before I go, to tell him I'll try. I'll do whatever it takes."

"WE GO NOW!"

I look up and the faces of the Rama leave little doubt that this visit is over. It's then I explode into hysterical sobs that come out of nowhere.

Over the heads of the natives, into the tangle of plant life, I hear myself screaming. "You bastard! You righteous bastard! You have always thought the world was about you! You self-centered bastard. I *will* tell them all that you're dead. As far as I'm concerned nothing could be better. I'm leaving do you hear? And you will never see me again. From now on you will be as dead as if I buried you. Do you hear me Nial? Do you?

The palms clap uproariously as I back out to the water, sobbing, screaming all the way. Roger lifts me into the boat, Nimo picks up the anchor.

As we head back to Bluefield, I am shivering despite the tropical steam laying across the water's face. Roger attempts to mollify me. He says Nimo can always let me know if there is a reason for me to return to Kukuloe. He must be reading my mind.

I was so hateful. Nial has obviously suffered a terrible trauma. He asked nothing of me but to let him go. How can I do that?

Roger asks if I want a warm arm around me.

"He's temporarily insane," I say, as I lean into his shoulder.

"He's changed, Gwen. He's one of those men I was telling you about. He can't go back in the box. He can't face the sales charts and streets with names and rules for every move he makes. It's a world of high maintenance and he's done with it. You are only part of the package he wants to throw out."

I listen to the river man and think of things I might have said. I could have left so differently. I could have told my husband I was leaving, not because love died, but because love still lives in me—in the memory of us. I should have said I'm leaving because the gift of freedom is all I have left to give.

Roger shifts in his seat. I feel his golden arm tighten around my shoulders. The hair on his forearm glitters. I inhale the familiar smell of maleness, listen to the pounding of his strong heart, and begin to allow a degree of comfort. Maybe, someday, I'll let myself go entirely in this man's arms, I think, and fall asleep.

184

Twenty
Serena

They've finally closed Jeffrey's Banks and every fisherman I know is up in arms. The Feds are being called Fascists and the president is less popular than Qadahfi. With the tight reins on the fishing industry, drugs are moving through the harbor faster than bluefish and trawlers are going down for mysterious reasons.

The fighting is loud and mean at the Fisherman's Council. It got physical when Tiny Haskell went after a *suit* the other day. It took three of his buddies to pull him off the poor guy. It makes me sick. No one wants to mention the healthy signs of sea bass and mackerel returning to the harbor. Or that the puffins are increasing along with the plover.

Last year, despite restrictions, we hauled over twenty million pounds of fish out of the sea into the Granite Shores fisheries. Multiply that times all the other ports along the Bay of Maine and it doesn't take the brightest light in the heavens to see we'll soon deplete the supply. But what fisherman can afford to give the waters a time out, time to breathe, to regenerate? They won't cooperate until the government pays them to stay home like it did the farmers in the mid-west. And while they wait for compensation, regulations without back-up is making for desperate fisherman, and it gets especially ugly where international fisherman are concerned. The locals hate the Japanese, the Russians, the Canadians, even the sport fishermen who they believe are fishing in their waters without any handicaps.

I have my own concerns. My catches are down and I take that as a sign. Not sure yet what it means, but, I think it's relevant to my future. I'm asking myself hard questions, like, is it time to quit? Time to ground myself?

Fish farming is the hottest topic on the table right now. Nevermind, that it's not even close to sensible. They've been experimenting with lobster farming for years and it's always been a disappointment. You can't deny nature its way. Of the thousands of eggs each female lays at a time, only ten survive for a reason. As Pop and Darwin said, it's the way nature protects herself —the backbone of nature's process. The meek and the weak do not inherit the earth, it's only the strongest who evolve and adapt. But what happens when the ten, who *should* make it, are disrupted? Do we bring on the death of the species instead?

St. Peter has been receiving a lot of prayers about the halibut and cod shortages. I'm more upset at how the so-called marine biologists are trying to replace them. They're scraping the edge of the banks clean for fish farming. Breeding fish in the shoals, where the shallows meet the deeps, has to put a warp in the eco-system. The whole world knows that when diversity is diminished, species are too. Emerson said it more than a hundred years ago: *Nature hates a monopoly.* It takes a lot of arrogance to disrupt systems created by an intelligence far more perfect than humans can imagine! When we homosapians get into the act, we almost always fuck it up. Weak shells, sick fish, imbalance, and then disaster.

My pots have been dropped in these waters for more than twenty years. I expect my catch's progeny to stay close to their spawning grounds. Just like seamen, no lobster leaves good clean water with great hiding places and familiar feeding grounds. So, where are my lobster?

You've got to hand it to lobster. They're a masterpiece of design; a highly evolved creature; a total sensory organ. Lobster antennae are so fine they can recognize more than the sex of their prey, they recognize their moods, too. It's capable of looking every which way at once, with its high-tech eyes. Grandma Bridget used to say she had eyes in the back of her head. Well, the lobster has 360° vision.

And it grows its own armor, protective mail as strong and indestructible as plastic. Who could conjure up an exoskeleton like the one a lobster sloughs off, once, sometimes twice a year? I've watched it happen; watched it carefully climb out of its own skin. With intrinsic agility, it extricates itself from a package that has grown too tight. Naked and vulnerable, it strengthens its new shell by ingesting the old one. If a body part falls off during molting, it generates another. Then, in a dark and private place, it waits until its transformation is complete. These waters, filled with rocky outcroppings, are ideal for that process.

I read in the paper the other day that a forty-two pounder was caught in Nova Scotia. Almost four feet long! Someone figured this monster lobster had to be over a hundred years old. In our business, we call five year olds, *mature*. But when you consider a huge specimen, one like this granddaddy, I'd say we abort their lives at a fraction of their full potential. It shouldn't bother me, not after the thousands of pounds I've delivered by now, but it does. Just as much as it bothers me to see larvae, unnaturally spawned, dumped into waters that will destroy nine hundred and ninety-nine out of every thousand of them.

There has to be another way.

Tim is out in the harbor whizzing around like a fifteen year old. He's making last rounds. Home for two weeks now, he's been tying up loose ends. Their house sold and I'm more upset about it than he is. It's as if it was *my* house, I've been so close to it and its people for most of my life. It was the house of my fondest dreams and worst nightmares. No matter how unencumbered he says it makes him feel, it's obvious he has more love for it now. He won't admit it, though. Says he wants the damn thing off their backs. Strange to hear that. Stranger to see him mowing the lawn and cutting back the fruit trees without Gwen around to whip him into shape. When I saw him taking off the storm windows and putting up screens, I knew he'd taken ownership just in time to give it up.

She's in Nicaragua again. Bought sixty hectares of land in a place where mahogany trees and old pine stumps make forests that can be cut or just used for seeds or resin or nothing at all. Tim says animals like armadillo and anteaters, jaguar and capuchin monkeys run wild all over the place. The woods smell like the juices of swamp water and the air sits on your skin, velvet as rose petals. He calls it God's country, even though his mother seems to be in charge. Only one road travels to and from its edge, connecting them with Matagalpa on the southeast and Managua far to the west. There's no blacktop, but Tim says it's the rivers and streams you can rely on in a land that empty. Two nearby towns, Alamikamba and Prinzapolka are all she has for neighbors.

I was afraid she'd lost her mind when I heard what she'd done. I mean, sixty hectares is something like six thousand acres. But Tim says no, she's found it. He's so excited about her work you'd think it was his idea. He stays at the collective farm with a bunch of displaced peasants, who earn very little. His job is to facilitate shipping the crop back to the rope company, where it's being marketed as Townsend's gift to the sea. "Eco-conscious cordage." It's one answer to the barrage of non-degradables harbors have to deal with now.

"So far, so good," he says. "The factory is up and running-- we've had great press in a couple of environmental magazines..."

He isn't the same Tim. He's changed for the better.

Funny 'cause he says I haven't. I'm his *home*, he says, the one person who he can count on. But I know the only thing that's really the same is that we were kids together. So much has happened since Camelot, I can hardly remember those perfect days of starfish watching; days when life was mostly dreams and fascination and that was all it took to be happy. A time when I was young enough to think happiness could wind up being a permanent condition.

It won't be long before I leave for Woods Hole. I'm going to spend August in a laboratory, as an apprentice with a team of marine biologists, before I enter the University of Rhode Island's program. So far, the decision has been as easy as crossing the street. When Tiny Haskell's trawler sank and he asked me if I'd consider selling the Serena Marie, I knew it was time to let her go. The thought of her sitting right in Townsend's Cove on the old wharf, where she should be, felt exactly right. She was my childhood home, and she knows her place as well as her name. Besides, it means a part of me will remain here, too.

Gwen wants me to take the break between my internship at Woods Hole and the start of school, to visit Nicaragua. She's coming home next week for the house closing. They'll be moving to a smaller house on Portugee Hill, a good half mile from the water and yet high enough to have views of the entire harbor. The house is a New England Classic, a two-story Queen Ann with a date on it, and lots of windows with little diamond-shaped panes. It has an old barn in the back that Tim is renovating into a place of his own. Should be a great place for a guy.

Simon and I still see each other. I think he's not too happy with me. He wants a soul-mate, someone to do good works at his side. But my good works aren't his. I did bring a group together with his help, and they're already raising money to make Gwen's home for girls, the Casa de las Ninas, a success. Gwen seems satisfied at any rate. She says her little girls are opening like buttercups on a spring lawn.

I think Nial's death freed her up to become this new person. Her seaside garden was pretty impressive, but forests and rivers and animals and kids really go the distance. It's hard to imagine; I suppose I will have to go to see for myself. Gwen said she and Penny have a sign on their wall, *Nicaragua ain't no place for sissies*. She and this Penny person travel all over eastern Nicaragua looking for girl babies and young women who need help. She's like a Mother Superior, hiring people, training them, coming and going as she pleases. But I don't think I get the whole picture. All I know is the last time she came here she had never looked better.

Nothing stays the same. Nial and Gwen Townsend being gone changes Townsend's Cove. Tim and I talked about that a couple of weeks ago when we met on the dock and I invited him into the shack for a cup of tea.

"What will become of Townsend Cove without the Townsends?" I asked Tim.

"They're going to change its name to Serena's Cove," he said.

"I don't think so. You know, I told your mother I lived here."

"You've never lived here. Why did you tell her that?"

"To shock her, I suppose. I figured she'd never given a damn who came and went. I guess I wanted her to notice me. Anyway, it is sort of my home."

He smiled. He understood. "Heard you and Mother have become friends," he said. "That's a surprise."

My breath stopped. Only she could have been the carrier of news like that.

"It's true." I waited for the ax to fall.

"Damn. And I thought you were all mine! I never thought you and Mother would get on. How much does she know?"

"I didn't tell her about past history, if that's what you mean. I didn't tell her you and your perverted friends did drugs and sex on our sacred ground. That you broke my heart."

"Serena, I was an asshole. What more can I say?"

What more could he say? What could I say? If he ever knew what happened between myself and his father —

"You could say, I'm sorry," I suggested.

"More than you'll ever know." He tried to take my hand but I found another place for it. I'm afraid of his touch. Why open healed wounds?

He pretended not to notice. "How did you and Mother meet?"

"I met her on the beach one night. I decided to talk to her when I realized you'd left and I saw how lonely she was. I felt guilty, somehow."

"Why guilty?"

I spoke clumsily. "Just seeing her alone day after day, knowing you were gone, your Dad missing. It was a pretty bad time for her." A bad time for me was more like it.

"I'd never have put you and mother...thought that you and Mother, well..."

"No. I didn't think so, either, but it turned out that we like each other very much. She's more than a friend to me, actually."

"What does that mean?"

What does that mean? I had to ask myself. What was it that happened this year between Gwen and me?

"I admire her too much for her to be a friend. She's good. I think she's a really good person."

"And you're not?"

"I'm no Gwen Townsend! I'll admit I didn't understand her at first, thought she was stuck-up, selfish all the rest, but getting to know her, well, she's got a lot of courage, Tim. Things scare her and she does them anyway. She's a survivor."

"She's changed. You've rubbed off on her. You know, you're a bit of a survivor yourself, Serena. Are you ever afraid?"

"Of some things, yes. Not as much afraid as unsure."

"What is it you're not sure about?" he asked, moving closer to me, his voice showing signs of the old Tim. I felt the warmth of his breath, the familiar heat of his body.

"Tomorrow. It has to be different than today. I've been thinking about what comes next, what to do with myself that means something. I'd love to do research, become a scientist. It would mean a big change, of course, but I think I can do it."

"Of course you can do it! You can do anything you set your mind to do. You topped out on the SATs. Remember?"

"That was a hundred years ago."

He threw up his hands. "Shit! You've been doing research for twenty years now. Who else knows more about lobster than you do?"

"Considering they've been my livelihood I should know a lot more."

"Remember when we were in high school? Your scores were higher than mine by a long shot. I was humiliated when I heard Whitey bragging to my father. You still have those scores. You can name your school."

"Well, I'm not going to some place where the average age is twenty. It's got to be a university. I don't know where, but I do know what I want to do."

"And that is?"

"I want to be there when the politicians decide the future of the ocean. I want to have the facts and make sure someone hears them."

"Jesus, Serena, it's just what you should be doing! It's what you love and know, and you should go for it. Find the best damn marine biology program in the country and apply. Right now, while you have the vision. They won't know what hit them."

"You think?"

"I think."

I resisted throwing my arms around his beautiful neck.

189

Simon wasn't quite as excited as Tim about my plan. He wondered how many years I was willing to put into a course of study that was overpopulated and at the mercy of public funding.

I told him I didn't care. I took out my Ouija board and asked it whether I should go to school. It said, B E F U L L.

"You see," I said, "it says *be full*. I have to go fill my mind with everything I can, and then go out and save the ocean, or at least try."

"*Be full* could mean, be full of good food. Why not become a chef?" he teased.

"I don't cook," I reminded him.

"What if the Ouija board can't spell and it meant to say, BE AWFUL."

Very funny. "Ouija boards are guides, not critics!"

"Maybe it meant be-u-tiful. And you already are. Or maybe it was trying to tell you to *be full* of baby, my baby."

I didn't know for sure if he was serious. We had just started sleeping together. Does he really want a baby? Diapers, crying, high chairs and nursery rhymes? I am mortified by my feelings.

"What are you saying?" I asked.

"Serena, if you go to school, you're married to it for four maybe five years."

"I know."

"I feel... I feel that we have work to do. We can do it together and start the world over. I'm not a kid. I'd like to have another child, maybe two."

"But, I don't want to start the world over. A new world is an empty world. I want to save what's here. I want it to survive. I want to have my say, be a woman of science who can teach others, to back up what I already know with evidence and find strategies that work. You should understand, being a man of science yourself."

"What if I tell you, what if I say that I...I think I love you?" he said, as if it hit him at that very moment.

I was hearing words it seemed I'd waited my entire life to hear. I was sure that if they were said to me by a good man, a man who would make me one of two, place me in the world of couples and family and Sunday picnics it would make me whole. To my surprise, it was not enough. Words escaped me for a minute or two.

"I'm complimented, Simon. I really am. I know you'll have a hard time understanding this, but I have to go to school."

And Grandma Bridget, if you're up there shaking your red head at me, I think you should know, I like him. I like him a lot. Maybe, someday, I could make his babies and support his work, but not now; now I'm headed somewhere else. Look, if the ocean dies so do we.

Twenty-one
Gwen

At night, I sit on the porch and watch moths the size of birds compete for airspace with fleets of sonar-driven bats. The air here is more alive at night than during the day, definitely more mysterious. Most of life in this jungle of wood and vine is nocturnal. I have become more nocturnal, too. Actually, it's the edges of day I love most. Early mornings, when misted light turns purples into blues and then illuminates the crests of trees. Evenings, when the process is reversed, and what seems too much and too hot becomes less overwhelming. I've learned the meaning of siesta and discovered that sleep in the middle of the day provides me with two days instead of one.

Yes, I have two days instead of one now, and my life is more than twofold. I am in a constant state of discovery in this chattering home for little girls. The varieties of language and dialect gradually seep in through osmosis, as does my affinity for the smell of hot rain on banana leaves, the music of tree frogs singing and occasional spottings of coatimondi and parrot and wild pigs. Nothing tastes better than an avocado still warm from the bough. I cheer for the raptors who successfully target quick-footed mice. Who would not admire the patient iguana, splayed on a sun-baked wall for hours awaiting his meal? I am in love with wild orchids, cascades of yellow trumpet vines and spreading carpets of verbena.

Hot pink bougainvillea cover the garden walls; purple clematis clamber up the trellis. Edible nasturtiums make carpets for them both. I smile at the spread of sunlit yellows and oranges at my feet. These are colors that suit me. The world is fertile no matter where I turn. It is a sensual life with my self happily part of the feast.

Serena arrives today, and I will have a chance to share our bounty with her. She and Tim are driving from Texas all the way through Mexico, Guatemala and Honduras. He wanted to have a new truck at the ranch, so they flew to San Antonio, bought a Ford pickup, and took their chances with the Central American highway system.

He's bursting with enthusiasm—more and more involved with the farm, and even more surprisingly, with the cordage business on Granite Shores. He's had two articles published, one in *Sailing Away Magazine,* the other in *Wood & Boats,* arguing the case for biodegradable line. I've learned it's best if I stay out of his way, although he says he wants me to lean on him and insists the truck will make regular deliveries to and from the casa. It makes me feel the best when he comes to me on his own and shares spontaneously.

For example, when Roger and I identified a grove of rubber trees, Tim became more excited than either of us. He began to do research about their genus and found these particular rubber trees are "exclusively" South

American; proof positive that our land was settled long ago, and not just by tribes from the north. But that wasn't all. Soon after, he invented a new product. He took the sap of the chicle trees and mixed it with the latex of the rubber trees to just to see what would happen. When it dried on the stick he'd used for mixing, he saw the mixture of saps conform to the stick's shape and adhere to the ground. He'd concocted a simple but effective type of glue--one that's soft and pliable at first, like rubber cement, and then as hard and impenetrable as plastic when it dries. My son the alchemist created a glue that we intend to translate into a saleable item. Using abaca and glue, we're making sandals to be sold for very little money. We'll send them to Managua with Tim; from there, Father Joseph will do his best to put shoes on every child who needs them.

Tim's positivism suggests there's more going on in his life than abaca. Then again, what do I know? He has never confided in me about love. I won't deny the yenta inside me hoping he and Serena have discovered each other. His ready response when I suggested he bring her here whet my curiosity. I couldn't resist and asked if anything was going on between them. He said only what I know to be true, "Serena is her own woman right now. She's all ambition and, as far as I can see, her goals don't include a relationship." I almost had to seal my lips with electric tape to keep from suggesting the two of them might have something worth exploring.

It will be such fun to show Serena what her efforts have brought about. She should be proud of the group she organized at the little church in Granite Shores. They helped outfit the casa, dress the children with appropriate clothes, bed them in good sheets, and supply them with boxes of pencils, crayons, and paper. It's impossible to buy such things at the mercado. Even shipping is unreliable; the precious packages might not have reached us if it weren't for our connections. Thank God for the river and the river man. He's our faithful conduit and advisor. A man I like to serve who serves me back.

We have a windmill and a battery-run generator for emergencies. We even have a battery charger. With limited energy resources. We use everything consciously. Sometimes we allow ourselves a movie on our VCR, but it's the radio we depend on.

The children have photographs of themselves and the Casa de las Ninas, a la Penny's Polaroid. They have written thank you notes to all the Americanos who have made their lives safer and richer. It is only right that the notes and illustrations were drawn on the first paper we received, colored with Crayolas considered nothing less than miraculous by children who had never held a crayon before. Mail travels faster by hand than with the precarious postal system, so Serena will be responsible for bringing all our thank yous back with her.

When the children first got their crayons, we tried to demonstrate the wonderful things the point of a crayon could do. We emphasized not to press too hard or the points would break. Each child received her own box.

They might just as well have held rare jewels. The colors were organized in upright order and the lid carefully closed whenever they were put away. Even the rubber bands we provided were treated like gifts.

One of our special occasions here at casa is the loss of a tooth. When a child loses a tooth, she gets a wooden Scrabble letter. If anyone loses enough teeth and forms a word with her letters, she gets a bow for her hair. Our only concern is that the children may start yanking their teeth out for the prizes because the excitement is so intense. Meanwhile, poor Penny lost a molar the other day. I will not accuse her of being overly dramatic about it, but everyone in the house knew that gray-haired Penny was losing her teeth just like a seven year old.

We had explained the wonder of losing baby teeth to make way for the grown-up teeth that follow, teeth meant to last forever. It was most disconcerting, therefore, to have Penny wailing about her missing tooth. The event elicited at least one small person's sympathy. That little girl decided to be a tooth fairy for Penny, and, somehow during the night, sneaked a gift wrapped in a nutshell bound with a rubber band and placed it under her pillow. Penny found it in the morning when she made her bed. It was a treasure trove of crayon points sacrificed from the child's crayon box. What greater love?

Knowing a new truck would be arriving soon, we created a contest to see who could guess what color it would be. Each girl chose a color and wrote the color word on a badge before we pinned it to her blouse. I couldn't choose negro, knowing Tim's predilection for all things black, so I choose azule. Blue. After all, it wouldn't look right if I won. Most of the children want it to be red. It seems to be their favorite color.

As we hear the truck climbing up the long road to the hacienda, I realize the girls are more excited to see its color that the people it carries. When the dusty machine pops into view and there's no doubt that the children have guessed right, they shout joyfully. *Rojo!*

I am sure this red truck will be the envy of every Nica and famous in all the villages through which it passes.

There are more squeals of delight and hands clapping as Tim and Serena pull up to the building. Tim cuts the motor and the two of them emerge with smiles for everyone and black plastic bags strung over their shoulders like Santa's helpers. A little girl runs up to Tim, he grabs her and swings her up on his hip. Rosita offers her tiny hand to Serena.

Rosita's mother was killed in a senseless massacre of women who had organized themselves to sew blouses for an American company. Nine women died because they were organizing, claiming their independence. Senseless murders, leaving eighteen children motherless. No one has been arrested.

I have never seen Serena look so well. She is strikingly beautiful, tall, strong and healthy in this world where beauty ends too soon and suffering takes its toll.

Tim, lean and blond, his beard gone and his hair tied back, has an air of genuine confidence, not unlike Nial's.

I will not tell him the truth about Nial. Never. I may be breaking laws and defying chance, but he doesn't need to know. If there are truly scales of justice, I see no pans move. Tim's better off loving a father who stays on a pedestal, a father that love and time make finer than reality allowed. His son works as hard as he does because he believes he is completing something for the man he could never please, winning his approval posthumously. It is a beautiful thing to see his commitment and pride; I won't take these away from him. When I say Nial's in Paradise, I do it without guilt; he named it himself. He has found his Paradise and, most peculiarly, we're all surviving quite nicely, thank you, in the place I least expected.

Our lodgings are spacious but spare. The house has a generous living room with double doors and panes of glass leading to a large screened in porch. It's on this porch that we make our shoes and gather for songs and stories. It's furnished with picnic tables and benches made of the same mahogany that creates the ceiling over our heads. The porch has become the center of most of the activities for the children and our staff. By staff, I actually mean the four teenage girls we have working here. I honestly don't know how long we can keep them. They had little choice but to join us because pregnancy or poverty or both were their only alternatives. We're teaching them to read, to care for themselves, to cook, and to understand the world around them. They in turn, teach us the names of things in their native tongues and help us with the children. They're sweet, appreciative, yet secretive girls who talk much more to each other than to Penny or me.

On my last trip, I brought back pharmaceuticals from the doctors at Granite Shores Hospital. We decided to be as prepared as possible to treat the variety of diseases we may face. So far we've been lucky; the worst problems we've had to deal with are colds and scratches. Penny and I are hoping to diagnose illnesses through self-help books and instinct. We're focusing on preventative medicine to minimize the possibilities of cholera, fungal infections, and malaria by teaching about hygiene. There's not much we can do about the mosquitoes other than sleep with netting and boil water long enough to kill any larvae.

From the swell in her belly and her gray face in the morning, I think we are facing the possibility that the youngest of our teenagers, Carlita, is going to have a baby. If so, we'll need midwifery training before too long.

It's only months since all this has transpired, but it's working. The house has three wings. I think it's fair to say there's an adult wing and two children's wings, although the teenage girls who live in them would be very insulted to be called children. Our young women came from a camp that was once inhabited by Contra soldiers paid to carry guns they hardly knew how to load. These girls must have been *las queridas*, their girlfriends. They were abandoned and frightened when Nimo discovered them. He asked Roger to bring them here.

They all came—Roger, Nimo and the four girls—and we set about building the rooms in which they now sleep. We worked from dawn to dusk for weeks. It was the most satisfying project. We took the earth beneath our feet and mixed it with concrete. The mud was poured into wooden forms and shaped into bricks. While the blocks were still moist we reinforced them with rebar twisted by our own hands. We dried the blocks under Heaven's sweet sun, then laid one upon another until walls and windows appeared. They look strong enough to last a millennium. Truly a work of love.

Nimo Suarez has proven to be our friend. Little did we know the man we chose to take us to the out islands, had chosen us first. Nimo was our shadow guide from the time we arrived in Bluefields. The woman with the boy whose leg I had sown, saw to it we were protected by this man who is a legend in his own time. He knows all of the indigenous people and makes peace wherever he goes. But Nimo, with such remarkable personal power among his people, still remains shy and quiet around me. Roger says it's because he thinks I'm a witch. Imagine! Roger has not discouraged his perception, either. He says he, himself, is helplesssly drawn by the spells I've cast on our place. But, I would say it's quite the reverse. Roger has been the magnet for me to be here. His Casa de los Ninos was inspirational; his love for this land, and his urging me to invest in it, all combined to turn my life around. I am not beyond thinking about Nial, not without wondering about him, but I *am* given to blocking his image more and more, and often it is Roger's face that replaces his. Is this true love? I don't ask such questions. I'm happy with Roger's arms around me and his easy presence. He's reaffirmed my womanhood, and at the same time, given me wings.

Tim and Serena are a dilemma to house. They seem familiar with each other. He, mussing her hair. She, with a hand on his knee as we chat on the verandah. She talks about the world's changing climates and fish farming, but I don't miss her fingers holding on to his pinky, how she strokes it with it her thumb and forefinger. He's distracted by it, too, poor boy. It would be good to let whatever chemistry they have be free to express itself. I decide to leave the sleeping arrangements up to them.

Rosita has not left Serena's side since she arrived. She shows Serena her room and her bed and asks if she will sleep beside her. "Is this allowed, Gwen?" Serena asks. "It would be all right with me," she adds.

I tell Rosita it will be okay for one night. Her six and seven-year-old roommates clap with glee.

Tim, meanwhile, decides on the room adjacent to Penny's. He is an appreciated commodity, a male in this female environment. The teenagers giggle and flirt, and we watch him encourage them. Serena's little fan club grows as the children take her on a tour of the ranch. As if they invented it themselves, they show her the water basin where we capture rain for our showers, and when they bring her to our new outhouse, they proudly display the fourholer and the soft toilet paper it contains.

Three of the children have discovered the joy of gardening. The trio persuades Serena to come with them, pulling her away as they chatter about beans and chipotle. We have peppers and avocado in abundance. There's a sixty foot chicle tree at the far end of the garden. They offer her some brown fruit to eat and she doesn't miss a beat. Into her mouth it goes and she exclaims how sweet it is. All of them talk at once and Serena laughs at her own helplessness with the language.

I look at Penny and see her laughing, too. This friend of mine who showed up at the right time and continues to do so. Tim has loved Penny from the first, and my guess is, it will be the same for Serena. Penny, who had no children of her own, is basking in this experiment of ours. Her great big heart is open enough to hold all of us inside. Except for Roger. I've felt a glitch between Penny and Roger; they just don't seem to take to one another. It makes it hard when he comes to visit or when we are a threesome on the boat to Prinzapolka. He will say something lightly and she invariably makes it heavy. The other day he mentioned a mixer between the boys from Los Mission de Paulina and our girls, and she reacted as if he'd proposed an orgy. She went into a militant diatribe about liberating our girls from the machismo culture. How it was male thinking that had turned them into victims. I suspect our girls would be more forgiving about it, but decided not to say anything at the risk of prolonging her harangue.

Penny is more in touch with the sisters of the Mission de Paulina than I am and perhaps they have prejudiced her against Roger. We haven't discussed it, except I do try to remind her that, with so few people in our world, we must learn to include as many as possible. Besides, Roger is our willing go-between when it comes to sharing supplies and human resources. What I don't say, what I can't say, is that he is my confidant; my conspirator. He has made it possible for me to live with the duplicity concerning Nial's *death*. Roger saw with his own two eyes what I saw, and named it for it was. It's a powerful link we share. That, and a bed when it's possible. He's a far more gentle man than his frame might lead you to believe, and a tender lover.

When I have thoughts of Nial, Roger reminds me that we could go to Kuku if I so choose; but he also insists the Rama will treat Nial well. Well, because they believe the soul of a rescued person is sent from the gods. In their eyes, he has already transcended death and therefore is considered holy.

Time has begun to make real what was at first unbelievable—that my husband, the man I thought I knew, is lost to such a bizarre reality. I try to remember Nial as any other widow might remember her husband. I tell myself, at least we once knew the magic of youth and now with that gone, we are spared the pain of seeing one another grow old. No crippling slow deaths for us to watch. No cruel disappearances of life or limb. No vagaries. It has ended this way—two people letting go. I gave him himself, and I have taken myself back. Now I am interested in who else I may become. I need no longer wait for his truths.

Roger and Penny are gifts. They're my teachers in a world where rules bend like rivers. It was Roger's wisdom that kept me from investigating the

Cessna's crash from the beginning, and that now looks all the wiser. Living here, I understand it could have exposed information we'd be better off not knowing. Something to give the CIA an excuse to reenter Bluefields and create more international tension than already plagues the area. Something that could have made life unbearable for Nial or Tim or me or an innocent boy who had no idea of the power of his gun. We will never know what happened. The plane may have been brought down by Nacionales or the Rama. I can see how messy the facts may be, why Trainor Steele saw so little hope, why Father Joe worried for our safety. I can't think of any better conclusion than to allow the notion that Nial was downed by fate.

When Roger brought me to this vast untamed property and walked me through it, identifying the trees and describing the animal kingdom they support, he introduced me to a world I wanted to save. It hurt when he said the mahogany forests we walked through faced extinction. These (Swietenia macrophylla) precious trees, six hundred years old, were so popular throughout the world that lumberers came and raped the land with careless mining and blind eyes to the future. Walking under the high domes formed by the trees' broad red leaves, and rubbing my hands on the bark of their tough old trunks, I felt a calling. I would make sure they continued to live for no other reason than life itself.

Then I brought Penny to see the place and her eyes saw beyond my own. We walked and examined almost every inch of the property while I told her my thoughts. It was as if we were Eve and Eve in the original garden; we knew beyond knowing, this was a place where dreams could come true.

Penny had already adopted the mission of the Casa de los Ninos in her heart. Talking her into starting a sister home for girls took almost no effort at all. She immediately saw the need and knew it was right. Now, every day brings a harvest of unexpected challenges and satisfaction. Like the garden we have planted in a clearing near the house. The only hope we have for its success is the contraption we built of sticks draped with acres of netting. It looks like an awkward bridal tent which is fine. We're not concerned with looks here, strictly substance. Sometimes the work is grueling, but Penny has no problem setting priorities and organizing our workdays. She's a tireless soul, bound and determined to make this experiment work.

Sustaining us is the reality that life goes on.

The first morning after Tim and Serena arrive, I am at the chicken coop where I've gone to check the egg supply. From inside the shed, I inadvertently overhear them at the water pump. She is crying and Tim is trying to comfort her. I remain covered even though I feel her tears as if they are my own.

"I can't tell her about us, Tim. She would feel betrayed. I kept so many secrets from her. I don't know how she'll react."

"She'll love it. She loves you. Thinks you are an amazing woman. Serena, the past is the past. We can't keep going back there. I did some dumb things, my mother did, too."

197

"Tim, you don't understand, there's more to it than that. It's worse than you know...there's stuff I haven't told you."

"I don't care. You're my girl, you've always been and always will be."

"But that's just it."

"You're not? I know better."

Her voice becomes muffled and I imagine he is holding her. I don't need to hear any more.

After breakfast I drive Serena to the "forest" of mahogany in the northeast sector where we will find ten to twenty trees on every acre —an uncommon number and perhaps the densest stands left on earth. We pass ebony and cacao, chicle and catalpa trees as we jiggle along in Tim's new red truck over the battered dirt roads and undulating hills. I slow down in front of my crudely carved sign, the one I spent many evenings tooling. It reads, *Hope is the Anchor of the Soul.* She turns sideways to look at me instead of observing my hard work.

"How do you do it? What happened that you could move here?" she asks.

I reach in my pocket and pull out the blue piece of glass she'd handed me over a year ago. I want to say something glib like, *I was lost and then found*, or maybe, *Life happened,* or more appropriately, *Death happened.* But I know she is asking more from me. I could say that I didn't know I had closed myself up and stopped asking questions. That I was afraid of life from the day my Sabrina died. That all those years, I had only been pretending to be alive—pretending that Nial was enough, that the house was important, the labels, the Bridge Club, the endless days of creating illusions. I pretended so well, I didn't know I was doing it. It took something devastating, something totally irrational and demanding, for me to wake up. It took the despair of a wife, the goodness of a river man and innocent children's needs, combined with the courage of a selfless friend. It took a trip into a tortured scarred land for me to find beauty—a deep profound beauty in life itself, a beauty that teaches me everything I need to know.

"It simply happened. I saw an opportunity to do something meaningful and did it. That's all I can say."

"The little girls? Are you going to adopt them?"

"Oh no. In this part of the world we don't need papers. I'm simply a caregiver. I will do what I can, and when their wings spread, I will let them go. Sabrina taught me that. I'll give them what I can and remember that the most important thing we can give our children is themselves."

"But this ranch, where do you go from here?"

"I don't need to go anywhere. I'm here. I'm letting the forests go to seed. You know, they're trying to cultivate mahogany in the States and on lands in Mexico. They can't succeed because they don't have the natural adversity for the trees to grow. Without other species for them to compete with, they die. The fight for survival is what makes them grow strong; they have to have fires to rise above, room to spread their boughs and dig their roots, and then time, lots of time, for them to become the grand hard wood they are."

"Just like the lobster!" Serena says.

She is so funny. "Lobster? Comparing a lobster to a mahogany tree seems a stretch!"

"Not when you think in terms of one system versus another; not when you remember that it's all a connected web," she says.

"Of course. And I suppose you plan to share that wisdom with the rest of the world?"

"That's my plan. To find a way to make the web safe, to heal it, make it work.

"Just like the two of us," I say.

"What do you mean?" she asks, strangely cautious.

"I mean, when you showed up in my life you made a difference, and that difference has taught me how connected we all really are, even when we don't know it."

"Connected, despite ourselves!"

"Yes." I am flooded with tenderness and reach over to her. I hug her and she hugs me back. "You are quite the young woman. I'd be proud if you were my daughter."

"You're quite a woman yourself, Mrs. Townsend. And considering all the obstacles that have come our way, it would be quite a miracle if I ended up your daughter. Well, daughter-in-law."

"Perhaps it's best not to see difficulties as obstacles. Perhaps each obstacle is a step forward. Don't you think that is a better way to look at it?"

"I want to think it's possible."

"Isn't everything?" I search her glistening gray eyes. "Remember our whale?" I ask.

"I remember."

"Who would have thought?"

"Who would have thought?" we say at the very same time.

About the Author:

As a woman of words, and mother of four daughters, St. John has an invested interest in the evolving state of women. In *Anchors of the Soul,* she draws upon her own adventures in post-revolutionary Nicaragua and the time she spent as an artist on the North Shore of Massachusetts. Her characters and their circumstances, however, are pure fiction.

Born in Brooklyn, educated in upstate New York and Boston, St. John currently paints and writes in Tubac, Arizona.

www.ingramcontent.com/pod-product-compliance
Lightning Source LLC
Chambersburg PA
CBHW030318290526
45785CB00001B/411